# REVOLUTIONARY ROMANTICISM

### EDITED BY MAX BLECHMAN

*A Drunken Boat Anthology*

CITY LIGHTS BOOKS
San Francisco

Cover design by Nicholas Blechman
Book design by Elaine Katzenberger
Typography by Harvest Graphics

Library of Congress Cataloging-in-Publication Data

Revolutionary romanticism : a drunken boat anthology / edited by Max
Blechman.
    p.   cm.
Includes bibliographical references.
ISBN 0-87286-351-4 (pbk.)
1. Romanticism. 2. Civilization, Modern. I. Blechman, Max.
PN603.P48    1999
808.8'0145—dc21                      99-17522
                                            CIP

City Lights Books are available to bookstores through our primary
distributor: Subterranean Company, P.O. Box 160, 265 S. 5th St., Monroe,
OR 97456; 541-847-5274. Toll-free orders: 800-274-7826. FAX: 541-847-6018.
Our books are also available through library jobbers and regional
distributors. For personal orders and catalogs, please write to City Lights
Books, 261 Columbus Ave., San Francisco, CA 94133. See our Web site at
www.citylights.com.

CITY LIGHTS BOOKS are edited by Lawrence Ferlinghetti and Nancy J.
Peters and published at the City Lights Bookstore, 261 Columbus Avenue,
San Francisco, CA 94133.

# CONTENTS

# PREFACE – "THIS IS OUR HIGH ARGUMENT"

And the creation (by no lower name
Can it be called) which they with blended might
Accomplish:—this is our high argument.

— *Wordsworth*

When the storm finally subsided, I scrambled around the apartment for my keys, threw on a raincoat, and tore out to the boulevard. The gates of Père-Lachaise were going to close in a few hours, and I wanted to lose myself among the tombs. As I crossed the Canal de Paris, I felt unusually sure on my feet. Everything was somehow charged with meaning, as though an angel had passed and sprinkled the streets with allegorical light. At Père-Lachaise the fading leaves breathed in unison, forming a rustling blur of color, like a continuous sigh. But the sigh was all my own, my reason for being there, for musing in the fall, for freeing my thoughts to the rhythm of the autumn wind, for honoring the dignity of life within death, for apprehending the sublimity of death within life, for recalling the poets under the mossy stones, the Communards beneath the ivy wall, the ruins of philosophy, the legends of Resistance, the desperate utopias, the triumphs and the betrayals and the hatred and the love. . . .

An unexpected presence distracted my contemplations; from behind, some broken footsteps gave the impression of a hesitation, and when I turned the young woman had chosen a path that forked from mine. Her red hair fell in waves around her hips, her thin leather gloves suggested a musical fragility, and the proud defiance of her violet suit provoked my curiosity. I was ill-disposed for an adventure, but seeing how an alternative path could soon meet hers, I accepted destiny. We agreed on a café not far from the cemetery, and as we walked she began an interview. "Revolutionary romanticism?" she chuckled and lit a Gauloise. "That's a tautology—romanticism *is* revolutionary."

The mysterious woman is, of course, essentially right. Set against the current of modernity, the romantics raised the resounding question: "What is the good life?" And whether they revived the Scriptures, the myths of the Orient, Dionysian Eros, the sagas of chivalry, the Athenian *agora*, or the guilds of the Middle Ages, their disparate journeys to the past communicate a common urgency to bring *news from nowhere*. Romantic hindsight pierced through the gains of industrialism and the market economy to what in the process was being lost, and its melancholic gaze remains revolutionary to the extent that it shatters the very notion of progress. If we bear Michelet's new religion of liberation in mind, if we heed the metaphysical standpoint from which Blake applauded the events of 1789, if we at all understand the mythological pantheism of the *Athenaeum* circle, we can appreciate how the romantic ideal of a redeemed humanity that would live in harmony with nature partook of the revolutionary spirit—on its own passionate terms.

Yet the title of this book has a fundamental justification that makes it more than a tautology. Whereas romantic nostalgia gave way time and time again to tendencies severed from its revolutionary roots, the revolutionary movements in romanticism consistently redirected the longing for precapitalist modes of life back to the project of emancipation, making the romantic worldview conscious of its original import. As a synthetic force within modernity, revolutionary romanticism brought the quest for a new relationship with nature to cohere with the enlightenment quest for liberty. The romantic vision of organic community here unites with the vision of an outstanding political revolution, and the revolutionary principles of equality and fraternity are in turn buttressed by the romantic imperative for *the poetry of life*. Revolutionary romantics were pioneers in the battles for feminism, ecology, genuinely expressive culture, community-oriented economy, and radical political freedom; they were enlightened revolutionaries not in spite of their romantic fantasies but as a sophisticated extension of them.

I edited this anthology with a definite viewpoint as to what revolutionary romanticism is and as to what it may yet be. The strength of *Revolutionary Romanticism* lies in the power of its perspective as much as in the quality of the individual essays. There is an idea that brings the parts into a whole, and my hope is that the reader will discover a genuine coherence from chapter to chapter, right up to the concluding "Reflections on Revolutionary Romanticism," which outline "the blended might" of revolutionary romantic idealism, and look forward to a renaissance of revolutionary romantic struggles in the new millennium.

When in the late 1970s revolutionary romantics were accused of "moral paternalism" (or was it "bourgeois sentimentalism"?) by the Althusserian "alternative terrain of scientific knowledge," E. P. Thompson warned:

> It may have been thought once that those of us who acknowledge our continuing relation to the transformed romantic tradition could simply be read out of the intellectual Left: we belonged somewhere else. But that attempt has failed. We are still here. We do not mean to go.

We *are* still here, and given the current disarray of the Left, I dare say maybe it is only now that our time has come. The world of fact has long stood the romantics on trial for their dreams—but the tribunal of history alone will determine who in the unfinished play of modernity are the real protagonists of illusion.

*— Max Blechman*
*Paris, March 1999*

# EDITOR'S ACKNOWLEDGMENTS

My essay on the early German romantics is based on a talk delivered at the Université Pierre Mendès France conference on "La Culture Libertaire," March 23, 1996. Annie Le Brun's essay was originally delivered during Michel Le Bris' broadcast on romanticism on France Culture, June 6, 1978. Peter Marshall's essay is a romantic spin on his book, *William Blake: Visionary Anarchist*, 2d ed. (London: Freedom Press, 1994). Arthur Mitzman radicalized—in fact, restored—his essay first published in the *Journal of the History of Ideas* (December 1996). Miguel Abensour romanticized his essay featured in *L'Imaginaire Subversif* (Paris: Atelier de Création Libertaire, 1982). Earlier versions of Christopher Winks's "Erich Mühsam: In Defense of Literary High Treason" and his translation of Erich Mühsam's "The Artist in the Future State" were first published in *Soup* 3 (1983); the German original, Erich Mühsam, "Die Künstler in Zufunktsstaat," was first published in *Die Fackel* 8 (1906) and reprinted in *Fanal: Aufsätze und Gedichte 1905–1932*, ed. Kurt Kreiler (Berlin: Verlag Klaus Wagenbach, 1977). Martin Green operated a romantic return to his *Mountain of Truth: The Counterculture Begins* (Hanover: Univ. Press of New England, 1986).

Jim Fleming and Peter Lamborn Wilson encouraged this project from the outset. André Bernard was pivotal in providing early production. I am indebted to sharp remarks from Arthur Mitzman and René Moerland. Michael Löwy offered vital criticism and direction. Marie-Christine and Marianne Enckell of the C.I.R.A. library magically assisted my penchant for making research a time of romance. Nicholas Blechman functioned as my Apollonian better half at crucial moments. Daniel Blanchard and Helen Arnold stimulated the subject of this book through many late-night conversations and countless glasses of superb wine. I owe much to Lawrence Ferlinghetti and Nancy J. Peters for having glimpsed reason amidst the drunkenness and to my editor at City Lights, James Brook, for having made key suggestions and important revisions from beginning to end. Finally, without the combined support of R. O. Blechman and Philippe Brugnon, *Revolutionary Romanticism* (which constitutes *Drunken Boat* 3) would never have materialized.

# CONTRIBUTORS

*Miguel Abensour* teaches philosophy and political science at L'Université de Paris-XII and was president of the Collège International de Philosophie from 1985 to 1987. He is the author of many articles on utopia, political heroism, and modern political philosophy. His *Democracy Against the State: Marx and the Machiavellian Moment* is forthcoming from Verso.

*Daniel Blanchard*, former member of Socialisme ou Barbarie, is the author of several books of poems and two novels, *Halte sur la Rive Orientale du Lac Champlain, Vermont* and *Fugitif.*

*Max Blechman* is the editor of the *Drunken Boat* anthologies on politics and art. Living in France since 1994, he is working on his doctorate in philosophy at the Sorbonne.

*Martin Green* is professor of English at Tufts University. His books on cultural history include *The Von Richtofen Sisters, Children of the Sun,* and *The Mountain of Truth: The Counterculture Begins.*

*Maurice Hindle* teaches literature at The Open University. Among his published works are his study, *Mary Shelley, Frankenstein,* and editions of *Frankenstein,* Godwin's *Caleb Williams,* and Stoker's *Dracula.* He is currently working on the poetry and prose of Humphry Davy.

*Annie Le Brun* is a poet and prolific author of books and articles on surrealism, romantic literature, and cultural politics, including *A Distance, Les Châteaux de la Subversion,* and *Sade: A Sudden Abyss.*

*Michael Löwy* is a research director at the CNRS and teaches at the Ecole des Hautes Etudes en Sciences Sociales. His books include *Georg Lukács: From Romanticism to Bolshevism, Redemption and Utopia: Libertarian Judaism in Central Europe,* and *Révolte et Mélancolie: Le Romantisme à Contre-courant de la Modernité.*

*Peter Marshall* is the author of *William Blake: Visionary Anarchist, Nature's Web: Rethinking Our Place on Earth,* and *Riding the Wind: A New Philosophy for a New Era,* among other books.

**Marie-Dominique Massoni** is a member of the Paris Surrealist Group and the author of several collections of poetry, including *Tout Filet Perdu* and *Toujours à Retardement*.

**Arthur Mitzman** is Emeritus Professor of History at the University of Amsterdam where, between 1971 and 1996, he taught nineteenth-century cultural history. Among his many works on modernist culture and politics is *The Iron Cage*, a historical interpretation of Max Weber. His *Michelet ou la Subversion du Passé* has recently been published.

**Michael Richardson** is a translator and the editor of several collections of surrealist writing, including *Refusal of the Shadow: Surrealism and the Caribbean*.

**Christopher Winks** is managing editor of *Black Renaissance/ Renaissance Noire*, a Pan-African journal of culture and politics. He has taught Caribbean, African-American, African, and other literatures at New York University and the City University of New York, and is currently working on a study of utopias and dystopias in Caribbean literature.

# THE REVOLUTIONARY DREAM
# OF EARLY GERMAN ROMANTICISM
## *Max Blechman*

*Collage by Knickerbocker, after* The Traveler Above the Sea of Clouds
*(1818) by Caspar David Friedrich*

A solitary man stands on the edge of a cliff contemplating a sea of clouds. The traveler in Caspar David Friedrich's painting suggests, by his heroic posture, an existential courage, as if the sight before him were the site of his own being. The clouds that in waves overtake the mountain peaks seem to constitute for the lone spectator a natural drama, a story of his own condition. They overflow and withdraw, revealing and eclipsing the abyss they hide, inspiring both a sense of omnipotent grandeur and fragmented limitation. The movement in the painting is both outward and inward: from the light of the sublime scenery to the darkness surrounding the figure in the foreground, the lofty sea that flows over the free-fall reflects like a mirror the inner ocean of the traveler's consciousness. One is tempted to see the traveler as emblematic of idealism's marriage of nature and mind, a portrait, perhaps, of the visionary who has traveled the earth as a free man, contemplating nature with a gaze at once candid and proud, remembering that the ancient Freya was both goddess of earth and of freedom. But there is a melancholic, almost tragic aura to Friedrich's romantic hero; indeed, he might just as easily be the prophet who could already say with Nietzsche: "If you stare too long into the abyss, the abyss also stares into you."[1]

Friedrich's painting epitomizes the romantic reaction to what Max Weber would call "the process of disenchantment."[2] In the dominant criticism of enlightenment thought—the intellectual backdrop against which Friedrich's work is set—truth that does not survive the analysis of reason was considered irrational dogma, and accordingly truth liberated from dogmatic illusion defined rational thought. Friedrich's *oeuvre*, on the contrary, strives to communicate a form of thought antithetical to the rationalization of experience. It represents a world shrouded in mysteriousness, and suggests the urge to feel at home again in a nature demystified by the advances of critical reason.

What is the rationalization of experience that so concerned the romantics, and what is its relationship to the enlightenment? For Max Weber "intellectualist rationalization" means that "there are no mysterious incalculable forces that come into play, but rather that one can, in principle, master all things by calculation."[3] While a facile comparison, it is instructive to compare Weber's definition of rationalization with Christoph Martin Wieland's definition of enlightenment:

> Representations of men become enlightened when the true is separated from the false, when the entangled is disentangled, when the complex is dissolved into its simple components, when the simple is pursued to its origin, and, above all, when no representation or claim passed off by men as true is granted a reprieve from unrestricted scrutiny.[4]

Put simply, the scientific rationalism of much enlightenment philosophy was grounded in a Cartesian principle: the deconstruction of all experience and its reconstruction based on what subsists once all prejudice has been cast aside.

The paradox of this principle, as the early German romantics argued, and as Max Horkheimer would reiterate in our own century, is that a new prejudice was instituted: "nature lost every vestige of vital independent existence, all value of its own. It became dead matter—a heap of things."[5] Moreover, like the young Hegel the early romantics were concerned that the critical philosophy of the German enlightenment was turning the Cartesian principle of knowledge into a lifeless ethics: just as Cartesian reason can know only a nature that is fundamentally dead and mechanical, Kant's conception of human freedom affirmed the domination of impulse and passion by rational moral principles, making freedom an abstract regulative idea. However, if all forms of spontaneous feeling and action are only occasions for error, what is left to human freedom other than a calculating substance that has the power to refuse illusion, maintaining its independence from all natural inclination, suspending judgment from every uncertainty?

The early German romantics wanted to broaden the enlightenment's conception of human freedom by rethinking its relationship to nature. Against the modern process of disenchantment, they tried to imagine how human freedom could be more than rational independence, how autonomy could also express a belonging to the natural world. Although Germany would not have a fully industrial economy until the end of the nineteenth century, many of the problems that came with free trade and urbanization were already visible at the turn of the eighteenth century. Significantly, the romantics did not view the new dehumanizing methods of production and the anomie of individuals in society as a side effect of modern civil society; rather, they believed this was the consequence of a modern ideology based on rationalization, economic self-interest, and a purely instrumental view of nature.

The deficiencies of the French Revolution pushed the early German romantics to also ask pivotal questions concerning social change. While they criticized the absolutist and the liberal traditions for undermining community and popular political participation for the sake of centralized authority, they also believed this dynamic resurfaced in the Revolution itself, and that therefore the idea of revolution needed to be rethought. If the romantics were enthusiastic spectators of the French Revolution and believed that true community consists in the liberty, equality, and fraternity of a republic, they eventually took their distance from Jacobinism after the Terror, and drew their own conclusions, emphasizing as had Schiller in his *Aesthetische Briefe* the need for a positive development of freedom through cultural formation (*Bildung*), for organic culture as transformative egalitarian creation.

For the early German romantics the crisis of the enlightenment was therefore more than the question of reason's power and limits, it also implied a broad critique of the mores of their day. As will be seen, even the seemingly politically irrelevant realms of religion and aesthetics were reformulated by the romantics in the context of their demand for organic community and a new relationship between society and nature. The early German romantics at once spearheaded the critique of modern civil society by developing an aesthetic theory of the political sphere and anticipated the modern ecological movement by relating the idea of democratic social organization to an organic philosophy of nature (*Naturphilosophie*). To reconsider the origin of political romanticism as it first emerged in Germany is, then, also to reexamine an early critical response to modernity as a whole, one that involves fundamental political questions that remain radical today.

## Political Romanticism and Its Critics

> The first kiss is the principle of philosophy—the origin of a new world—the beginning of absolute chronology. Who would not like a philosophy whose germ is a first kiss?[6]
>
> —*Novalis*

> Much seeming stupidity is really folly, which is more common than one might think. Folly is an absolute wrongness of tendency, a complete lack of historical sense.[7]
>
> —*Friedrich Schlegel*

The main romantic thinkers here considered are Friedrich von Hardenberg (best known by his pen name, Novalis), Friedrich Schleiermacher, Friedrich Schlegel, and Friedrich Hölderlin, a poet who wrote on the fringes of the romantic group but who shared many of their ideas. The literary and philosophical work of the first movement in history to be called *Romantik* (*Frühromantik*; literally, romanticism "of the first hour," or early romanticism) took place between 1796 and 1801 in Jena and Berlin, after which the romantics' "symphilosophic" journal, *Athenaeum*, came to a conclusion and the original group disbanded. Although the writings of later German romanticisms (*Hochromantik* and *Spätromantik;* literally, "high romanticism" and "late romanticism") would obscure this fact, the early romantic writers did not impatiently reject enlightenment philosophy; they wanted on the contrary to radicalize enlightenment thought by making criticism assess its own activity. Far from being regressive, the original romantic circle's religious and aesthetic thought was the recognition that the vacuum created by critical reason could not be filled by it. Whereas the *Frühromantik* viewed critical reason as a liberating modern force, they considered aesthetics and religion a creative counterpart to the destructive force of criticism, one that could positively respond to the call born with the French Revolution for universal equality and freedom. The early romantics' aesthetic and religious outlook was born of a desire to push critical philosophy to embrace its affirmative twin, to elaborate a worldview that would emphasize the metaphysical and reconstructive power of freedom. The original romantic circle is the first avant-garde group that, like the German expressionists of the 'teens of the century or the French situationists of the 1960s, conceived the auto-formation of poetic activity an apt metaphor for spiritual renewal and political change. The early romantics were revolutionaries: not because they believed in a political insurrection in their homeland—among them only Hölderlin was directly affiliated with insurrectionary groups—but because through public expression they hoped to redefine the meaning of progress and revolutionize the values of modern civilization. As Friedrich Schlegel dramatically proclaimed, "The revolutionary desire to realize the kingdom of God on earth is the elastic point of progressive civilization and the beginning of modern history."[8]

Why then has political romanticism been seen by historians and critics as politically irrelevant or reactionary? Romanticism in Germany (as in France and England) was a protean movement, and the writings of formative romantics were contradicted by those of late romantics, some of whom broke with the early romantics' idealism for various forms of conservatism. However, there were also important political ambiguities and differences among the early romantic thinkers themselves. While many of the early romantics were inspired by the invention of democracy in Ancient Greece—Schlegel, for example, was deeply interested in the ancient republics—and were eager to rethink the idea of democracy in the context of the French Revolution, what this revolutionary Hellenism actually meant varied. If Hölderlin believed the State-form was an outmoded mechanism of domination that should as such be abolished, this movement of negation was for Novalis not necessarily the best means to realize the ideal, noncoercive State—what he called "the poetic state." Whereas Hölderlin expressed stridently antistatist sentiments in his writing, Novalis developed complex theories on how republicanism might ultimately be compatible with a reformed monarchy. Moreover, Schlegel came to share Novalis' belief in a reformed monarchy in the early romantic period itself. Although Schlegel continued to espouse political autonomy as a means toward the ideal of a stateless society (*Anarchie*) as late as 1801, his early revaluation of monarchy problematizes any strict dichotomy between early (revolutionary) and late (conservative) romantic thought.

Yet a distinction between revolutionary and conservative tendencies in romanticism can nonetheless be made; for the extent to which the early romantics reinterpreted along conservative lines their own principles of democratism (*Demokratismus*) is the extent to which they cleared a path for a movement of antidemocratic nationalism in the *Hochromantik* period.[9] It is precisely the complexity of this transition from revolutionary to conservative thought that has allowed critics, from Heinrich Heine's *Die Romantische Schule* onward, to carelessly attribute ideas to the early romantic school that were not theirs, to ignore or downplay their revolutionary convictions, and to make anachronistic generalizations. What most of the critics of the *Frühromantik* have in common, despite divergent motives, is an ignorance or a rejection of the romantic synthesis, formulated in the 1790s, of aesthetics and democratic politics.

Among the most serious modern critiques of political romanticism is that of Carl Schmitt, who argued in *Politische Romantik* that romanticism is politically irrelevant.[10] For Schmitt, romanticism is essentially apolitical because its main orientation is toward aesthetics; it is a subjectivist retreat into an ideal world of the imagination wherein political commitment has no meaning outside of artistic inspiration. The essentially aesthetic nature of romantic political commitment explains the political somersaults of the romantics, and it shows how they can be pro- or antirevolution, depending on how much the idea of revolution stimulates their imagination. Romantic irony, in this light, is little else than a fear of genuine commitment, a fear intrinsic to the aesthetic attitude that, as Kierkegaard had argued before Schmitt, is as unstable as the stimuli on which it depends.

What Schmitt overlooks is that the romantics' idea of irony, far from being an aesthetic absolute that avoids political commitment, was inspired by their political idealism. The romantics' belief that there are intrinsic limits to artistic creativity was a recognition of the inadequacy of artistic activity in relation to the ideal social harmony sought through creation, and it is this recognition of finitude that is constitutive of irony in romantic creativity. Schmitt, who by the 1930s had become a leading theoretician of Nazi ideology, saw in romanticism—which like him was critical of the liberal view of the State—a theoretical contender to his goal of a hegemonic National Socialist philosophy. As Schmitt revealingly stated elsewhere, to declare that a political movement is apolitical is the best way to render the movement politically irrelevant.[11]

Alternatively, many Nazi thinkers appropriated romantic ideas in their effort to gain political legitimacy. Rather than emphasize the total irrelevance of political romanticism, they made it compatible to National Socialist doctrine by differentiating an early and decadent romanticism ("subjective" romanticism) from a later and veritably German romanticism ("objective" romanticism) and they called this latter "true romanticism." For Walther Linden, editor of the pro-Nazi *Zeitschrift für Deutschkunde*, German romanticism is the breakthrough of German organic spirit, the long-awaited overcoming of the rationalist enlightenment transmitted by liberal Jews. Linden attacked the liberal interpretations of romanticism that saw Schlegel as its representative, and believed that the early democratic ideal of organic society was an immature version of the true romantic theory of the "organic State," developed by the late romantic Adam Müller.[12] Although Müller's concept of an organic State, as we shall see, is for early romantic theory a contradiction in terms, just how successful the Nazi appropriation of romantic organic theory was can be measured by the continued association of romanticism with National Socialism by modern thinkers.

Politics as aesthetics: Is this not the synthesis of Nazism? Was it not Wagner who composed the glory of Nazism, and the infamous Goebbels who defined Nazi politics as "the plastic art of the State"?

Was not, as Philippe Lacoue-Labarthe has cogently argued, "the aestheticization of politics the program of National Socialism"? Is not the romantic ideal of "political organicity" capable of being turned into a "biologism," wherein one can "substitute the race for the nation (or the language community)"? Did we not see that this is what happens "once physis comes to be interpreted as bios on the authority of a 'science'"? While these are real questions to which we must affirmatively respond, we can take issue with Lacoue-Labarthe's conclusion that this "is merely a consequence of the organic interpretation of the political," and that "racism—and anti-semitism in particular—is primarily, and fundamentally an aestheticism."[13] These conclusions are not unusual in contemporary political philosophy, and they testify to the need to make our terms clear when considering the pertinence of early romantic thought.[14]

First, for the romantics aesthetics is the sensuous sphere of the unknown; it is at once the other of reason and inextricable from it, whereas racism is the irrational fear and hatred of the unknown and has nothing to do with romantic thought on aesthetics. That fascists and Nazis gained power by making use of romantic ideas on aesthetics and by manipulating sensuous feeling indeed points to the need to understand the importance of aesthetics in politics and its dangerous potential. However, this what the romantics implicitly did by emphasizing Eros, by maintaining that only love makes up the whole, by insisting that love is the "magic" principle that connects the visible with the aesthetic invisible, that unites organic beings in their different modes of being, anticipating Freud's speculation that it is love that assures the cohesion of our elements. In the context of early German romanticism, racism has less to do with aesthetics than with mechanism, "the evil principle in philosophy and in reality," in the words of Schlegel.[15]

Second, romantics such as Schleiermacher believed in a renaissance of all native cultures, the enrichment of particular cultures through the traditions of others, and, like Herder, they criticized the chauvinism of a hypocritical enlightenment that supported a politics that had conquered two-thirds of the world.[16] It is the romantics' organic theory that, far from being a stepping stone to racism and totalitarianism, in fact informed their political pluralism. The romantics believed that German rootedness, if it is to be enlightened, is also the opening to the rootedness of all cultures. When in current political thought we speak of multiculturalism and social diversity, we are returning to forms of expression characteristic of the early romantic generation.

Third, the theory of *Bildung* championed by the romantics is pitted against both the supposed objectivity of science and the destructive potential of a Promethean *techne*. Whereas Hitler harnessed the rise of a new spiritual Germany to the progress of Germanic technology, the romantics believed that science and technology reflect the sensibility or the presuppositions of the subject and should not be conceived as having any objectivity or as capable of causing any progress in themselves.[17]

Fourth, and contrary to the fundamental organization principle of fascist and Nazi ideology, a significant dimension of early romantic thought was opposed to the impersonal hierarchy of State formation and believed that eventually political domination should be completely superseded. This is a point that is easily ignored when the romantic synthesis of art and politics is associated with an instrumental model of politics and when "political organicity" is *prima facie* understood as synonymous with the so-called organic State.[18]

Beyond these historical arguments, and as elementary as this may be, it is important to consider that every concept and sign developed in a given context by certain individuals can have a contrary meaning in another context in the minds of others. Is this not the inherent ambiguity of the instrument of language? The deceptive potential of the signs of language was noted by the romantics, who feared what could happen to any concept or sign, and this is one reason why they greatly valued the autonomy of poetry and why they insisted that all politics is necessarily aesthetics, that there is no antecedence of politics over aesthetics, that politics is less rational organization than the sensuous relations among people. This too was a motivating factor for their emphasis on difference, irony, individuality, and interpretation as a necessary complement to tradition and positive meaning. It is the "mania for the One, one country, one truth, one way," the arrogance that imposes a definitive fiction, that Hölderlin called "the root of all evil" (*Wurzel alles übels*).[19] The romantics' belief that there is an inevitable discrepancy between the sign and the meaning it attempts to convey was an integral part of their hope that signs would not passively be accepted according to the meaning attributed to them but would instead be the object of individual scrutiny and creation, as Schleiermacher ardently expressed in the *Monologen* of his youth:

> The spirit must search for a long time in the great abundance of words before it finds a trustworthy sign, so that under its protection it can transmit its innermost thoughts. Quickly though the enemy snatches it away, giving the sign a foreign meaning, so that a listener will doubt from whom it originally came. Probably many replies will come from afar to the lonely spirit; but he must question their meaning. . . . This is the great struggle.[20]

That romantics considered language (as much as culture and politics) a fragile common world of meaning points to the problem with attributing a teleology to romantic terms or seeing the germ of National Socialist ideology in the ideas of the *Frühromantik*. For the romantics, linguistic activity consists in poetically inventing a world, creating a world of meaning to which the signs of language refer. This implies that the signs do not *a fortiori* live from generation to generation in conformity to the meaning originally intended. On the contrary, the signs as such are merely the skeleton of a previous process of active formation and foundation, perpetually in need of new interpretation. Manfred Frank has insisted on this creative aspect of signification in relation to romantic thought:

> The social dimension of language only records and establishes initiatives that are originally individual: before circulating into social language the meaning was first produced by individuals interpreting the varied in their singular experience: and this act is a creative operation. . . . It is not sufficient that one generation communicates by means of the signs of language for the signs to automatically have meaning for the following generation: rather meaning must be constantly attributed to these signs. This means that the meaning signified is itself reinterpreted.[21]

In romantic philosophy the same applies to the life of the mind in general: reason is formed only in and by way of orientating ideas that are established as norms. Concepts are configurations; they depend on a synthetic operation that assembles the variety of experience into a representative unity according to certain criteria of selection, and this assembling is essentially creative.

One must therefore bear the romantic critique of signification in mind given the argument, still current in contemporary political philosophy, of an almost rational genesis that leads from romantic notions of cultural belonging and aesthetic politics straight to Auschwitz. A radical reconsideration of political romanticism demands that the original ideas of the romantics be removed from the shadow of their historical determination and understood in light of their initial formation; that is to say, in the context of the *Frühromantik*. A fresh look at the spirit motivating early romantic political thought can thus show in what ways we would be making a serious historical and intellectual error to consider romanticism a purely regressive or reactionary tendency of German culture. As should now be evident, the very opposite is the thesis of this essay: early German romanticism was an essentially utopian movement that aspired to give greater depth and meaning to the cosmopolitan ideal of universal freedom and equality; and as Thomas Mann believed, it even "may be permitted us to consider romanticism the most revolutionary and the most radical movement of the German spirit."[22]

## Romanticism and the Reenchantment of the World

> Mere intellect produces no philosophy, for philosophy is more than the limited perception of what is.[23]
>
> — *Friedrich Hölderlin*

> Philosophy is actually homesickness—the urge to be everywhere at home.[24]
>
> — *Novalis*

> But whenever I find a spark of that hidden fire that will sooner or later consume the old and create the new, I am drawn to it with love and hope, regarding it as a sign of my distant home.[25]
>
> — *Friedrich Schleiermacher*

When in 1796 Schlegel proclaimed "republicanism is necessarily democratic," he not only took a stand against the antidemocratic perspective of Kant's republicanism, he also implicitly announced the radical and ambitious character of the literary and philosophical group he would found two years later.[26] Under Schlegel's lead, the *Athenaeum* circle aimed for the transformation of all aspects of social life. The early German romantics struggled to enrich and radicalize the enlightenment ideal of autonomy, to envision a republicanism that would be a power of people's free expression of their culture, their sensibility, and their belonging to the world, and thus counterbalance those aspects of modernity that had, from their perspective, become a veritable movement of alienation.

*Athenaeum* was in many respects a journal of opposition. Schlegel reacted against a mechanistic model of science and modern philosophy that would, as he saw it, increasingly dominate the incommensurability of nature, destroy the diversity of traditional cultures, and iron out all the mystery, art, and passion that live outside the legislating power of rational reflection and its progress. For Schlegel, the emergence of bourgeois culture was an unprecedented leap in human organization and thought that contrasted sharply with everything that preceded it. He deplored the abstract organization of economic activity by civil society and saw the enlightenment's no less abstract comprehension of the earth and of human freedom as dehumanizing. With the development of bourgeois society, he argued, human beings are molded into mere gears of the machinery of social organization. Not only had workers become cogs in the mill of industrial production, the very character of prosperity in civil society often deteriorated the quality of life rather than constituted progress. According to Schlegel's laconic description of the bourgeois ethic, "the bourgeois man is first and foremost fashioned and turned into a machine. He is happy even if he has become only a number in a political sum, and he can be called in every respect perfect if he has transformed himself from a person into a cipher."[27]

Like Schlegel, the more outspoken members of the *Frühromantik* were afraid that collective life would become a meaningless bond of atomized individuals when political freedom is one-dimensionally defined as universal independence and rational judgment, when economic life means the systematic division of labor and the isolation of the individual's multifaceted powers, and when notions of spiritual belonging to community and to nature are considered unenlightened remnants of irrational mythology. Whereas the romantics saw modernity as the historical possibility for a new emancipatory freedom, they also believed it announced a new form of slavery, a perversion of humanity's most profound determinations. They feared that the Cartesianism of the enlightenment and the epistemological empiricism of thinkers like Locke reflected political and economic forces that created an unreal world deprived of life, in which people could discover only artificiality and were condemned to a life of doubt and routine, performed without love, art, or honor. The universe as such could not be humanity's home, charged with meaning and mystery, it could only be uniformly opaque, indifferent to the all-too-human desire for shared culture and individual adventure, natural belonging and imaginative discovery.

The criticism of modern rationality is particularly present in the writings of Novalis. He viewed subjectivity as more than self-founding reason; for him consciousness is secondary to a spirit that transcends it. By contrast to the subjectivity of modernity that limits human action to consciousness and will, he believed the world of consciousness is inscribed in a higher world that overflows it. For Novalis all consciousness is riddled with the unconscious, "all that is visible clings to the invisible . . . the thinkable to the unthinkable"; in other words, subjectivity is always dependent on a spiritual nature that precedes and bypasses it.[28] This is one of the reasons why for Novalis human nature is linked to aesthetics. He believed that all people are artists if only because, like artists, people cannot only be rationally autonomous; they are also inspired, propelled by a force that is never fully transparent. Human creativity is not capable of being purely circumscribed to will or consciousness because humans are not their own foundation—there is always an inexplicable origin to thought and action by virtue of nature's transcendent and constitutive relation to being. Novalis argued that the modern world is increasingly absurd because of the attempt to explain this transcendence away or to ignore it by identifying freedom with certainty and construction, reducing the realm of nature and the sensuous to sheer matter. Everything operates in the modern age as if human reason were somehow above the world or exterior to its enigmatic lifeforce—as if the living dynamism of the earth had no end other than the goals established by the discipline of economics and no other truth than the certainties determined by analytical science.

Novalis challenged this modern prejudice by showing how aesthetic experience points to the difference between explanation and comprehension. Modern science can explain various facts about the world, but it gives no sense to these various facts or to our being in the world. On the contrary, the logic of functional explanation, by rejecting any sense to the world, renders the world incomprehensible. Not that scientific explanation is invalid as such, but by establishing scientific reason as the sole criterion of truth, by suggesting that what we spontaneously perceive and understand is an illusion, modern science divides human experience in two, debasing sensibility and situating truth in a purely analytical sphere. For Novalis, the mathematician may know the world "as an inventor knows the mechanics of his creation" because he "plays with nature like one plays with a gigantic instrument." However, the mathematician "will not understand nature," because the understanding of nature is not his concern; it is alien to his very methodology.[29]

Similarly, Schleiermacher sought to defend the diversity of culture and the legitimacy of traditions rooted in their particular comprehension of the world by affirming the primacy of sensuous experience over rational reflection. Instead of subordinating particular ways of life—considered by the enlightenment as so many prejudices—to the ideal of universal autonomy, Schleiermacher believed in seeing universal autonomy as the autonomous development of humanity in the diversity of its manifestations. Only in this way does the ideal of universal autonomy make sense, because only the consideration of the living diversity of cultures makes the ideal more than an empty abstraction. As Schleiermacher put it, "every person presents humanity in his own unique way, by his own mixture of elements, so that humanity reveals itself in every possible manner, and so that everything diverse realizes itself in the fullness of infinitude."[30] The universal as such is not achieved despite cultural diversity but is expressed through the process of humanity's natural diversification.

The emphasis on culture grew from the romantics' belief that only the simultaneous maintenance and renewal of tradition allows for the development of people as a whole, as both natural and spiritual beings. Tradition is a mediation between the legalities of the natural and the human world; tradition is that which allows the spirit of human life to be continuous with the spirit of natural life from which it stems, whose mystery and beauty traditions seek to express. The poetry that expresses the heartbeat of a living tradition is the "aesthetic legality" of this connection, the opening to a spiritual world of primary sense that speaks to people and makes them truly human by its speech. Against the idea that tradition is the domination of local prejudice, the arbitrary imposition of particular norms, and the closure of autonomy, the romantics envisioned tradition as the opening of a people to the spirit of their culture and the ongoing expression of this spirit through tradition. Tradition is thus a collective discovery, it is the struggle to animate and reanimate human life in its relation to the universe, as if the world were a vast text wherein every hieroglyph awaits new expression. For the romantics, authentic tradition undermines rather than buttresses claims to absolute authority because there is no authority capable of containing or commanding the flux of people's cultural expression and their feelings toward life and nature.

By seeing community as a sort of "aesthetic creation," the romantics sought to imagine how politics could merge with culture and community life, and thus embody an alternative to the abstract determination of society by impersonal political hierarchies. Taking the idea of a free community to its anarchist extreme, Hölderlin refused to subscribe to the quintessential enlightenment view that saw the constitution of the rational State as the highest goal of a free humanity. Instead, Hölderlin hoped that politics would directly reflect the "inspiration" and deliberation of people in their communities. His novel, *Hyperion*, abounds with such utopianism:

> What love and spirit give cannot be extorted. The State has always been made a hell by man's wanting to make it his heaven. The State is nothing but the coarse husk around the seed of life, the wall around human fruits and flowers. Yet what good is a wall when the soil of our garden is parched? . . . O inspiration!, you will bring us the springtime of peoples again. The State cannot command your presence, but if it does not obstruct you, you will come.[31]

One may find an equivalent to Hölderlin's idea of "inspiration" in Schlegel's notion of "fantasy," which he defines as understanding that is the spontaneous "influence of the higher on the finite." In ways analogous to Hölderlin's belief that inspiration is the necessary ground for genuine freedom, Schlegel held that fantasy can be the positive expression of freedom and that it is not incompatible with reason as such. Drawing similar utopian conclusions as Hölderlin,

Schlegel theorized that a community that harmoniously unites fantasy with rational judgment and free will is

> anarchy—one may call it the kingdom of God, or the golden age. The essential point is that it will always be anarchy. This freedom is the capacity of man; it is the final goal for everyone. It is the highest good—but it is an ideal, which can be found only through approximation. These conditions are to be found in an opposition, not in an absolute but a relative opposition. Namely, freedom is the ideal; we approach it through lawfulness. But does that lawfulness not conflict with freedom? The contradiction is resolved when lawfulness is decided by freedom, so that a relative freedom arises. Whoever gives himself laws is relatively free. And this is the condition of approximation.[32]

The idea that fantasy or inspiration is compatible and even necessary to autonomy indicates a radical break with Kant's practical philosophy. An implicit project common to Hölderlin and Schlegel was to bypass the fundamental dualism between nature and freedom articulated by Kant in his first two critiques. Kant had made it clear that one can only know the world as it appears to us subjectively by the synthesis of sense data. Nature as an object of truth can only be located in the structure of the consciousness that perceives it. As a result, perception is limited to the subjectivity of consciousness; the world as it is in itself, as it exists independently of consciousness, can never be known. In a radical Cartesian move, Kant argued that cognition does not follow the object, but rather the object as such is determined by the subject who constitutes it in his consciousness. The fundamental point of this distinction between things in themselves and appearances is that it provides the necessary space for moral action that Kant sought to establish in his system. If the laws of nature were properties of the object world "in itself," then these laws would mechanically determine us as natural beings. In this case, we would be completely determined by natural causality and there would be no possibility for autonomous action.

The inevitable problem that arises is how this chasm between nature and freedom can be surmounted. How can freedom be realized if it is necessarily in conflict with natural inclination? Kant's dualism may have made room for autonomy by freeing human will from natural determination, but this autonomy militates against human nature. If Kantian autonomy is essentially independent of passion and impulse, then how can it coincide with human activity, since human action is never fully separate from sensuous determination?

The romantics found a solution to this problem by appropriating and reformulating the Kantian concept of the organism, and by using it as an analogy for human freedom. It was in the law-like character of the causality of the organism that romantics such as Hölderlin and Schlegel found a political analogy for their ideal of a self-organized society that could render obsolete external force and the legal machinery of the State, and that could allow for a more than abstract determination of freedom. Kant had suggested the use of the natural organism as an analogy for political freedom when, inspired by the French Revolution, he added a footnote to the "Analytic of the Teleological Judgment" in his *Kritik der Urteilskraft*:

> In a recent complete transformation of a great people into a state the word organism for the regulation of magistracies, etc., and even of the whole body politic, has often been fitly used. For in such a whole every member should surely be an end as well as a means, and, while each contributes to the whole, each is determined as regards place and function by the Idea of the whole.[33]

Hölderlin and Schlegel wanted to go further than Kant in the analogy. Since their idea of the whole is anarchy, the means must be consonant with that whole ("lawfulness decided by freedom"). This meant that the State apparatus itself is inherently at odds with the idea because its legal machinery is inconsonant with the whole. By virtue of excluding lawfulness decided by freedom (autonomy), by being in fact a political heteronomy that imposes law rather than letting law be the expression of its members, the State can only function to the detriment of freedom, understood in both its absolute and relative forms. Whereas Kant had characterized monarchist rule as a grinding machine, Hölderlin saw in the terror unleashed by the French revolutionary state the unsaid truth of the State as such, be it monarchist or revolutionary.[34] One must consider the relationship of the organism to aesthetics in order to understand how the Kantian theory of the organism contains the kernels for a more far-reaching interpretation.

Kant defined the organism as a self-organizing being, a relation of parts to the whole in which the activity of each member has an intrinsic purposiveness, founded in the realization of a common end. The causality of nature is inherently teleological; it has as its ground final causes that are invisible to the understanding but that may be represented by transcendental judgment, a judgment that has as its principle the purposiveness (the finality) of nature. If one represents nature in the light of final causes, it appears as if it were the result of an idea that gives it its purposiveness, as if all its parts were propelled by the idea of their end. In other words, from a transcendental perspective it appears that nature's end is intrinsic to the whole of nature's members in such a way that every effective cause is an effect through final causes. For Kant, such a perspective can account for why not only every part functions by means of the other parts, as in a watch or any other mechanical instrument, but why, miraculously, as an ontogenetically organized and self-organizing being (as a being endowed with intrinsic purposiveness) its parts are all organs reciprocally producing one another. A watch wheel cannot produce other wheels or adapt itself to changing circumstances because, unlike nature, the parts of a machine are devoid of formative power of a self-propagating kind. The power of a machine is a strictly moving power, each part within it operates by way of an external force that extrinsically causes the motion of the parts. The machine part is a fragment that has no internal relation to either what precedes or follows it; it cannot be both cause and effect of its movement like the members of a natural organism. Indeed, for Kant "the organization of nature has in it nothing analogous to anything we know."[35]

Yet if the purposiveness of nature is in itself necessarily mysterious to us, Kant postulated that nature nonetheless communicates its purposiveness to us when we take pleasure in its beauty. In a passage that contains a key idea for the romantic philosophy of nature, Kant fancied that

> one can regard it as a favor which nature has felt for man that, in addition to what is useful, it has so profoundly dispensed with beauty and charm, and one can therefore love it (*und sie des halb lieben*) . . . just as if nature had established and adorned its splendid theater with precisely this in view.[36]

That the inclination of love (*Liebe*) should surface in Kant's thoughts on the teleology of nature is striking, considering that it has no determined role in the faculty of judgment or in providing a passage between the realms of *Natur* and *Freiheit*. And yet it is precisely by means of a philosophy of love that the romantics, developing Kant's parenthetical remark into a concept, would seek to throw a bridge over the abyss separating nature and freedom. For the romantics, the extrinsic force of mechanistic organization described by Kant epitomized the alienation of the State, and, alternatively, the organization of nature symbolized the "love" of an "organic community" whose politics allow each member to be intrinsically active in its elaboration, participating in the whole of public life. "We accuse the poets of exaggeration," wrote Novalis four years after the publication of *Kritik der Urteilskraft*, "but it seems to me that poets exaggerate too timidly, that they only obscurely suggest the marvels of that language of nature." The true thinking of nature's productivity, Novalis continues, the "feeling for the history of the generation of nature" even, is nothing less than a return to the original meaning of humankind's being, "an inner auto-conception," a "new manifestation of the genius of love" (*eine neue Offenbarung des Genius der Liebe*) capable of creating a "new connection between the you and the I."[37]

## Freedom and the Causality of Love

> You have lost all faith in anything great; you are doomed, then, doomed to perish unless that faith returns, like a comet from unknown skies.[38]
>
> — *Friedrich Hölderlin*

> All representation rests on making present that which is not present and so on—marvelous power of fiction. My faith and love rest on representative faith.[39]
>
> — *Novalis*

> In its ultimate origins, all life is not natural, but divine and human; for it must spring from love, just as there can be no intellect without spirit.[40]
>
> — *Friedrich Schlegel*

The social dimension of the romantic philosophy of love is most explicitly expounded in Schlegel's *Lectures on Transcendental Philosophy*. While Schlegel may agree with Kant that the mysterious causality of the natural organism is not analogous to any causality we objectively know, he nonetheless argues it is analogous to an equally mysterious causality that we subjectively know: love. For Schlegel, "freedom is the opposite of mechanism" because the causality of freedom derives from a higher form of force, to a form of love that alone can organically connect the individual to community and the community to nature.[41] Just as nature organically strives toward the end that unites all its parts in harmony by a mysterious principle, so too for Schlegel in the human world "love relates to the highest good" and "the highest good is freedom." (151, 155)

At once appropriating and subverting Kantian philosophy, Schlegel believed that the highest end of nature and the highest end of humanity find a point of unity in the human feeling for beauty, a feeling of pleasure that comes from love and that ennobles our spirits by producing love. For Schlegel the mysterious causality behind the beauty of organized nature analogically exists in us as "the causality of love." (150) By taking aesthetic pleasure in the forms of nature, we are encouraged to judge these forms beautiful and to love them, and the love of nature's beauty is a symbol for human freedom. Love, according to Schlegel, is a "precept borrowed from nature, and says: follow nature." (152) And how does one follow nature? "Follow nature means: just as nature is organized, so organize yourself." (152) Just as in nature every individual member strives toward the whole, love understood as self-disclosing freedom "is the core of ourselves," it is a human principle analogous to the principle of organic formation in nature. (151)

As idealist as this idea first sounds, what the "core" of love means puts Schlegel's philosophy in an individualist context, leaving the abstractions of Kantian moral autonomy in favor of a sensuously grounded ethics. Paradoxically, romantic moral universalism is the belief that, as Schlegel says, "there is no universal vocation of man, because every person has his own ideal; and only the striving after this ideal will make him moral." (143) Like enlightenment philosophy, romantic philosophy is universalist; it is "concerned with the universe, and therefore with unity." (155) In so far as philosophy is the love of truth, all philosophy is concerned with unity, the unity of truth that makes things true as such. However, rather than separating the multiplicity of phenomenal appearance from truth, the romantics argued that what is true may be true in the multiplicity of finite forms, and they therefore tried to make their moral and political philosophy consistent with their belief that the difference of forms as they appear may constitute the true. For the romantics, the flourishing of forms of truth is the real ground for unity in moral life no less than in the natural world. It is not a determinant principle that makes a harmonious whole, as in Kantian moral philosophy, because that goes against the nature of things that has as its rule that all truth manifests itself as difference and exception. In political terms this means that social unity should not be a preconceived mold to which members conform, but that "the whole" (the end of politics) comes from the love of individuals, so that in a different way each individual presents the whole. For Schlegel the science of politics should be founded on the higher life of all people, and this "end of all ends" is manifest in the single person "as something subjective and that relates to the whole: this is love." (146, 149)

One of the chief aims of Schlegel's ethic of love was to stress the importance of community as much as individual freedom. Against the contractualist tradition in political theory that viewed human nature as basically asocial and that believed a contract between self-interested individuals is the ground for political freedom, Schlegel held that all people, as political animals, are inherently interested in communicating their ideas of "the whole" among others. For Schlegel, a person is not a person without expressing "the whole" to others, so much so that each member of "the whole" makes the other member human: "a person can be a person only among other people"; a person is a person only by means of active engagement among the different members of "the whole." (145) If the concept of society "lies immediately in the concept of community and the concept of freedom," if organic society is "unity in multiplicity and multiplicity in unity," it is because every different ideal, every different person's "inspiration," is one way of expressing the eternal "higher life of the human being [that] relates to the whole." (145, 149) It is the multiplicity of ideals, the diverse forms of love and its different presentations, that simultaneously makes every person an independent person and a community free. Freedom in a community is the effect of this humanizing process of every person's ideals, of "inspiration" made visible by its diverse presentations, so that love in the community is analogous to the Kantian effect through final causes in the organism: it is a causality of love that is also a causality of freedom.

Schlegel's ideal of a free community is therefore both aesthetic and organic; every member of a community is analogous to a single poem in an infinite poem, for each member expresses an autonomous meaning while simultaneously expressing the meaning of the whole of which it is a part, just as the meaning of the whole depends on the autonomy of its members, and is expressed in different ways by the different members. Thus for Schlegel the vocation of humanity is above all a discovery; it is characterized by an unpredictable mobility that, ideally, would reveal a unity:

> The new gospel will appear as a Bible, as Lessing prophesied, but not as a single book in the customary sense. Even what we call the Bible is only a system of books. And this is no arbitrary usage! Or is there another word besides "Bible," say "the Book," "the absolute book," to distinguish the idea of an infinite book from a common one? Surely there is an eternal, and even a practical difference if a book is merely a means to an end or an independent work, an individual in its own right, a personified idea. A book cannot have such status without the divine, and here our esoteric concept agrees with the exoteric; moreover, no idea is isolated but is what it is only among all other ideas. An example will explain my meaning. All classical poems are connected and inseparable, forming an organic whole; seen properly, they are only one poem, the only one in which poetry appears in perfection. Similarly in a perfect literature all books should be one book; and in such an eternally developing book the gospel of humanity and culture will be revealed.[42]

To understand this famous and easily misinterpreted *Athenaeum* fragment, it is important to not lose sight of the complexity of early romantic thought on organic society. The implicit question of the fragment is not simply how there can be cultural rootedness and unity as opposed to mechanism and discord, but more fundamentally how such organic unity can be compatible with the irreducible autonomy of individual vocation. In a fragment that reformulates Kant's belief that true moral action is its own end, Schlegel stresses the spiritual individualism inherent to every person's vocation: "You live only insofar as you live according to your own ideas. Your principles are only the means, your calling the end in itself."[43] However, in the immediately following *Athenaeum* fragment Schlegel makes it clear that individual vocation is not merely defined by one's ideas but, above all, by the transcendent passion behind them: "Only through love and the consciousness of love does a person become a person."[44] Therefore, love is simultaneously at the heart of the particular (individual calling) and the universal (humanity's vocation) and the mobile link between the two; it is love that draws the individual to realize his or her calling in a community, and it is love that pushes a community to realize its vocation to be free. And perhaps, if we follow Schlegel's logic, it is also love that transforms meaningless repetition into personified expression by virtue of being true communication—the condition for the "absolute," "infinite," and "divine" book: the "gospel of humanity."

### Aesthetics and the Mythology of a New World

In the past everything was an appearance of the spirit. Now we see nothing but dead repetition that we do not understand.[45]

— *Novalis*

No poetry, no reality. Just as there is, despite all the senses, no external world without the imagination, so too there is no spiritual world without feeling, no matter how much sense there is.[46]

— *Friedrich Schlegel*

There is no greater obstacle to religion than this, that we have become slaves, and a slave is anyone who must perform something that could be performed by an inanimate power.[47]

— *Friedrich Schleiermacher*

The symbiotic relation elaborated by the *Frühromantik* between art and politics is based on the hypothesis that only culture reshapes human sensibility and that only a new sensibility can make freedom a political reality. The French Revolution had a decisive impact on the romantics' ideas about social change. Whereas they consistently maintained that love is the transcendent impulse that unites human beings in a free community, toward the turn of the eighteenth century they increasingly argued that when there is no culture that allows ideals to be integral to public life, all attempts at social change that do not first cultivate love in a community will be unable to produce political freedom. The violent failure of the French Revolution provided the best proof for the quintessential romantic "high argument" that true revolution is synonymous with a change in the human condition, one that makes freedom a virtue and radical political freedom a possibility.

This is indeed why artistic activity was posited as a revolutionary principle. Art educates people by making them conscious of their love for beauty and by encouraging them to pursue this love collectively. By becoming conscious of their own love for beauty, people strive to create beauty, to realize it in their community, and this is how a community becomes autonomous, a community of love that everyone can recognize as their own.

How does artistic activity make freedom conscious and a community autonomous? To put it simply, autonomy is the principle of the artistic yearning for beauty, in the same way that autonomy is the principle of self-organizing nature in its beauty. Just as natural beauty is an end in itself because it is beautiful, art is an end in itself by virtue of its beauty. Art, as Schlegel says, "must be complete in itself like a porcupine."[48] People realize the principle of autonomy by being conscious of themselves as autonomous creators, by being conscious of their love for beauty, and by creating for its own sake, for the end of beauty itself. Following Kant's distinction between pure art (autonomous art) and applied art (instrumental art), the romantics' theory of *Bildung*, or cultural formation, sought to transform all applied art into pure art, all instrumental action into autonomous action, all subordination into creation, and all static creations into mobile creations, by constantly introducing new creations and new relations among different forms of beauty. The romantic ideal of beauty is the imperative for all forms of human action to be an aesthetic *praxis*, an autonomous activity that is the activity of beauty in its realization. Therefore, autonomy cannot define artistic activity and not language, or language and not social relations, or social relations and not the relationship between society and nature. Since action is never spontaneously autonomous, action in its totality must be the conscious development of beauty, the merging of unconscious freedom through conscious freedom: art. Art restores what has been lost with the mixed blessing of critical reason; it points to how freedom can transcend the modern antagonism of human construction and natural beauty. Through art, autonomy is more than independence, it is also the expression of a belonging, it reanimates the beauty of natural life by bringing the principle of natural beauty into human life. The expression of beauty makes community the natural home of people and nature the spiritual home of community. If nature is the wholeness of beauty produced by spontaneous powers, art can be the translation of this wholeness into culture and political freedom.[49]

The modern degradation of art to a form of entertainment is for the romantics a consequence civil society's utilitarianism, the inevitable result of a modern economy based on the division of labor and the quest for profit. Instead of realizing our humanity to the full in work by making works of beauty, the modern work ethic demeans production and social relations by subordinating them to economic interests; work becomes the means for mutual advantage and benefit instead of an end in itself. Similarly, the French Revolution's failure to create a free republic is the outcome of neglecting the importance of autonomous creation. By overruling community spirit through the authority of secret committees, by destroying the symbolic institutions that hold people together in independent fraternity, the revolution could only discourage people from realizing their ideals themselves. Instead of being the confidence of people in their own creative capacities, the revolution became a demonic machine, as impersonal and removed from the imagination of people as the technology of modern industry.

The romantics' theory of *Bildung* was a strategic alternative to the problems of both civil society and modern revolution. By radicalizing the notion of art, by arguing that all history is creation and that people must make this creation conscious and participatory, the romantics created a new political philosophy. Instead of art being a form of leisure after a day of alienation, instead of revolutionary politics being an elite rule of self-appointed politicians, Novalis insisted that "every person should be an artist."[50] For Schlegel, this necessitates that every person be both radically independent and engaged: "No artist should be the only, the sole artist among artists, the central one, the director of all the others; rather, all artists should be all of these things, but each one from his point of view."[51] Indeed, "the artist should have as little desire to rule as to serve."[52] All artists must be as autonomous as a porcupine, they must relate to the whole by their own perspective, and everyone should participate in the whole because everyone should pursue his or her individual ideals like an artist. Romantic culture is the democratizing of political life by egalitarian participation and liberal tolerance; it "means being almost unaware of being free in all directions and from all sides; means living one's whole humanity; means holding sacred whatever acts, is, and develops, according to the measure of one's power; means taking part in all aspects of life and not letting oneself be seduced by limited options."[53] The ideal of *Bildung* is the harmonious development of all humanity's powers in a community, a community in which each person expresses his or her powers in a different way and participates in the community distinctly, individually, according to that capacity. The central aspect of such a community is that it makes beauty universal through the uniqueness of its members; it is the work of every person who in his or her own way makes the "love for beauty" visible. The aim of romantic art is thus to revive the sense of community that is corrupted by the struggle to survive in the modern economy, and to strengthen the feeling of autonomy that comes through artistic activity.

This reenchantment of the world by art is the political dimension of the romantic "invisible church," a pantheistic religion that believed in God's immanence and presence throughout the beauty of creation.[54] Art for Hölderlin is "the first child of divine Beauty" and "Beauty's second daughter is religion."[55] The collective love for beauty defines the romantics' ideal of a new folk religion, their hope for a spiritual renaissance that would transform culture into a common creation individuals would recognize as the work of their own higher spirit. Religion does not replace *Bildung*, still less is it subordinate to *Bildung;* rather, religion is the love that is expressed through *Bildung.* "Religion is not a part of culture, a limb of humanity," Schlegel wrote, "it is the center of all things; it is always first and foremost. It is originality per se."[56] Religion is more than love made conscious, it is also the consciousness of freedom; it activates the imagination, inextricable from reason, into a transformative power so that reason is no longer a purely theoretical activity but the practical activity of realizing the higher life. Like the poet, the priest makes the invisibility of love in the world a visible invisibility by elevating the mundane in life to the ideal of the imagination, by giving the things of the world a higher meaning through faith. Different forms of artistic beauty are so many forms of realized ideals, and one should devote oneself to them with the absolute independence of spirit that makes a true priest devote himself to a god. Thus Schlegel's verdict that "there are as many gods as there are ideals."[57] Faith in the ideal that inspires art is the same religious faith in God; God is the universal spirit of freedom that inspires the realization of individual freedom and thus the realization of new gods in their manifold forms. The romantics' humanist pantheism, their conception of divinity as the *hen kei pan* (or, "one and all") is their belief that if God is immanent in his creation, then he is present in everyone equally alike. As Novalis wrote in a fragment with the suggestive title of *Politics:* "Only pantheistically does God appear wholly—and only in pantheism is God wholly everywhere, in every individual."[58]

The romantics' pantheistic faith points to how art and religion are fundamentally one and the same activity. For is not art the desire to see the real in the ideal, to enliven the ideal behind the real, to transform unconscious idealism into conscious idealism—and is this not done through faith in the ideal? Is not the experience of art above all the experience of freedom in making the ideal real, the experience of the ideal within the real, the ideal that needed only faith to show its reality? Religion thus is not only love for the beautiful but the discovery of freedom by faith. Religion is the self-revelation of freedom, the discovery of the power to raise the mundane to the ideal. It is by faith in the beautiful that one has the assurance to realize the beautiful, as if faith were nothing other than the process in which higher life becomes real. It is this radical faith that explains the stubborn intransigence of the artist who, according to Schlegel, "does not suffer any law that is above himself," because the artist's faith is such that no arbitrary law is more true than the inner law of inspiration that demands the artist's faith.[59] The glory of the artist is not in itself the love of beautiful things, but the inspiration that makes the artist feel the freedom to realize the beautiful. In this context, then, the romantics' goal is not primarily the perpetual recreation of beauty, but primarily the revival of a faith in humanity's capacity to realize beauty: it is a love of freedom, the love that sees in the beauty of the world the beauty of freedom in action.

The political significance of pantheistic faith rests on the need to bridge the gap between political ideals and individual expression so that everyone is as engaged and as free as an artist. For the romantics, this necessitates a shared mythology, some common symbolic source that inspires all persons to be independent agents of their ideals while also uniting individual idealism in a common idealism. Whereas love for the beauty of an artwork is individual to the extent that it is a particular expression, mythology can make the beauty that inspires art appeal to the heart and imagination in a popular form; it can inspire faith in the practical reality of radical ideals by using common and readily accessible imagery. Seen in this light, the romantic call for a new mythology is nothing less than the attempt to make the high ideals of revolution the democratic idealism of all. A new mythology, the romantics argued, could render faith in a new world an integral part of common culture; it could restore to individuals a sense for the integrity and the reality of their ideals, and thereby catalyze a revolutionary process that would unite the sensuous and the political toward the end of universal freedom.

What would such a new mythology look like? The romantics were adamant about not determining what above all is indeterminate. A new mythology, precisely because it is to be a mythology of humanity, can only be realized by the imagination and the ideals of future generations, adopting an infinite number of forms and combining with the traditions of different peoples. In his famous lecture on mythology, Schlegel described mythology as the hieroglyphic expression of the beauty of the world, transformed by fantasy and love.[60] The idea behind Schlegel's notion of a new mythology is to take a critical step beyond the designated limits of enlightenment theory and seek the harmony of the ideal and the real that only isolated poets have succeeded in penetrating. As a folk poetry, mythology would be the presentation of this identity of nature and freedom in a popular idiom, so that revolutionary ideals could be part of culture. All thinking is a divination, Schlegel argued, and a new mythology would encourage this imaginative essence of thought to become conscious, merging critical thought with feeling and the voice of inner conscience, endowing life with moral meaning and purpose. A new mythology may be created from mythologies of the past, but more important, as Schlegel saw it, a living mythology would awaken the ideals of the present, and they would be realized in as yet unimagined ways.

While the most generous contemporary readings of the romantic new mythology view it as a charming utopianism, one need only consider the emergence of liberation theology in Latin America in the 1970s, or the recent synthesis of Mayan tradition with democratic humanism by the Zapatistas, to see that the romantics were grappling with ideas that can be emancipatory. The purpose of a new mythology is to make it possible for ideal freedom to be proper to everyone, or to present ideals that contain in themselves the idea of their autonomous realization, and to provide a communicable symbolism that is more than mechanical, in which every person's struggle for freedom is also the most individual struggle for freedom. The desire to bypass mechanistic organization and analytic knowledge is synonymous with the romantics' goal to make ideals democratic. The early German romantic idea of a new mythology distinguishes itself from all other mythologies by conceiving mythology as a complement to reason, a dissemination and extension of revolutionary values in an aesthetic form. However, such a synthesis of politics and aesthetics has little to do with what would today be called "realist" or "engaged" art; romantic thought on aesthetics and mythology was formulated in the perspective of the demise of the aesthetic realm once occupied by religion—it was more interested in the possibility of collective form than in any specific didactic content. As Andrew Bowie has argued concerning the new mythology of the early romantic and idealist period,

> The mythology demanded is a mythology of reason: the
> point is that it is up to us to make up the mythology. . . .
> The synthesis of aesthetics and reason in the name of radical
> democratic politics . . . points to the major difficulties that
> will be faced by Marxist theory in coming to terms with the
> significance of art in a world where the collective theological
> basis of society has disentegrated.[61]

Indeed, it remains an open question whether the spiritual need to relate the inner world to the outer world through faith could vanish with religion. The efforts of the modernist movements in art and literature to create a new world of the imagination, or the existential crisis of the isolated self and the widespread institutionalization of psychoanalysis—to cite but two obvious examples—indicate that the "romantic" desire to personally relate to society and to attribute sense to the world continues to be a poignant issue.

Hölderlin evoked the "darkness of the abyss" (*die Nacht des Abgrunds*) to refer to the growing division between nature and freedom, a spiritual crevice that would inevitably deepen so long as reason does not direct criticism to its own progress.[62] Redefining reason in the romantic context does not mean establishing boundaries to theoretical activity but reorienting reason toward a conception of freedom that would allow for genuine self-knowledge and liberation. While the romantics admired the enlightenment's successful critique of feudal ideology, with Schleiermacher they feared that the new enlightenment fetish of "laws, duties, uniform action" would go on to destroy any metaphysical dimension to action, and lose sight of the spiritual needs and possibilities of freedom itself.[63] Thus, the romantics' sometimes quixotic attempts to reenchant a dehumanized freedom through aesthetics and mythology, to create a metaphysical dimension to political life that could provide purpose without being irrational. A metaphysical dimension to political life: that is to say, a political activity that recognizes in human freedom the capacity to found a world of meaning—the free and conscious development of individual inclination with rational values that Hölderlin optimistically described as "a coming revolution in the way we think, feel and imagine that will eclipse the world as we have known it till now."[64] When today aesthetic life is increasingly defined by advertising and corporate culture, and democracy has more to do with the power of private interests than the power of the public imagination, the romantic insistence on the liberatory dimension of aesthetics and on radical democracy may yet prove crucial to contemporary efforts to envision a new political freedom.

### Notes

1. F. Nietzsche, cited in Stephan Zweig, *Der Kampf mit dem Dämon: Hölderlin, Kleist, Nietzsche* (Frankfurt am Main: S. Fischer, 1982) 274.
2. M. Weber, *From Max Weber: Essays in Sociology*, ed. and trans. H. H. Gerth and C. Wright Mills (New York: Oxford Univ. Press, 1958) 139.
3. Ibid.
4. C. M. Wielands, "A Couple of Gold Nuggets from the Wastepaper or Six Answers to Six Questions," in J. Schmitt, ed., *What Is Enlightenment?* (Berkeley & Los Angeles: Univ. of California Press, 1996) 84.
5. M. Horkheimer, "Reason Against Itself: Some Remarks on Enlighten-

ment," in Schmitt, *What Is Enlightenment?* 361. For example, compare Horkheimer's statement to Novalis' *Die Lehring zu Sais,* in Novalis, *Schriften,* ed. P. Kluchkohn, R. Samuel (Stuttgart: W. Kohlhammer, 1960) 7:84: "While the poets were above all interested in the fluid and fugitive aspects of Nature, others desired, by slogging away with a hatchet and pickax, to discover the interior structure of Nature and the relationship between the separate morsels. The spirit of our friend Nature dissolved in their hands, leaving nothing but throbbing or dead parts."

6. Novalis, *Logical Fragments I,* in *Philosophical Writings,* trans. and ed. M. M. Stoljar (Albany: SUNY Press, 1997) 58–59.

7. F. Schlegel, *Philosophical Fragments,* trans. P. Firchow (Minneapolis: Minnesota Univ. Press, 1991) 56–57.

8. Ibid., 48.

9. For the early romantic concept of *Demokratismus,* see F. Schlegel's 1796 critique of Kant's *Perpetual Peace,* "Essay on the Concept of Republicanism," in *The Early Political Writings of the German Romantics,* ed. and trans. F. Beiser (Cambridge: Cambridge Univ. Press, 1996). For an account of Schlegel's notion of democracy, see "Ein 'Strom des Demokratismus' in der griechischen Geschichte," in Werner Weiland, *Der junge Friedrich Schlegel oder Die Revolution in der Frühromantik* (Stuttgart: W. Kohlhammer, 1968).

10. See C. Schmitt, *Political Romanticism,* trans. Guy Oakes (Cambridge, MA: MIT Press, 1986).

11. For an interesting analysis of Schmitt's book, see F. Beiser, *Enlightenment, Revolution, and Romanticism* (Cambridge, MA: Harvard Univ. Press, 1992) 224, especially 403 n11.

12. See Beiser, *Enlightenment, Revolution,* 225–226.

13. P. Lacoue-Labarthe, *Heidegger, Art, and Politics,* trans. C. Turner (Oxford: Blackwell, 1990) 69 (originally published and better known as *La Fiction du Politique* [Paris: Christian Bourgois, 1987]). I obviously cannot here do justice to Lacoue-Labarthe's provocative book. My aim in citing *La Fiction du Politique* is simply to distinguish my understanding of the relevance of early romantic political philosophy from Lacoue-Labarthe's fundamental critique of that philosophy.

14. See, for example, Dana R. Villa, *Arendt and Heidegger: The Fate of the Political* (Princeton: Princeton Univ. Press, 1996) 248. According to Villa, with romanticism "a peculiarly modern version of the traditional conflation of art and politics is created. The organicity of the political, originally laid down by Plato's *Republic,* takes on a new and extreme form: the figure of the subject who is simultaneously artist and work absorbs that of the aesthetically integrated state. This subjectivization of the state as artwork trope culminates in the totalitarian will to self-effectuation." Hannah Arendt's thought on political romanticism, however, is more nuanced than Villa would lead one to believe. Villa here relies on

Lacoue-Labarthe's treatment of romanticism in *La Fiction du Politique* more than on Arendt's own analysis of the development of totalitarian ideology. For Arendt's views see, for example, *The Origins of Totalitarianism* (San Diego & New York: Harcourt Brace, 1973) 166–167: "Organic naturalistic definitions of peoples are an outstanding characteristic of German ideologies and German historicism. They nevertheless are not yet actual racism, for the same men who speak in these 'racial' terms still uphold the central pillar of genuine nationhood, the equality of all peoples . . . the genuine equal plurality of peoples in whose complete multitude alone mankind can be realized." It is noteworthy that there where Arendt does argue in *The Origins of Totalitarianism* the link between early political romanticism and the whimsical fashioning of fascism, her principle source of reference is, ironically, Schmitt's *Political Romanticism*, a work that as I pointed out, is extremely jaundiced by the author's political motives. For a fairly objective critique of antiromanticism in contemporary political philosophy, see Martin Jay, "What Does It Mean to Aestheticize Politics?" in *Force Fields: Between Intellectual History and Cultural Critique* (London: Routledge, 1993).

15. F. Schlegel, *Lectures on Transcendental Philosophy*, in Beiser, *Early Political Writings*, 150.

16. For Herder, see Beiser, *Enlightenment, Revolution*, 206; regarding the romantics, see 238.

17. For an account of the romantic critique of technology, see Michael Löwy and Robert Sayre, *Révolte et Mélancolie, Le Romantisme à Contre-courant de la Modernité* (Paris: Payot, 1992) especially 95–96.

18. See Beiser, *Enlightenment, Revolution*, 236: "It is customary to refer to the romantics' 'organic concept of the State' as if this marks a radical break with the 'mechanical concept of the State' of the *Aufklärung*. Yet such an interpretation is highly misleading in the case of the young romantics. Like Fichte, they believed that, in an ideal society, the State would disappear." Concerning the antistatism of Fichte's early philosophy, which was decisive for the romantics' political thought and which for reasons of space I have not here treated, one may refer to W. G. Fichte, *Early Philosophical Writings*, trans. and ed. Daniel Breezeal (Ithaca: Cornell Univ. Press, 1988) 156. The young Fichte was stridently opposed to Kant's belief in an ideal State: "Despite what a very great man has said, life in the state is not one of man's absolute aims. . . . The goal of all government is to make itself superfluous. There will certainly be a point when all civic bonds will become superfluous." When, in his "Essay on the Concept of Republicanism," Schlegel stated "The highest political freedom. . . . [is] completely independent of all coercive laws, ending all domination and dependency" (Beiser, *Early Political Writings*, 97), he was indeed only restating Fichte's teachings. Fichte and Schlegel, incidentally, belonged to the same lodge of the Free Masons.

19. F. Hölderlin, *Sämtliche Werke*, ed. F. Beissner (Stuttgart: W. Kohlhammer, 1946) 1:305.

20. F. Schleiermacher, *Monologues*, in Beiser, *Early Political Writings*, 195.

21. M. Frank, *Der Kommende Gott: Vorlesungen zur Neuen Mythologie* (Frankfurt: Suhrkamp, 1982) 146.

22. T. Mann, *Freud in Der Modernen Geistesgeschichte*, in *Leiden und Große der Meister* (Frankfurt am Main: S. Fischer, 1982) 889.

23. F. Hölderlin, *Hyperion*, in *Sämtliche Werke*, ed. F. Beissner (Stuttgart: W. Kohllhammer, 1957) 3:83.

24. Novalis, *General Draft*, in *Philosophical Writings*, 135.

25. Schleiermacher, *Monologues*, 194.

26. F. Schlegel, "Essay on the Concept of Republicanism," in Beiser, *Early Political Writings*, 102.

27. F. Schlegel, cited in Beiser, *Enlightenment, Revolution*, 234.

28. Novalis, *On Goethe*, in *Philosophical Writings*, 118.

29. Novalis, *Die Lehringe zu Sais*, 7:98–99. See also R. Legros, *L'Idée d'Humanité: Introduction à la Phénoménologie* (Paris: Editions Grasset, 1990) 79–130, for an interesting account of Novalis' and the early German romantics' criticisms of modern science.

30. Schleiermacher, *Monologues*, 194.

31. Hölderlin, *Hyperion*, 3:31–32.

32. F. Schlegel, *Lectures on Transcendental Philosophy*, in Beiser, *Early Political Writings*, 155–156.

33. I. Kant, *Kritik der Urteilskraft* (Hamburg: Felix Meiner, 1990) §65, 238.

34. See Frank *Der Kommende Gott*, 153–187, for an overview of the anarchist utopianism of early romanticism and idealism and the romantic critique of the French Revolution.

35. Kant, *Kritik*, §65, 238.

36. Ibid., §67, 244.

37. Novalis, *Die Lehringe zu Sais*, 7:101.

38. Hölderlin, *Hyperion*, 3:42.

39. Novalis, *General Draft*, 134.

40. Schlegel, *Philosophical Fragments*, 102.

41. Schlegel, *Lectures on Transcendental Philosophy*, 150.

42. F. Schlegel, *Ideas*, in Beiser, *Early Political Writings*, 133.

43. Schlegel, *Philosophical Fragments*, 101.

44. Ibid.

45. Novalis, *Fragments from the Notebooks*, in Beiser, *Early Political Writings*, 133.

46. Schlegel, *Philosophical Fragments*, 70.

47. F. Schleiermacher, cited in Beiser, *Enlightenment, Romanticism*, 233.

48. Schlegel, *Philosophical Fragments*, 45.

49. See T. Todorov "La Crise Romantique," in *Théories du Symbole* (Paris: Editions du Seuil, 1977) 179–260, for an in-depth discussion of how the

romantic philosophy of art opposes artistic production that is a "genetic imitation" of nature capable of revealing the spiritual in the natural to a "symptomatic imitation" of nature that is merely formal, and as such fails to express spirit. Todorov's argument is that the romantic philosophy of art is less interested in the appearance of nature than in nature's "artistic instinct," the mobile process of becoming as against the stasis of the already developed. In other words, the romantics viewed artistic activity as a productivity that has no end outside itself, in which the activity of spirit is given priority over the substance that symbolizes its presence.

50. Novalis, *Faith and Love*, in Beiser, *Early Political Writings*, 48.

51. Schlegel, *Philosophical Writings*, 104.

52. Ibid., 99.

53. Ibid., 91.

54. For Novalis, the invisible church is the "full yearning to see heaven on earth" and its essence "will be genuine freedom." See Novalis, *Christianity or Europe*, in Beiser, *Early Political Writings*, 78. Hölderlin conceives the church as the world's second age, when "there will be but one Beauty; and man and nature will be united in one all embracing divinity." See his *Hyperion*, 3:74. Schlegel describes the church as "a completely spiritual community" without laws or constitution. "It rests on absolute freedom and is progressive *ad infinitum.*" See his *Lectures on Transcendental Philosophy*, 146. The idea of the church was probably developed in the various associations of the Free Masons. Its two main tenets were faith and action, the idea being the inner development of spirituality as opposed to the construction of external institutions that represent and alienate this spirituality—thus the invisibility of the church. Amazingly, the original incentive came at least in part from Kant, who in *Religion within the Limits of Reason Alone* evoked a church that could realize the kingdom of God on earth. The romantic assumption is that if this kingdom has been lost, it is still present in us in the form of nostalgia.

55. Hölderlin, *Hyperion*, 3:79.

56. Schlegel, *Philosophical Fragments*, 95.

57. Ibid., 82.

58. Novalis, *General Draft*, 127.

59. F. Schlegel, *Athenaeum Fragments*, in Beiser, *Early Political Writings*, 117.

60. See F. Schlegel, *Rede über die Mythologie*, in *Schriften und Fragmente*, ed. E. Behler (Stuttgart: A. Kröner, 1956) 121–126.

61. A. Bowie, *Aesthetics and Subjectivity: From Kant to Nietzsche* (Manchester: Manchester Univ. Press, 1990) 52.

62. Hölderlin, *Hyperion*, 3:43.

63. F. Schleiermacher, *Monologues*, 179.

64. F. Hölderlin, *Briefe*, in *Sämtliche Werke*, ed. F. Beissner (Stuttgart: W. Kohlhammer, 1957) 6/I:229.

# ON THE SUBJECT OF ROMANTIC WOMEN
## *Annie Le Brun*

*Photo by Anne Sauser-Hall*

It is out of convenience that people have spoken and that we still speak today of romantic women since, in truth, there is no type of "the romantic woman." Furthermore, that is what is fascinating about this handful of young women who knew, I think, before Rimbaud's injunction, how to reinvent love.

For what strikes us first is the diversity of their characters, the differences in their behaviors: it is indeed impossible to find any resemblance between Bettina's turbulence, Suzette Gontard's passion, Caroline Schlegel's vivacity, Caroline von Günderode's despair, Sophie von Kühn's innocence, and Henriette Vogel's audacity. . . . Nonetheless, as dissimilar as they may be, these young women have in common a complete lack of pretense of playing a role. Not that it is a question of self-effacement—and the best example is Bettina, of whom Rilke wrote

> that strange Bettina has, through all her letters, created a space, one that is like a world of enlarged dimensions. From the start she threw herself into everything as if she had already overtaken her death. Everywhere she profoundly installed herself in being, she became a part of it, and everything that happened to her was for all eternity contained in nature. . . .

And, paradoxically, this evocation that fits Bettina so well could more or less fit all the women of romanticism to the precise extent that none of them takes pains to be: they *are*. And they *are* intimately, innocently, impudently, madly, scandalously, tragically, but always, always, superbly.

And it is above all in this sense that they completely escape the secondary role that is, and especially will be, usually reserved for women in various intellectual adventures. They are *the heart* and *at the heart* of romanticism in the same way as their friends, their lovers, their brothers. . . . In the tumultuous and desperate chronicle of the liberation of women, I see no other figures move so freely. A little as if these women were characterized by a *weightlessness* that could follow only freedom. A weightlessness that common sense soon caricatured as weakness. We know the cliché of the young romantic woman, diaphanous, evanescent—the opposite of what these young women were. For this weightlessness is the weightlessness of excess, of the game played to the point of death, of the intensity of the moment, of the impatience to live. . . . It is the weightlessness of life returned to itself, stripped of what holds it back, of what separates. "It's as if I were thrust into everything I look at," Bettina would say.

And here two questions arise:

(1) How, when the feminist idea had hardly begun to exist, did a few young women spontaneously find themselves risking their lives in the alarming freedom of being what they are?

(2) How is it that contemporary feminists, otherwise eager to find ancestors, have up to now literally censored the existence of these women of romanticism?

The two questions are in fact connected. And the silence shrouding these women of romanticism seems to me perfectly natural given that there is no attitude less irreconcilable with Bettina professing to "dream upright" than that of any contemporary feminist busy certifying the realities of her protest, not to mention her recrimination. How indeed could people who are in the process of creating an ideology based on the insurmountable difference between the sexes recognize themselves in lives bent on losing or finding themselves in the *lovers' quest?* Isn't it a question of choices that are not so much irreconcilable as incompatible? And is not every militant ideology inherently interested in warding off the "disturbing strangeness" that is at work in the depths of individuality? Is it not this that opposes the politics of profit and ideological productivity to the poetic prodigality of life? So the distinction becomes very clear: it is the withdrawal of the Same that resists the opening toward the Other; or, in other words, it is the enlistment under a uniform of thought, feminist or otherwise, that is opposed to an indomitable *inner desertion.* An inner desertion that can attain the absolute revolt of Caroline von Gürderode, who wrote just before she stabbed herself on the banks of the Rhine: "I was filled with a nostalgia that did not know the object of its desire, and I was always searching and never finding what I was searching for."

Of this revolt, without which the idea of freedom is reduced to being only a means of socio-economic development, without which love is reduced to an individual weakness; of this revolt, of this thirst for the absolute, one hears not a word in contemporary feminist discourse, and that is, as far as I am concerned, the definitive reproach that should be made of it. For I think it is by having had in common with a few young men this absolute revolt, this fierce refusal to adapt to banality, that the women of romanticism knew how to invent their freedom.

I am furthermore persuaded that it is this revolt in common—and specifically because this revolt is in common—that permitted Frederich Schlegel to decide, just as radically as naturally, the question of equality, hoping for "the complete destruction of the prejudices that have established between the two sexes an inequality of rights fatal to him who it favors." But it is also this revolt in common that incites them all to look to love as one of the privileged paths of this desperate quest of the individual beyond his or her self.

And this is why the women of romanticism merit the privilege of having, despite everything and against everything, reinvented love because they had searched for what women had never before searched for: love becoming knowledge and knowledge becoming love.

*Translated by Max Blechman*

# WILLIAM BLAKE
## Revolutionary Romantic
### *Peter Marshall*

*Collage by Art Hughes, after* Albion Rising *by William Blake*

Neglected in his own lifetime, considered mad by many of his contemporaries, William Blake is a mighty eagle who cannot be pigeonholed. There are those who stress his social roots and political commitment and those who celebrate his perennial philosophy, admiring his metaphysical and psychological insights. He has been called a mystic, a prophet, an idealist, a materialist, a humanist, and an anarchist. He has been the noble savage of the oversophisticated and the psychedelic guru of the Flower Power Generation. Both the political right and the left have hijacked his great poem "Jerusalem." And yet he continues to soar beyond the critics and commentators, riding the wind of his own imagination, cleansing the "doors of perception" and seeing that "everything that lives is Holy."

It is the main argument of this essay that the social and spiritual aspects of Blake are inextricably interwoven. That is his great strength and appeal. While he may have seen angels in the trees as a boy and listened to the voices of "Messengers from Heaven," he had his feet firmly on the ground in late-eighteenth-century and early-nineteenth-century England. Indeed, his unique attraction lies precisely in the fact that he combined the social and the spiritual with what we would today call the ecological.

Blake was rooted in his age as a revolutionary romantic, but he looked back to the gnostic heresies of the Middle Ages and anticipated modern anarchism and liberation ecology.[1] Despite the failure of the French Revolution, he did not abandon the radicalism of his youth and retreat into a craggy and misty wilderness in his later prophetic writings.[2] Throughout his difficult life, the "Liberty Boy" rebelled against authority, whether in the form of the State and King, Church and God, Master and Mammon.[3] He searched for social and spiritual freedom so that all humanity could free themselves from their "mind forg'd manacles," exercise the "Divine Arts of the Imagination" and become priests, monarchs, and artists in their own homes. Indeed, he set no limits to personal liberty: "No bird soars too high, if he soars with his own wings."[4] (151)

## The Tradition of Dissent

The most important influence on Blake's world view was his Protestant background. It was a radical libertarian Protestantism which rejected the repressive aspects of Puritanism. Excluded from public life in Church and State, the Dissenters in Blake's own day formed a separate interest and constituted a permanent undercurrent of social criticism. The Dissenting Interest, as it came to be known, encouraged individualism and self-examination and had an instinctive suspicion of all authority.[5] It pitted the right of private judgment against established beliefs and received opinions. Its culture produced the great radical thinkers Thomas Paine, Richard Price, Joseph Priestley, and William Godwin, who felt the same enthusiasm as Blake about the outbreak of the French Revolution.

But while sharing the libertarian assumptions of these rational Dissenters, Blake was also in touch with an underground heretical tradition which influenced his thought in a communitarian and chiliastic direction. It finds its roots in the mystical anarchists of the millenarian sects, especially the Brethren of the Free Spirit of the Middle Ages.[6] It reemerged in the extreme left amongst Anabaptists, Ranters, and Diggers of the English Revolution, who wanted to build God's kingdom on earth and live in perfect freedom and complete equality.[7] It continued in the sects like the Muggletonians and Taskites which survived in London in Blake's youth.[8] It was a tradition that expressed social aspirations in Biblical language, that wanted to replace the Babylon of existing Church and State with the Jerusalem of a free society in which people would live according to the Everlasting Gospel of mutual aid and forgiveness. Indeed, Blake was far from alone amongst the radical Dissenters in the 1790s in using the imagery of the Revelation to express his revolutionary aspirations, arguing about the rule of Antichrist and hoping for the millennium.[9]

When Blake added to this radical Dissenting tradition what he found in the esoteric tradition of the Cabbala, the Hermetic Tradition, and in the mystical writings of Swedenborg and Boehme, it became a heady and revolutionary brew, indeed. But whatever the influences at work on the young Blake, he made them his own. By the use of his creative imagination, he fashioned his own distinctive worldview: "I must Create a system," he wrote, "or be enslav'd by another Man's./ I will not Reason & Compare: my business is to Create." (629) The result was that where Godwin developed the rationalist tendency within Dissent to anarchist conclusions, Blake elaborated the mystical strand to the same end.

## Opposition Is True Friendship

T. S. Eliot, standing in a very different Catholic and monarchical tradition, commented on "a certain meanness of culture" in Blake's thought and rather disparagingly likened his philosophy to an "ingenious piece of home made furniture."[10] Although a largely self-taught thinker and primarily a painter and poet, Blake is more than a philosophical Robinson Crusoe, patching odd and esoteric bits of knowledge together. His philosophy does no creak and sway but has a solid, massive, and organic wholeness about it. It is more like a Henry Moore sculpture than a rustic tool. Moreover, it not only questions many fundamental assumptions in moral and political philosophy but threatens the materialist and rationalist premises of Western civilization itself.

The most striking and decisive aspect about Blake's thought is its dialectical nature. He rejected the mechanical and materialist philosophy which dominated the universities and schools. Like Lao-tzu, he saw reality as a constant process of flux and believed that change occurs through the dynamic interplay of opposing forces. Every substance has two inherent qualities which Blake called "contraries":

> Without Contraries is no progression. Attraction and
> Repulsion, Reason and Energy, Love and Hate, are necessary
> to Human existence.
> From these contraries spring what the religious call
> Good & Evil. Good is the passive that obeys Reason. Evil is
> the active springing from Energy.
> Good is Heaven. Evil is hell. (149)

This conflict between the contraries at the root of all things is not only inevitable but also beneficial; indeed, "Opposition is true Friendship." (157) The higher synthesis of wisdom, moreover, can emerge only from the conflict between innocence and experience, good and evil, liberty and authority. Intellectual and corporeal war is therefore an integral part of reality. This dialectical way of looking at things was as essential to Blake's vision as the cornea is to the eye. As his iconoclastic annotations show, he even engaged in a dialectical polemic with the authors he read.

In the end, however, Blake foresees a higher synthesis taking place in the new society of Jerusalem. In personal and historical terms, there comes a marriage of heaven and hell, a reconciliation between mind and body, imagination and reason, conscience and desire, rich and poor, humanity and nature. As in Marx's communist society, Blake believed that at the end of history there would be no longer any antagonism between man and man, and man and nature.

Blake's metaphysics may best be described as a kind of pantheistic idealism. He rejected the rationalism of Newton, the empiricism of Bacon, and the sensationalism of Locke which presented the external world as matter in motion governed by universal laws. For them, the world consisted of a finite quantity to be weighed and measured and classified. Blake was convinced that their mechanical philosophy, which shaped the dominant worldview at the time, made the cardinal error of separating the perceiving mind from the object of perception, the observer from the observed.

Blake, on the other hand, was a philosophical idealist, believing that the world is not made of matter but of organized spirit. The everyday world of apparent permanence and stability presented to the senses is illusionary but not the spiritual and visionary:

> A Spirit and a Vision are not, as the modern philosopher supposes, a cloudy vapour, or a nothing: they are organised and minutely articulated beyond all that the mortal and perishing nature can produce. He who does not imagine in stronger and better lineaments, and in stronger and better light than his perishing, mortal eye can see, does not imagine at all. (576)

For Blake, there is no difference between the observer and the observed for all things exist in the imagination: "To Me This World is all One continued Vision or Fancy or Imagination." (793) Since all natural phenomena exist only in consciousness, it follows that a person's perceptual apparatus will determine what he perceives: "As a man is, So he Sees." (793)

At the same time, Blake believes that the independent and separate existence of the physical world is ultimately a delusion. Like the contemporary Platonist Thomas Taylor, he distinguishes between the fleeting world of time and space presented to the senses and an eternal and unchanging world perceived by the imagination: "Accident ever varies, Substance can never suffer change nor decay." (589) This "vegetable Universe," as Blake calls it, is thus "a faint shadow" of the real and eternal world. It is the purpose of the artist, he believes, to use the "Divine Arts of Imagination" to depict this real world, depicting purer forms than those perceived by the mortal eye. (716–717)

Blake was also a nominalist, in that he believed that there are no universals or general terms but only particulars: "Every class is Individual." (460) This had important corollaries for his art, morality, and politics. In the first place, he hated the kind of generalized nature Joshua Reynolds tried to portray and insisted that the artist should see nature in terms of minute particulars: "To generalize is to be an Idiot. To Particularize is the Alone Distinction of Merit." (451) This approach was central to Blake's way of seeing the world. Some of his most beautiful images are of the minute objects in nature: wild thyme, meadowsweet, the pebble, the clod of clay, the ant, and the grasshopper. In addition, Blake's nominalism led him in the sphere of ethics and politics to anarchist conclusions. Like Godwin, he believed that every case should be considered a rule unto itself. As a result, he went on to reject all moral rules and man-made laws.

## Nature Is Imagination Itself

Blake's concept of nature follows from his dialectical and idealist position. On the one hand, he stresses that "Nature Teaches us nothing of Spiritual Life but only of Natural Life." (412) The science which only studies nature is therefore the "Tree of Death." (777) But Blake here is talking only of Newton's nature, the nature of matter in motion. If we accept that "Nature is Imagination itself" (793), then the "sweet Science" (379) of true knowledge is possible. Like modern ecologists, Blake adopted a holistic approach to nature, stressing its interdependence, its unity in diversity, and its organic growth. If we go beyond our five senses, if the doors of perception are cleansed, then we will see that "everything that lives is Holy." (160)

Human beings are not separate from nature like subject and object, but an integral part of it. Unfortunately, utilitarian and exploitative man has interfered with the beneficial course of nature: "The Bible says that God formed Nature perfect," Blake wrote, "but that Man perverted the order of Nature, since which time the Elements are fill'd with the Prince of Evil." (388) Men in their fallen state have therefore introduced self-interest and cruelty into the originally pure natural order. But this is not true of all men; a few like Blake are horrified by the callous treatment of other species. In *Auguries of Innocence*, he makes one of the most eloquent pleas for animal rights ever made:

> A Robin Red breast in a Cage
> Puts all Heaven in a Rage.
> A dove house fill'd with doves & Pigeons
> Shudders Hell thro' all its regions.
> A dog starv'd at his Master's Gate
> Predicts the ruin of the State.
> Horse misus'd upon the Road

Calls to Heaven for Human blood.
Each outcry of the hunted Hare
A fibre from the Brain does tear.
A Skylark wounded in the wing,
A Cherubim does cease to sing.
The Game Cock clip'd & arm'd for fight
Does the Rising Sun affright.
Every Wolf's & Lion's howl
Raises from Hell a human Soul.
The wild deer, wand'ring here & there,
Keeps the Human Soul from Care.
The Lamb misus'd breeds Public strife
And yet forgives the Butcher's Knife.

Further along the chain of being, Blake sees the plants and objects as having a spiritual and aesthetic quality. In his poems, clods of mud and pebbles talk, flowers feel. Blake's profound ecological sensibility also comes through in his letters where he laments the fact that in this fallen world dominated by the cash nexus to the eyes of a miser "a Guinea is more beautiful than the Sun, & a bag worn with the use of Money has more beautiful proportions than a Vine filled with Grapes. The tree which moves some to tears of joy is in the Eyes of others only a Green thing that stands in the way." (793) Blake speaks directly to those modern ecologists who argue that a forest cannot be merely seen in terms of an economic unit but as an integral part of the earth's ecosystem which nurtures animal life as well as the human spirit. When the sun rises, Blake did not see a round disk like a guinea but "an Innumerable company of the Heavenly host crying 'Holy, Holy, Holy is the Lord God Almighty.'" (617) He was one of those people who are able

To see a World in a Grain of Sand
And a Heaven in a Wild Flower,
Hold Infinity in the palm of your hand
And Eternity in an hour. (431)

## The Divine Image

The human species finds its place within the organic world of nature, but it is the most important species: "Where man is not, nature is barren." (152) Humanity is unique in that it is made in God's image, the Divine image. Like the Christian anarchist Tolstoy, Blake believes that the kingdom of God is within us: "All deities reside in the human breast." (153) There is no distinction between the creator and the created: "God is Man & exists in us & we in him." (775) Man is thus primarily a spiritual thing and is not bound by his physical body: "Spirits are organized men." (577) Blake calls this spiritual human essence the "Imagination" or "Poetic Genius" and insists that the "Poetic Genius is the true Man, and that the body or outward form of Man is derived from the Poetic Genius." (98) At the same time, Blake does not fall back on traditional dualism, separating the mind from the body, praising the one to the detriment of the other. He remains a thoroughgoing monist idealist. Body and mind are two aspects of a common spirit. The body is not only organized spirit but also the source of creative energy:

1. Man has no Body distinct from his Soul; for that call'd Body is a portion of Soul discern'd by the five Senses, the chief inlets of Soul in this age.
2. Energy is the only life, and is from the Body; and Reason is the bound or outward circumference of Energy.
3. Energy is Eternal Delight. (149)

Blake thus sees the unconscious and instinctual side of our makeup as a positive driving force. And like Godwin, who defines the will as the last act of the understanding, Blake insists "Thought is Act." (400)

Blake calls the human essence the "Imagination" but he also celebrates imagination as the most important creative faculty within us. Indeed, his theory of the imagination in which inspiration is contrasted with memory recalls Coleridge's distinction between Imagination and Fancy. At the same time, Blake is highly critical of the faculty of reason: "Man by his reasoning power can only compare & judge of what he has already perceiv'd." (97) But it would be wrong to conclude that Blake is irrational or anti-intellectual. He does not reject reason out of hand but only that kind of reason which controls the passions and serves self-interest: "He who sees the Ratio only, sees himself only." (98) Reason, in Blake's mythology, becomes Urizen, the "horizon," and is presented as a burdened, entangled, listless tyrant. Blake hates the kind of instrumental and analytical reason which can destroy what it dissects and which argues that ends justify means. He abhors the reason which acts as "an Abstract objecting power that Negatives every thing." (629) On its own, naked reason can only curb, govern, and destroy:

> The Spectre is the Reasoning Power in Man, & when
> separated
> From Imagination and closing itself as in steel in a Ratio
> Of the Things of Memory, It thence frames Law & Moralities
> To destroy Imagination, the Divine Body, by Martyrdoms &
> Wars. (714)

But Blake here is only talking about analytical and instrumental reason. It is the task of naked reason to recognize its own inadequacy, not to abolish itself entirely. Moreover, Blake makes no crude distinction between reason and the passions, "For a Tear is an Intellectual Thing" as well as an emotional one. If the understanding encourages the passions rather than curbs them, then the "Treasures of Heaven" can be "Realities of Intellect." (615)

In Blake's psychology, the whole person is made up of four essential components, which he calls the Four Zoas: body (Tharmas), reason (Urizen), emotion (Luvah), and spirit (Urthona). Blake does not suggest that one should exist without the other. Love, for instance, involves physical, intellectual, and emotional states, but in true sexuality the spiritual is needed to perfect the physical. Moreover, to achieve a state of heightened consciousness, to obtain full visionary awareness, it is necessary to reconcile energy, reason, emotion, and spirit. In his scheme of things, Blake calls this a "fourfold vision."

On the first level of consciousness, mechanical reason holds sway in darkness (which Blake calls heaven). The second level, associated with fire, is the realm of energy (hell). The third is a state of light which unites the first two into *The Marriage of Heaven and Hell*, as Blake's prose poem puts it. The fourfold vision is the inspired state of full light which brings together all the other levels of consciousness:

> Now I a fourfold vision see,
> And a fourfold vision is given to me;

'Tis fourfold in my supreme delight
And threefold in soft Beaulah's night
And twofold Always. May God us keep
From Single vision & Newton's sleep!

Beaulah is the country in Bunyan from which the pilgrims can see the city they are searching for.

Unlike other contemporary radicals, Blake believed in innate ideas. Writing against Reynolds, he maintained that we are born with a sense of ideal beauty and a moral conscience: "Innate Ideas are in Every Man, Born with him; they are truly Himself." (459) Where Godwin and Paine argued that we are products of our circumstances, Blake insisted that intelligence is genetic: "The Man who says that the Genius is not Born, but Taught—is a Knave." (470) Indeed, nothing important is acquired in a person's makeup for he brings all that he has into the world with him: "Man is Born Like a Garden ready Planted & Sown." (471)

Unfortunately, the growing child can forget his innate knowledge as he becomes lost in the cave of the five senses. The grown adult, absorbed in external nature, easily becomes cut off from his or her innate universal ground. For this reason, Blake believes that children, who have not had their visions clouded by sensuous infatuation and worldly interest, are more capable of appreciating and elucidating his visions.

Although we have an innate moral sense or conscience that we can rely upon as the "voice of God," it is no easy task to adopt the right course of action. (385) Within all of us, there is a constant struggle between our good or bad side, between our Emanation and Spectre. The Spectre represents for Blake everything that is negative in the world: tyranny, empire, false reason, conventional religion, and self-hood. It is associated with the Jehovah God of the Old Testament. The Emanation, on the other hand, stands for all that is positive: creative energy, imagination, forgiveness, and Jesus. The struggle between the two forces takes the form of corporeal and mental war:

My Spectre around me night & day
Like a Wild beast guards my way.
My Emanation far within
Weeps incessantly for my Sin. (415)

Nevertheless, the conflict between the forces of good and evil are not eternal as in the Manichean universe. Good can triumph over evil, the Emanation can defeat the Spectre when the individual realizes his or her divine potential:

> Each man in his Spectre's power
> Until the arrival of that hour
> When his Humanity awake
> And cast his own Spectre into the Lake. (421)

Out of this dialectical struggle between the Spectre and Emanation should emerge the higher synthesis of Divine Humanity which will reconcile all the opposing forces. This is the ultimate goal of Blake's visionary humanism which insists: "The worship of God is: Honouring his gifts in other men, each according to his genius, and loving the greatest men best: those who envy or calumniate great men hate God; for there is no other God." (158)

Blake's contemporary radicals like Paine and Godwin rejected the notion of innate ideas because they believed that it could be used to justify social inequality. Blake, however, felt that a belief in innate intelligence offered no grounds for social discrimination. Not everyone is born a genius, but for Blake everyone is equally made in the divine image and has a divine potential. This led Blake to talk in terms of Universal Humanity while recognizing local differences: "As all men are alike (tho' infinitely various), So all Religions &, as all similars, have one source." (98)

While the lawyers of the French Revolution were prepared only to extend political rights to property-owning white males, Blake made an impassioned plea for racial and sexual equality. He deplored slavery and knew of its cruelties directly. He depicted the horrors of the slave trade for his antislaver friend Stedman and was so horrified by his drawing of the "A Negro on the Rack" (1796) that he left it unsigned. He thought the African as capable as the European of spiritual enlightenment and social freedom. In "A Song of Liberty," Blake calls on the citizen of London "enlarge thy countenance!" and exclaims: "O African! black African! (go, winged thought, widen his forehead)." (159) In a "Little Black Boy," Blake at first seems to link the black and white boys with good and bad angels, but he goes beyond this moral dualism by presenting the black boy as teaching the white:

When I from black and he from white cloud free,
And round the tent of God like lambs we joy,

I'll shade him from the heat, till he can bear
To lean in joy upon our father's knee;
And then I'll stand and stroke his silver hair,
And be like him, and he will then love me. (125)

Color is therefore superficial and unimportant: black and white skins are merely the outward appearance of the physical bodies of children which will eventually vanish like clouds.[11]

When it comes to sexual equality, Blake's position might at first sight appear more ambivalent. On the one hand, he saw like his friend Mary Wollstonecraft that women were enslaved in the institution of marriage as the slave was enthralled in the plantation and that loveless marriage was no different from prostitution. Blake and Wollstonecraft not only collaborated together—he illustrated her *Original Stories from Real Life* (1788)—but were also close friends. At the end of her novel *Mary* (1788) the heroine longs to enter that "world *where there is neither marrying*, nor giving in marriage."[12] Many years later Blake echoed her sentiments in *Jerusalem* where Albion tells Vala "In Eternity they neither marry nor are given in marriage." (660) *In the Visions of the Daughters of Albion* (1793), he condemns the cruel absurdity of enforced chastity and marriage without love:

Till she who burns with youth, and knows no fixed lot, is
bound
In spells of law to one she loathes? and must she drag the
chain
Of life in weary lust? must chilling, murderous thoughts
obscure
The clear heaven of her eternal spring; to bear the wintry rage
Of a harsh terror, driv'n to madness, bound to hold a rod
Over her shrinking shoulders all the day, & all the night
To turn the wheel of false desire, and longing that wake her
womb
To the abhorred birth of cherubs in the human form,
That live a pestilence & die a meteor, & are no more. . . .
(193)

To end this state of affairs, Blake calls for an end to patriarchal posses-siveness and defends the right of women to complete self-fulfillment.

Nevertheless, while Blake advocates "Love! Love! Love! happy happy Love! free as the mountain wind!" a degree of ambivalence arises when he describes such freedom in terms of constraint: "silken nets and traps of adamant will Oothoon spread" to catch "girls of mild silver, or of furious gold."[13] Is he suggesting that Oothoon should supply her lover with girls so that she can watch them in "happy copulation" on a bank and draw the "pleasures of this free born joy"? (194) Or is he referring symbolically to instincts which should not be mutually exclusive? Again, although Blake clearly loved his companion Catherine deeply, she acted as if her chief role was to be his supporter and handmaiden.

In the prophetic books, Blake also often presents the female figure in the traditional role of the cunning temptress or the passion-ate destroyer. Los's female Emanation, in the guise of Enitharmon, is opposed to the imagination, embodying both the indulgence and repression of the passions. She comforts Los but also emasculates him. However, this is only half the story. Later in the guise of Jerusalem, the Emanation of Albion, woman represents liberty, the desire to unite with Jesus, and becomes one with Albion.

Blake in reality thought that the male and female principles are not separate and lodged in bodies of different genders, but are within us all: when Enitharmon is divided from Los, for instance, man becomes divided and jealousy comes into being. Ultimately, Blake believed that sex belongs only to the divided world of time and space: true "Humanity knows not of Sex" (656) and "Humanity is far above/ Sexual organization." (721)

## Things as They Are

Blake's politics are not presented as a coherent system or in a consis-tent manner. He had a very low opinion of traditional political philos-ophy, associating it with the mechanical and utilitarian mind of John Locke whose defense of government as the protector of private prop-erty had become the dominant Whig ideology. Blake even put down the wretched state of the arts in Europe directly to the "wretched State of Political Science, which is the Science of Sciences." (600)

It has been suggested that Blake came to despair of politics after his trial for sedition at the turn of the century.[14] Certainly, he wrote around 1810, "I am really sorry to see my Countrymen trouble themselves about Politics." (600) Yet Blake despaired of politics only in its conventional sense of factions and parties jockeying for power. His position can be called antipolitical only if politics is defined in its narrow sense of the art of government. Blake was not frightened from politics but he reached the anarchist conclusion that conventional politics in the form of governments is a denial of life and an insuperable bar to human freedom.

Blake never rejected politics in the broader sense of the relationships between human beings in society. His political views are not presented in isolation, for they form an inseparable part of his religious thought: "Are not Religion & Politics the Same Thing?" he asked, adding, "Brotherhood is Religion." (689) And just as his political and religious beliefs are intertwined, so they are both in turn based on his particular view of nature, society, and the self.

There is a critical and a constructive dimension to Blake's politics. He offered both a devastating critique of existing society and a powerful alternative vision of a free society. Although he pictured transformed humanity living in the new society of Jerusalem in the future, he drew inspiration from the mythical past. Like the Brethren of the Free Spirit, the Diggers, and the Ranters whom he resembles so closely, he wished to restore humanity to its original state. He assumed like them that in the Garden of Eden man and woman lived in a state of innocence and wholeness, without private property, class distinctions, and human authority: "When Adam delved and Eve span, who was then the Gentleman?" Indeed, Blake seems to have felt that "The primeval State of Man was Wisdom, Art and Science." (621) After the Fall, men and women were condemned to toil, poverty, and suffering. They became weighed down by positive institutions, mangled by Church and State, oppressed by Lord and King: "A Tyrant" Blake declared, "is the Worst disease & the Cause of all others." (402) As private property developed, and the State was established to defend it, people became divided against each other and classes came into direct conflict. With the loss of human innocence, experience thus created a world of contradictions, between Man and Nature, State and Society, Capital and Labor, Church and Christianity.

As always with Blake, there is a close parallel between psychology and politics: the state of the individual reflects the state of society in which he lives. Within man himself, a conflict developed between reason and imagination, conscience and desire, body and soul. The sleeping soul fell into "its deadly dreams of Good & Evil when it leaves Paradise following the Serpent." (614) But this state of affairs is not inevitable. Revolutionary energy is also at work in the individual, and history can transform things as they have become.

Blake saw it his express purpose to try and recreate the lost age of innocence and freedom which he supposed had once existed at the beginning of time. "The Nature of my Work is Visionary or Imaginative," he wrote. "It is an Endeavour to Restore what the Ancients called the Golden Age." But in the fallen world of experience it is impossible to go back to an original state of innocence; the only way is forward to create the whole person in a new society in a higher synthesis of innocence and experience. In *The Book of Thel* (1789), Blake implies that when the virgin hears of the dangers to which her own five senses will expose her, she is wrong to fear the world of experience and withdraw. There can be no genuine innocence which has not been tested by knowledge of the world since "Innocence dwells with Wisdom, but never with Ignorance." (380)

Blake lived in an age of revolution and like most of his fellow radicals experienced the extremes of hope and disappointment. He lived at a time when the Nation State in Britain oppressed and exploited the people who came under its way both at home and in the colonies in India and America. He witnessed the Industrial Revolution which not only threatened his craft as an engraver but was turning England's green and pleasant land into a polluted desert of dark satanic mills. In the new cities, he saw "turrets & towers & domes/ Whose smoke destroy'd the pleasant gardens, & whose running kennels/ Chok'd the bright rivers." (361) To the north, the new factories of England belched smoke and fire and consumed workers; from the south came the din of revolutionary war and the stench of rotting corpses on the battlefields of Europe.

And yet as a boy, Blake had been thrilled by the news of the American Revolution and as a young man had greeted with wild enthusiasm the French Revolution, convinced that it would inaugurate a new reign of peace, prosperity, and freedom on earth. He became deeply disappointed when the Revolution degenerated into the Terror and horrified when Britain went to war with France. In 1800, he recalled how in his life a "mighty & awful change" threatened the earth and despaired how it ended in war:

The American War began. All its dark horrors passed before
    my face
Across the Atlantic to France. Then the French Revolution
    commenc'd in thick clouds,
And My Angels have told me that seeing such visions I could
    not subsist on the Earth. . . . (799)

But Blake never lost in his darkest moments his vision of a free society which the two revolutions had inspired. While most of his radical contemporaries went over to the reaction or fell by the wayside, Blake remained faithful to his libertarian and egalitarian ideals. He always believed that "When the Reverence for Government is lost it is better than when it is found." (401)

## The Golden Age Restored

Despite his devastating critique of his contemporary world, Blake did not despair. He offered an alternative system of values and believed that it was possible to create a new society which would be both free and fulfilling. The first thing to do was to get rid of repressive religion, loveless marriage, and war. As "An ancient Proverb" has it:

Remove away that black'ning church:
Remove away that marriage hearse:
Remove away that man of blood:
You'll quite remove the ancient curse. (176)

Blake does not elaborate a comprehensive and rigid moral code. Like the Brethren of the Free Spirit, he goes beyond conventional definitions of good and evil to suggest Divine Humanity is incapable of sin.[15] As an antinomian and libertarian, he admires Jesus precisely because he rejected moral principles and broke the ten commandments. Nevertheless, Blake's fundamental values do come through in his writing. They are both simple and sublime, available to every person regardless of wealth or rank or intelligence.

Jesus personified what Blake valued most: forgiveness, energy, and creativity. Blake shaped Jesus in his mythology to his own subversive and revolutionary ends and argued that he rejected all hierarchies and tyrannies: "The Kingdom of Heaven is the direct Negation of Earthly domination." (407) Even the summation of Jesus's teaching in the golden rule of loving one's neighbor can be applied too rigidly: "He has observ'd the Golden Rule," Blake writes, "Till he's become the Golden Fool." (540) The key to Christianity for Blake is not to be found in the threat of punishment but in forgiveness: "The Gospel is forgiveness of Sins & has No Moral Precepts." (395)

Blake is totally opposed to a stoical or repressive approach to life; in a marginal note to Lavater; he observes that "True Christian philosophy" teaches the "most refined Epicurism" and the maximum amount of enjoyment. (75) And while accepting the claims of both sensual and intellectual pleasure, Blake believes that the highest degree of enjoyment comes from creative energy: "Energy is Eternal Delight." (149) He knew of no other Christianity and no other Gospel than the "liberty both of body & mind to exercise the Divine Arts of Imagination." (716–17)

Just as Blake refused to develop a rigid moral code, so he declined to elaborate a formal blueprint of a free society. He does, however, suggest what direction a free society might take. Early in his life, the experience of the American and French Revolutions had filled him with hope. In the *Songs of Innocence* (1789) he sketched a picture of how things might be: caring elders look after children playing on the echoing green; chimney sweepers leap and laugh in the sun; black and white children respect and love each other; and thousands of little boys and girls sing together in the presence of wise guardians. All is infant joy. The "Divine Image," Blake was convinced, could shine through humanity.

> For Mercy has a human heart,
> Pity a human face,
> And Love, the human form divine,
> And Peace, the human dress.
> Then every man, of every clime,
> That prays in his distress,
> Love, Mercy, Pity, Peace. (117)

Two years later, Blake in *The French Revolution* (1791) looked forward to the imminent realization of heaven on earth:

> "Then the valleys of France shall cry to the soldier: 'Throw down thy sword and musket,

And run and embrace the meek peasant.' Her Nobles shall
    hear and shall weep, and put off
The red robe of terror, the crown of oppression, the shoes of
    contempt, and unbuckle
The girdle of war from the desolate earth; then the Priest in
    his thund'rous cloud
Shall weep, bending to earth, embracing the valleys, and
    putting his hand to the plow,
Shall say: 'No more I curse thee; but now I will bless
    thee. . . .'" (144)

Even as the Revolution in France was degenerating into the Terror, Blake could end *The Marriage of Heaven and Hell* (1790–1793) with "A Song of Liberty," in which the fiery spirit of revolution is born. He overthrows the jealous king, and stamping the "stony law" to dust, cries: "EMPIRE IS NO MORE! AND NOW THE LION & WOLF SHALL CEASE." (160) The Chorus prophesies a time of sexual and social freedom:

Let the Priests of the Raven of dawn, no longer in deadly
black, with hoarse note curse the sons of joy. Nor his
accepted brethren—whom, tyrant, he calls free—lay the
bound or build the roof. Nor pale religious letchery call that
virginity that wishes but acts not!
    For every thing that lives is Holy. (160)

The crabbed and compressed Urizen, symbol of authority and tyranny, will be replaced by Albion who, rising "from where he labour'd at the Mill with Slaves," will dance in joy and freedom, naked and open-armed. (160)

In his *Visions of the Daughters of Albion* (1793), Blake further called for a sexual and political revolution which would bring an end to the "mistaken Demon" whose rigid patriarchal code divides mind and body and turns women and children into objects to be possessed. He yearned for the realization of love through freedom and for the whole of creation to behold "eternal joy." (195) In the same year, he summarized his love of freedom and his affirmation of life in a notebook:

He who binds to himself a joy
Does the winged life destroy;
But he who kisses the joy as it flies
Lives in eternity's sun rise.

Unfortunately, historical developments were to prove that Blake's confidence in imminent revolution was ill-founded. When Britain declared war on revolutionary France, the party of Church and State triumphed. By the turn of the century, Blake and Godwin both fell with liberty into one common grave. Blake's *Songs of Experience* (1789–1794) showed graphically how terrible things had become. But while he came to see life more tragically, he still lived in the hope of rebuilding Jerusalem and ending the divisions in humanity and society. He held firm to the Divine Image in times of darkness and strife. Born in an age of revolutions, Blake never lost his confidence that out of the dialectic of innocence and experience, liberty and authority, reason and imagination, a higher synthesis of the whole person in a free society would emerge.

With Pitt's "Gagging Acts" soon introduced after the outbreak of war with France and Church and King mobs ready to hunt down the mildest radical, Blake realized that "To defend the Bible in this year 1798 would cost a man his life." It was a time, he wrote, when "The Beast [of the State] & the Whore [of the Church] rule without control." (383) But he did not silence himself. Instead, he chose the same path as the persecuted Ranters in the English Revolution who developed a secret language to carry on a wary and clandestine propaganda.[16] He was aware of what Paine called "the Bastille of the word," the tyranny of language with fixed meanings, and sought to create a language of private meaning so that he could express his thoughts through his own symbols.[17] He therefore disguised his revolutionary and libertarian message in prophetic allegories to escape the censor and the hangman. To those who are ready to make the effort to find the key to his language and mythology, his message in plain enough. For all the complex symbolism and misty rhetoric of the prophetic writings, Blake's Jerusalem is not a religious fantasy or political utopia but the vision of a free society which he believed would be realized on earth one day.

In the *Book of Urizen* (1794), Blake first developed his own creation myth of the material world and humanity, in which Urizen, the

God of Reason, is the Creator. It offers the starkest account of the Fall of Man. The creation involves Los, the central figure in Blake's thought, who represents the poetic genius or imagination. From Los emerges his Emanation, Enitharmon, his female counterpart. But the world does not remain under the eternal rule of the tyrant Urizen who tries to entangle humanity in the net of religion, for the offspring of Los and Enitharmon is Orc, the spirit of revolt. In *The Book of Los* (1795), the myth is continued with Los creating the sun and forcing Urizen to create the material world, thereby compelling him to define and act so that he can be overcome. In *The Book of Ahania* (1795), Urizen casts out his Emanation, or Pleasure. The theme continues in *Europe: A Prophecy* (1794), with the coming of war between England and France heralded by Enitharmon imposing her dominion on the world. But terrible Orc is still ready waiting for the coming revolution: "And in the vineyards of red France appear'd the light of his fury." (245)

Although Blake began to express himself increasingly in the convoluted allegories of his prophetic writings, his libertarian vision shone as brightly as before. In swelling rhetoric, he may have presented the revolution in the apocalyptic language of the Gnostic sects, in terms of a Last Judgment bringing about the Everlasting Gospel in Jerusalem, but the celebration of moral, sexual, and social freedom is as vigorous and enthusiastic as ever. *Vala, or the Four Zoas*, written between 1795 and 1804, is full of prophetic gloom, but at the end Los and Enitharmon build Jerusalem. With the sound of the trumpet of the Last Judgment

> The thrones of Kings are shaken, they have lost their robes & crowns,
> The poor smite their oppressors, they awake up to the harvest,
> The naked warriors rush together down to the sea shore
> Trembling before the multitudes of slaves now set at liberty:
> They are become like wintry flocks, like forests strip'd of leaves:
> The oppressed pursue like the wind; there is no room for escape. (357)[18]

Out of the inevitable struggle of heaven and hell, innocence and experience, intellectual and physical war, Blake was convinced that

Jerusalem, the city within and without, could be built. In his preface to *Milton*, written between 1804 and 1808, when radical political hopes were at a nadir in Britain, Blake exclaims

> Rouze up, O Young Men of the New Age! set your foreheads against the ignorant Hirelings! For we have Hirelings in the Camp, the Court & the University, who would, if they could, for ever depress Mental & prolong Corporeal War. (480)

He recommits himself to the intellectual and social struggle:

> I will not cease from Mental Fight,
> Nor shall my Sword sleep in my hand
> Till we have built Jerusalem
> In England's green & pleasant Land. (481)

Milton foretells that the Children of Jerusalem will be saved from slavery. They will be redeemed from the tyrannic law of "Satan, the Selfhood," the creator of natural religion and the legislator of moral laws which curb the passions. But in order for the "Eternal Man" to be free, it will first be necessary to destroy the "Negation of the Reasoning Power" in man by self-examination. In Blake's dialectic, it is necessary to negate the negation. Milton, the inspired man, declares

> "There is a Negation, & there is a Contrary:
> The Negation must be destroyd to redeem the Contraries.
> The Negation is the Spectre, the Reasoning Power in Man:
> This is a false Body, and Incrustation over my Immortal
> Spirit, a Selfhood which must be put off & annihilated alway.
> To cleanse the Face of my Spirit by Self-examination,
>
> To bathe in the Waters of Life, to wash off the Not Human,
> I come to Self-annihilation & the grandeur of Inspiration,
> To cast off Rational Demonstration by Faith in the Saviour,
> To cast off the rotten rags of Memory by Inspiration,
> To cast off Bacon, Locke & Newton from Albion's covering,
> To take off his filthy garments & clothe him with Imagination,
> To cast aside from Poetry all that is not Inspiration,

That it no longer shall dare to mock with the aspersions of
    Madness
Cast on the Inspired by the tame high finisher of paltry Blots
Indefinite, or paltry Rhymes, or paltry Harmonies,
Who creeps into State Government like a catterpiller to
    destroy. . . ." (533)

In Blake's great culminating statement, *Jerusalem*, completed in 1820, the oppression of Church and State is at last cast off. Humanity realizes its divine potential and lives in peace and love. The moral law, imposed as a curse, is no longer valid. The division between the sexes ceases and the Eternal Man bearing the stamp of the Divine Image stalks the land from Amazonia to Siberia. Within every person, Blake insists, there is Jerusalem:

In great Eternity every particular Form gives forth or Emanates
Its own peculiar Light, & the Form is the Divine Vision
And the Light is his Garment. This is Jerusalem in every Man,
A Tent & Tabernacle of Mutual Forgiveness, Male & Female
    Clothings.
And Jerusalem is called Liberty among the Children of Albion.
    (684)

In his old age, Blake's revolutionary views inevitably made him an outsider. A republican and an anarchist, he could hardly feel at home in Tory England. Apart from Godwin and Hazlitt, nearly all the old radicals of his generation had died or lost their way. In 1827, he wrote to a friend, "since the French Revolution Englishmen are all Intermeasurable One by Another, Certainly a happy state of Agreement to which I for One do not Agree." (878) In the same year, in his annotations to Thornton's *New Translation of the Lord's Prayer*, Blake offered his own liturgy. It shows that for all the complexity of his imaginative world and the depth of his alienation from the everyday world, he was still calling for economic justice and social freedom to prevail on earth. He continued to pray for an end to capitalist exploitation (Price), repressive morality (Satan), and political authority (Caesar). Praying to Jesus, not God, he declares

Give us This Eternal Day our own right of Bread by taking away Money or debtor Tax & Value or Price, as we have all Things Common among us. Every thing has as much right to Eternal Life as God, who is the Servant of Man. His Judgment shall be Forgiveness that he may be consum'd in his own Shame.
Leave us not in Parsimony, Satan's Kingdom; liberate us from the Natural man & [*words illegible*] Kingdom.
For thine is the Kingdom & the Power & the Glory & not Caesar's or Satan's. Amen. (788)

Blake's prophetic vision is not merely that of a spiritual New Age. His view of paradise has its roots in the "sunny side" of eighteenth-century London life as well as in the hills, sky, and sea of the Sussex coast.[19] He is undoubtedly a visionary, but he combines mysticism with social radicalism and common sense. He valued above all bread, music, and the laughter of children. He asked for a fair price for the depiction of ideal beauty. Like the Brethren of the Free Spirit and the Ranters before him and like Godwin in his own day, his vision is of a free society which transcends conventional politics and the struggle for power and which ensures that every individual is "King & Priest in his own House." (879) It is a society based on mutual aid, for "Brotherhood is religion," (689) and complete forbearance, for "What is Liberty without Universal Toleration?" (413) It is a society which would allow communal individuality to flourish, combining voluntary cooperation with personal autonomy. Men and women would live in sexual equality and enjoy free love. Human relations would no longer be corroded by the cash nexus. Workers would receive the product of their labor and all would enjoy the fruits of the earth in common. Human beings would be able to realize their creative natures and be free to exercise the "Divine Arts of Imagination." (716–17)

While Blake dramatically pictures transformed humanity in a free society in harmony with nature, it is not a utopian dream or a mystical fantasy. "Every thing possible to be believ'd is an image of truth," he reminds us, and "Truth can never be told so as to be understood, and not be believed." (152) He may have been a visionary but he was not content with passive contemplation. He interpreted the world in his own way but he also wanted to change it.

Blake made no shallow distinction between theory and practice since "Thought is Act." (400) At the same time, he believed that one could begin to realize a free society here and now. It is not necessary to wait for a cataclysmic upheaval or divine intervention. Everyone can begin to change society by changing their own lives: "Whenever any Individual Rejects Error & Embraces Truth, a Last Judgment passes upon that Individual." (613) If one cleanses the doors of perception, one will see everything as it is, infinite, living, and holy. Blake believed that the political is the personal, and called for individual rebellion in everyday life even while working for a total transformation of society.

In his own life, Blake was an outsider, an eccentric living in virtual internal exile. He lived in a State of "Empire or Tax" (777) in which on his own account all visionary men were accounted madmen. Yet we can now see him at the center of the Age of Revolution in which he lived and as a key figure in English romanticism. He is the quintessential revolutionary romantic.

We continue to live in a very similar world, with warring nation states threatening to engulf the whole planet in an unimaginable cataclysm. Instrumental reason, unchecked by feeling and uninformed by the imagination, coolly plans the total annihilation of humanity and the complete destruction of the earth. The machine still dominates human beings who are divided within, from each other, and from nature. The agents of Urizen are still at large.

For this reason, Blake's message remains as potent and relevant as ever. He offers the prophetic vision of a free community of fully realized individuals who act from impulse and who are artists, kings, and priests in their own right. Neglected in his own day, distorted by posterity, Blake's star is beginning to rise as the third millennium dawns.

### Notes

1. See my *William Blake: Visionary Anarchist* (London: Freedom Press, 1988) and *Nature's Web: Rethinking Our Place on Earth* (New York: Paragon, 1993).
2. For Blake's alleged change of heart, see Kathleen Raine, *William Blake* (London: Thames & Hudson, 1970) 52.
3. For Blake as a "Liberty Boy," see Alexander Gilchrist, *The Life of William Blake*, 2 vols. (London: Cambridge, Macmillan, 1863).
4. All quotations are take from Blake: *Complete Writings*, ed. Geoffrey Keynes (London & New York: Oxford Univ. Press, 1972). The number

given in parentheses after each quotation in the text refers to the page number in this edition.

5. For an account of the radical aspects of the Dissenting tradition, see my *William Godwin* (London & New Haven: Yale Univ. Press, 1984) chapter iii and *passim*.

6. See Norman Cohn, *The Pursuit of the Millennium: Revolutionary Millenarians and Mystical Anarchists of the Middle Ages* (London: Paladin, 1984).

7. See Christopher Hill, *The World Turned Upside Down: Radical Ideas During the English Revolution* (Harmondsworth: Penguin Books, 1978).

8. See A. L. Morton, *The Everlasting Gospel: A Study in the Sources of William Blake* (London: Lawrence & Wishart, 1958) 35.

9. See E. P. Thompson, "London," in *Interpreting Blake*, ed. Michael Phillips (Cambridge: Cambridge Univ. Press, 1978) 13–14.

10. T. S. Eliot, "Blake," in *William Blake: Songs of Innocence and Experience*, ed. Margaret Botrall (London: Macmillan, 1970) 96–97.

11. See May Raine, *Blake and Tradition* (London: Routledge & Kegan Paul, 1969) I:11.

12. Mary Wollstonecraft, *Mary and The Wrongs of Women*, ed. Gary Kelly (London & New York: Oxford Univ. Press, 1976) 68.

13. See Edward Larrissy, *William Blake* (Oxford: Blackwell, 1985).

14. See David N. Erdman, *Blake: Prophet Against Empire: A Poet's Interpretation of the History of His Own Times* (Princeton: Princeton Univ. Press, 1977) 113–14.

15. See my *Demanding the Impossible: A History of Anarchism* (London: HarperCollins, 1992) 87–89.

16. Ibid., 102–107.

17. See Olivia Smith, *The Politics of Language 1791–1819* (Oxford: Clarendon Press, 1984) 139.

18. For the political nature of this poem, see my review of the French translation by J. Blondel, *Oeuvres IV* (Paris: Aubier Flammarion, 1983), in *Etudes Anglaises* XXXVII, 2 (1985) 235–236.

19. Erdman, *Blake*, 3.

# REVOLTING LANGUAGE
## British Romantics in an Age of Revolution
### *Maurice Hindle*

*Portrait of William Wordsworth*

The English poet Lord Byron wrote to his admirer Goethe on October 14, 1820:

> I perceive that in Germany, as well as in Italy, there is a great struggle about what they call "Classical" and "Romantic"— terms which were not subjects of classification in England, at least when I left it four or five years ago. . . . Perhaps there may be something of the kind strung up lately, but I have not heard much about it, and it would be such bad taste that I shall be sorry to believe it.[1]

Byron's disdain for what he evidently saw as fruitless quibbling over definitions serves to remind us that although we think of most of the great writers of English literature who flourished around 1800 as "the Romantics," the term itself is anachronistic. The English poets concerned did not use it of themselves and it was not until the 1860s that "the Romantics" became "an accepted collective name for Blake, Wordsworth, Coleridge, Scott, Byron, Shelley and Keats."[2] The closest that contemporary commentary got to naming a movement was when Francis Jeffrey repeatedly attacked what he called the "Lake School" of poets, which included Wordsworth, Coleridge, and Robert Southey.[3] The reason for his attacks goes significantly beyond the fact that they all lived in the "romantic" Lake district of Northumberland, and emerges in his review of Southey's *Thalaba the Destroyer* in the *Edinburgh Review* for October 1802. Jeffrey there referred to "a *sect* of poets, that has established itself in this country within these ten or twelve years," and described them as "*dissenters* from the established systems in poetry and criticism." He sees their dissent as deriving from the "antisocial principles, and distempered sensibility of Rousseau—his discontent with the present constitution of society."[4] The "Lake Poets" then, are being attacked for publishing writings which are perceived by Jeffrey as having an underlying "revolutionary" purpose, since it was the idealist political writings of Rousseau that had inspired leaders of the French Revolution "ten or twelve years" before.

Readers of Wordsworth today tend to think of him as the "nature poet" *par excellence*, so that the accusation of revolutionary purpose may seem amazing. But considered in the context of a British society and culture not only at war with France but deeply afraid of being invaded and overwhelmed by republican revolution, such a response to Wordsworth's writings in 1802 is not at all amazing. The political climate out of which Jeffrey wrote was deeply reactionary, and any publication that suggested dissent from "the present constitution of society" (i.e., monarchy) was viewed suspiciously as a potential source of incitement to political revolution. And this anxiety would persist beyond the end of war in 1815, a time when Regency England faced "the most widespread, persistent and dangerous disturbances, short of actual revolution and civil war, England has known in modern times."[5] In this essay I shall discuss writings of some of "the Romantics" whose work has been deemed "canonical" since the mid-Victorians began investing English literature with the kind of religious reverence usually reserved for the Christian Bible, but which, when re-read in the context of revolutionary threat, reveals a use of literary language that was *culturally* as well as politically revolting to the sensibilities of those who operated the "established systems in poetry and criticism" of the early nineteenth century.

### Wordsworth and the "Revolution" of *Lyrical Ballads*

An explicit connection between the Revolution in France and the new British poetry to which Jeffrey took such exception was made by the essayist William Hazlitt in his lecture "On the Living Poets," published in 1818:

> Mr Wordsworth is at the head of that which has been
> denominated the Lake school of poetry. . . . This school of
> poetry had its origin in the French revolution, or rather in
> those sentiments and opinions which produced that
> revolution. . . . Our poetical literature had, towards the close
> of the last century, degenerated into the most trite, insipid,
> and mechanical of all things, in the hands of the followers
> of Pope and the Old French school of poetry. It wanted
> something to stir it up, and it found that something in the
> principles and events of the French revolution.[6]

For Wordsworth and many others in the early 1790s the French Revolution had seemed to promise a new epoch of liberty, equality, and fraternity for the monarchist-dominated countries of Europe. He later recorded his own youthful visionary hopes in *The Prelude* and remembered how:

> Bliss was it in that dawn to be alive
> But to be young was very heaven.

Wordsworth was twenty-two in 1792 and on the point of offering himself as a leader of the Girondin revolutionary faction in Paris when he was recalled to England. Here he wrote "A Letter to the Bishop of Llandaff," fiercely attacking this prominent churchman's defection from reformism, and signing himself "a Republican." By

1795 he had been persuaded by William Godwin's philosophical arguments for society without government in *Political Justice* (1793) that it was possible to

> Build social freedom on its only basis,
> The freedom of the individual mind,
> Which (to the blind restraint of general laws
> Superior) magisterially adopts
> One guide, the light of circumstances, flashed
> Upon an independent intellect.[7]

In a world where reactionary governments increasingly imposed "the blind restraint of general laws" on a beleaguered British population at war with France, Wordsworth continued to cherish the freedom of an "independent intellect" and the "noble aspiration" to "spread abroad the wings of liberty."[8] Yet Godwin's rationalistic enlightenment philosophy soon began to feel inadequate for a man whose soul thirsted for deep spiritual assurance. It was therefore lucky that in 1795 he met and soon developed an important poetic collaboration with Samuel Taylor Coleridge, the man whom Wordsworth confessed "didst lend a living help/ To regulate my soul" at this crucial time.[9] This artistic collaboration and friendship resulted in the publication of what many still see as the book that marked the beginning of British "romantic" poetry, the 1798 *Lyrical Ballads*. Disillusioned by a French Revolution that had become aggressively nationalistic and militarily expansionist, Coleridge and (especially) Wordsworth now sought to pursue revolution "by other means," going their own way and becoming poetic "inner emigrants" of England[10] whose work addressed what they saw as the common concerns of people in a language that Wordsworth soon described as "the real language of men in a state of vivid sensation."[11]

He used this phrase at the beginning of the preface written for the second edition of *Lyrical Ballads* in 1800, referring mainly to Coleridge when he went on to say that

> Several of my friends are anxious for the success of these
> Poems . . . and on this account they have advised me to
> prefix a systematic defence of the theory, upon which the
> poems were written. But I was unwilling to undertake the

task, because I knew that on this occasion the Reader would look coldly upon my arguments since I might be suspected of having been principally influenced by the selfish and foolish hope of *reasoning* him into an approbation of these particular Poems. . . . For to treat the subject with the clearness and coherence, of which I believe it is susceptible, it would be necessary to give a full account of the present state of the public taste in this country, and to determine how far this taste is healthy or depraved; which again could not be determined, without pointing out, in what manner language and the human mind act and react on each other, and without retracing the revolutions not of literature alone but likewise of society itself.[12]

Wordsworth's seeming reluctance to dwell on the poetry's theoretical underpinnings (even though he went on to write a preface of substantial length!) is not because he thinks it "bad taste" to do so in the haughty Byronic spirit already noted. Far from it. He is concerned rather to foreground what he perceives to be the morally and (thus socially) "redemptive" capacities of poetic language itself, when its subject matter and diction are chosen with the common concerns of humanity in mind. He wants his readers (quite literally) to be *affected* for the better by reading this poetry, at a time when the political culture of which he finds himself a part divides society through its "blind restraint of general laws," alienates, and creates disaffection among the people it exploits. In 1793 his republicanism had been "theoretical and absolute,"[13] but now such abstract *reasoning* would be associated in English minds with a French revolutionary materialism seen as being driven along by principles of "selfish and foolish" atheism. The clue to Wordsworth's "revolutionary" aim in *Lyrical Ballads* is conveyed by his determination to deal with "the revolutions not of literature alone but likewise of society itself," and he will conduct such dealings with the canniness of one who has considered very carefully how "language and the human mind act and react on each other."

Wordsworth's new purpose then was to effect a moral revolution in the hearts and minds of his readers through poetry that refused the abstract discourse of philosophy in favor of "the real language of men in a state of vivid sensation." Such poetic language would convey both perceptions of a healing nature and the real concerns of everyday life, to engage with, inform, inspire, and uplift the human spirit of readers. There is good reason why twentieth-century readers of Wordsworth tend to regard him as a "nature poet," and it is certainly clear from the poems "Expostulation and Reply" and "The Tables Turned" (to name just two examples from *Lyrical Ballads*) just how vital an active, feeling response to living nature is in this poet's moral imagination:

> One impulse from a vernal wood
> May teach you more of man;
> Of moral evil and of good,
> Than all the sages can.
>
> Sweet is the lore which nature brings;
> Our meddling intellect
> Mis-shapes the beauteous forms of things;
> —We murder to dissect.
>
> Enough of science and of art;
> Close up these barren leaves;
> Come forth, and bring with you a heart
> That watches and receives. ("The Tables Turned" ll. 21–32)[14]

But what (it may be asked) is so "revolutionary" about turning one's focus from books to nature? Had not Shakespeare already recommended to us in the amplest terms the advantages of a nature "More free from peril than the envious court" and a life that "Finds tongues in trees, books in the running brooks,/ Sermons in stones, and good in everything."?[15] The difference in Wordsworth's understanding of nature is that the life he sees in it, he feels is in us, too. We are not apart *from* nature but a part *of* nature, which *lives*, and in living, is an element of divinity and the divine creation. That is why we can nowadays see Wordsworth as an early "green." It is also his sensitivity to the lived experience of ordinary people that from an early stage sets Wordsworth's verse apart from the poetry of late-enlightenment "humanitarian protest," with which it can to some extent be aligned.[16] Such sensitivity to the plight of the socio-economically oppressed and politically marginalized is registered in

"The Female Vagrant," a "lyrical ballad" that Wordsworth developed from the earlier "Salisbury Plain," written during his republican period in 1793/4. This poem is suffused with indignation at the social injustices resulting from an already exploitative economic system that in times of war (the setting of the American War of Independence is used to attack the English warmongers of the 1790s) creates even more suffering for ordinary people.

The first-person narrator of "The Female Vagrant" begins her "artless story" by recalling the happy days of her youth, when she lived with her father, "a good and pious man,/ An honest man by honest parents bred." She remembers the charms of her garden "stored with peas and mint and thyme" and how her spirit was enlivened by the "gambols and wild freaks at shearing time" of her father's small flock of sheep. For her

> The suns of twenty summers danced along —
> Ah, little marked, how fast they rolled away![17]

She remembers how all began to change:

> Then rose a mansion proud our woods among,
> And cottage after cottage owned its sway;
> No joy to see a neighbouring house, or stray
> Through pastures not his own, the master took.
> My father dared his greedy wish gainsay:
> He loved his old hereditary nook,
> And ill could I the thought of such sad parting brook.
>     (ll. 39–45)

The daughter now tells how her father was unwilling to sell his small-holding to the "master"—and must suffer the consequences:

> . . . when he had refused the proffered gold,
> To cruel injuries he became a prey —
> Sore traversed in whate'er he bought and sold.
> His troubles grew upon him day by day
> Till all his substance fell into decay:
> His little range of water was denied,
> All but the bed where his old body lay,

All, all was seized, and weeping side by side
We sought a home where we uninjured might abide.
      (ll. 46–54)

This cruel deprivation is the first of many recorded by the poem, until
by the penultimate stanza, by which time she has been robbed of
family, friends, possessions, and home by the circumstances of economic exploitation and war, the material destitution suffered has
tainted her spirit:

The fields I for my bed have often used:
But, what afflicts my peace with keenest ruth
Is, that I have my inner self abused,
Foregone the home delight of constant truth,
And clear and open soul, so prized in fearless youth.
      (II. 253–61)

As Nicholas Roe has observed, by registering the impact of material
deprivation on the narrator's "inner life," in the world of poetry these
words represent "a new insight into the nature of suffering."[18]

But neither the language used in the poem nor its subject-mat-
ter is of the kind that the poets whom Wordsworth attacks in his preface would have considered appropriate for poetry. The speech of
"low and rustic life" he chooses to base his poetic diction on and
which he claims is superior to the neoclassical poetic forms, is of
greater worth because "in that situation the essential passions of the
heart find a better soil in which they can attain their maturity, are less
under restraint, and speak a plainer and more emphatic language."[19]
The political animus with which Wordsworth invests this preference
for more everyday language is apparent in his explanation that it is a

more permanent and a far more philosophical language than
that which is frequently substituted for it by Poets, who think
that they are conferring honour upon themselves and their art
in proportion as they separate themselves from the sympathies
of men, and indulge in arbitrary and capricious habits of
expression in order to furnish food for fickle tastes and fickle
appetites of their own creation.[20]

The use of the word "arbitrary" here would for a contemporary reader connote the "arbitrary power" that critics of monarchs and aristocrats in the eighteenth century accused them of wielding against the vast majority, those who were *without* any political power at all.[21] And the metaphor for self-orientated greed that Wordsworth applies to the fickle language and taste of "arbitrary" poets and their readers, both of whom he evidently despises, is used to set against his "plainer," "emphatic," "simple," "unelaborated," "far more philosophical language," more real because it draws on the "language of the people," convincingly conveying the pressures and pleasures of life as they experience it, because spoken in their own language, from their own point of view, and conveying the feelings of their "inner selves."

## Shelley, Keats, and Byron

I have spent a good deal of time on Wordsworth, for the simple reason that it is inconceivable to think of the younger, "second generation" of British romantic poets having established themselves without Wordsworth to respond to. Whether they loved him or loathed him, in so many ways his poetic example made their work possible, even in the case of Byron, among the British romantics the least enamored of Wordsworth's work (the feeling was mutual, as we shall see).

Percy Bysshe Shelley was born in 1792 (the year that Wordsworth was in revolutionary Paris) and of the younger romantic poets was perhaps the most overtly political. Like Wordsworth, he was influenced by the idealistic philosophical anarchism of William Godwin, who became his father-in-law in 1816 when he married Godwin's daughter Mary (she was then in the middle of writing the radical Gothic novel *Frankenstein*). But unlike Wordsworth, Shelley sustained an atheistical commitment to revolutionary political change, driven by what Mary Shelley later called his "theory of the destiny of the human species [which was] that evil is not inherent in the system of the creation, but an accident that might be expelled."[22]

A major "accidental" evil afflicting the human species that Percy Shelley wished to see expelled from it, was one he seems to have noticed in Wordsworth's criticism of those poets who "separate themselves from the sympathies of men," and which he developed as the subject matter of his first important poem "Alastor; or the Spirit of Solitude," published in 1816. As the revolutionary in Wordsworth recognized, no political advance can be worthwhile if human beings have no genuine sympathy with and understanding of the lives of others. But rather than neglecting the sympathies of others and the world around him for reasons of smug, neoclassical class snobbery, the poet-narrator of Shelley's poem is a "politically incorrect" figure because of what the author in a preface calls his "self-centred seclusion." Preoccupied with the search for sublimity and perfection, the poet-narrator falls into a profound "dream of hopes that never yet/ Had flushed his cheek," held spellbound by the vision of a "veilèd maid," whose voice was "like the voice of his own soul/ Heard in the calm of thought," and by

> Her glowing limbs beneath the sinuous veil
> Of woven wind, her outspread arms now bare,
> Her dark locks floating in the breath of night,
> Her beamy bending eyes, her parted lips[23]

When the poet wakes in the cold light of day to find the beautiful phantom has vanished, he continues to pursue his narcissistic vision and eventually dies in the pursuit. As Richard Holmes has pointed out, Shelley was at pains in his preface to draw "a clear judgement *against* the experience of the Poet, condemning it as limited and destructive," the poem being an attempt "to come to terms with and reject tendencies which [Shelley] had found in his past life."[24] Given the merry dance that Shelley would now lead his new wife Mary as he continued his poetic "pursuit" across Europe so convincingly described in Richard Holmes's biography, it is doubtful that Shelley did really exorcise his own solipsism by writing the poem.

Nevertheless, his poetry shows that he was intent on advancing the cause of political freedom at a time when the poetry of the mature Wordsworth and Coleridge was now seen by the younger writers as the product of a "self-referential, self-mystifying, self-transcendentalizing Romantic ideology." Aidan Day points to this "self-solemnization" in *The Prelude* where Wordsworth tells us how

> to my soul I say
> "I recognise thy glory". . .
> . . . in such visitings
> Of awful promise, when the light of sense

Goes out in flashes that have shewn to us
The invisible world.[25]

Unlike Wordsworth, an atheistic Shelley was not persuaded of "the possibility of a meaningful relation between earthly existence and the invisible world,"[26] seeing nature rather as evidence of an awesome but indifferent "Power," addressed in "Ode to the West Wind" (1820) as a "Wild spirit, which art moving everywhere,/ Destroyer and preserver, hear oh hear!"[27] In its address to an unseen, unstable, and yet terrifyingly real power behind the visible universe, Shelley's poem subverts the form of a hymn to the Christian God and repeatedly pleads with the "wild west wind" to animate the speaker with its power: "Be thou, spirit fierce,/ My spirit! Be thou me, impetuous one!" And in the Promethean imagery of the final two stanzas, the invocation acquires an uncompromising revolutionary edge as the speaker states his prophetic belief that through him the universal power will effect a rebirth among mankind as inevitably as the seasons follow one another:

Drive my dead thoughts over the universe
Like withered leaves to quicken a new birth!
And, by the incantation of this verse,

Scatter, as from an unextinguished hearth
Ashes and sparks, my words among mankind!
Be through my lips to unawakened earth
The trumpet of a prophecy! Oh wind,
If winter comes, can spring be far behind?[28]

John Keats is not a poet whom many have thought of as "political," until relatively recently. Increasingly, influential "new historicist" readings of literary texts have come to pay closer attention to the complex relationship between the language deployed in a literary work and the texture of the historical culture from which that language emerges. When applied to the work of Keats, conveyed to us for so long as "the apostle of 'beauty' and 'truth,'" the "stricken Romantic: a supersensitive soul, brought to an early grave by the hostile reviewers of *Blackwood's Magazine* and the *Quarterly Review*,"[29] he emerges as an antiestablishment figure whose work can suggest a deep responsiveness to the political and intellectual currents of his turbulent time. We have long known that just as the younger Wordsworth was attacked for his radical politics and poetic diction, Keats was also savaged by the critics, notoriously so in a review of his *Endymion* in *Blackwood's Edinburgh Magazine* of 1818, entitled "The Cockney School of Poetry," one of a series of articles deploying the "Cockney School" tag and aimed, as was made crystal clear in a letter by Lockhart and Wilson (the reviewers behind them) to the publisher John Murray, as "a thorn which will stick to them & madden them & finally damn them."[30]

So as Wordsworth, Coleridge, and Southey had gradually accommodated themselves to a society of political reaction, with the originally radical Southey having turned "apostate" by accepting the Poet Laureateship in 1814 (much to the disgust of the younger writers), the political animus that reviewers formerly reserved for the "Lake School" now turned on the "Cockney School." The word "cockney" had for centuries simply meant an ordinary townsman of London, but for the *Blackwood's* reviewers it was a term of political abuse chiefly applied to literary essayist and lecturer William Hazlitt and to the founder and poet-editor of the radical literary journal *The Examiner*, Leigh Hunt, promoter and publisher of Shelley's and Keats's early poems, and the man to whom Keats dedicated his first book of poems. At the root of the reviewers' attacks was their distaste for writers whom they saw as "uneducated." What they really meant by this was that their literary victims had not undergone the "orthodox grounding in literary culture" to be had at Harrow, Eton, Cambridge, or Oxford which would have "enabled Keats to become 'acceptable' as a writer."[31] The point, however, is that the progressive, science-based, nonconformist dissenting education that Keats received at Enfield school, together with his lengthy medical training, by *not* giving him a grounding in the dominant cultural ideology, actually facilitated those "bitter-sweet" features of his poetry that some have seen as "Shakespearean in their power."[32]

Whether the reviewer's assertion that Keats had "learned to lisp sedition" in *Endymion*[33] from Leigh Hunt was true or not, the really interesting question to ask is whether it is really possible "to entertain the possibility of Keats's harbouring genuinely revolutionary ambitions, of his holding an oppositional social perspective from within the historical structure," as Donald Goellnicht has claimed.[34]

On the face of it, Keats's famous ode "To Autumn" would seem unlikely to yield to a political reading. But by carefully reading the poem in the context of its historical genesis and moment, Nicholas Roe sees elements in the poem that seem to justify such a view. Whereas Shelley's "Ode to the West Wind" opens with its address to a natural power that the speaker finally hopes will animate his politically Promethean ambitions, Keats's appeal is more "disinterested," seemingly concerned only to evoke the capacity of the season and sun to yield an abundance of fruits for the benefit of humanity:

> Season of mists and mellow fruitfulness,
>     Close bosom-friend of the maturing sun,
> Conspiring with him how to load and bless
>     With fruit the vines that round the thatch-eves run;
> To bend with apples the mossed cottage-trees,
>     And fill all fruit with ripeness to the core. . . . [35]

The source for some of the images of the poem, first drafted on Sunday, September 19, 1819,[36] has long been recognized as the "September" stanza from Spenser's *Mutabilitie Cantos*. But as Roe points out, if one notices that Keats as an avid reader of Hunt's weekly *Examiner* would almost certainly have read or re-read the stanza at the beginning of Hunt's monthly column entitled "The Calendar of Nature" for September 5, 1819, then one is able to think about the poem in quite a different way. This is for three main reasons. Firstly, after giving the Spenser quote, the last line of which links the harvest month to Libra, whose zodiacal sign is the scales— "And equal gave to each as justice duly scanned"—Hunt comments: "The poet still takes advantage of the exuberance of harvest and the sign of the Zodiac in this month, to read us a lesson on justice." He then goes on to describe autumn as the month of "the migration of birds, of the finished harvest, of nut-gathering, of Cyder and perry-making [and when the] swallows . . . disappear for the warmer climates"—all of which elements reappear in Keats's poem.[37] The second point to note is that this September 5 issue of the *Examiner* was full of commentary about the "Peterloo Massacre," *the* major political attack upon politically frustrated working people to have occurred since the end of the war with France, and which had taken place less than a month before in Manchester on August 16. The St.

Peter's Field meeting attended by 60,000 working people and union representatives had been called to consider and support "the propriety of adopting the most *legal and effectual* means of obtaining Reform of the Commons House of Parliament."[38] When the local mounted militia were ordered to intervene and arrest Henry Hunt, the meeting's leader,[39] they attacked the crowd with sabres, and after ten minutes eleven were dead and many hundreds injured from sabre wounds or by being trampled underfoot. The third factor in drawing out this political reading is that Keats himself witnessed what E. P. Thompson has called Henry Hunt's "triumphal entry into London on 15 September 1819," writing to his brother George that "It would take me a whole day and a quire of paper to give you anything like detail [since] the whole distance from the Angel at Islington to the Crown and Anchor was lined with multitudes."[40]

If we then follow Leigh Hunt's view that September's "noblest feature is a certain festive abundance for the supply of all creation," seeing this "season of justice" as a "commonwealth,"[41] it is not difficult to read into the rich, resonant language of "To Autumn" both a celebration of the fruitfulness that autumn is capable of yielding to humanity and also, as "the gathering swallows twitter in the skies" announce the passing of the season in the last words of the poem, a lament for that same oppressed and divided humanity of 1819, whose harvest of justice has yet to be garnered and enjoyed. Certainly the quality that Keats thought that "Shakespeare possessed so enormously" and which he called "*negative capability;* that is, when man is capable of being in uncertainties, mysteries, doubts, without any irritable reaching after fact and reason,"[42] comes through powerfully in this poem. Its living language and robust natural energies, when read with the trials of contemporary struggles for political justice in mind, seem to demonstrate the claim that Keats's "whole civil creed was comprised in the master principle of 'universal liberty.'"[43]

If it was the love of universal liberty that animated Keats, then it was also a political sensibility that inspired the work of George Noel Gordon, sixth Baron Byron, for, although he admitted to being "a strange mélange of good and evil," Byron also said of himself: "There are but two sentiments to which I am constant—a strong love of liberty, and a detestation of cant."[44] It is the powerful uniting of these two "sentiments" in *Don Juan* (1819–24) that makes this epic masterpiece his most political poem. In what Jerome McGann calls "a comic panorama of the world's folly, evil, and self-deceptions,"[45] not only are the "canting" political, religious, and economic orthodoxies dominating postwar England and Europe attacked by Byron (he had left England for good in 1816 and was able to adopt a much more "Eurocentric" perspective as a result), but he also poured scorn on the older generation of romantic poets in a blasphemous parody of the Christian commandments:

> Thou shalt believe in Milton, Dryden, Pope;
>> Thou shalt not set up Wordsworth, Coleridge, Southey,
> Because the first is crazed beyond all hope,
>> The second drunk, the third so quaint and mouthy;[46]

Byron saw himself as maintaining the tradition of political satire of Dryden and Pope rather than stressing "the break from them advocated by Wordsworth and Coleridge."[47] He also shared with these earlier poets a willingness to be direct about sexual matters, something the mature "Lakers" tended to avoid as they retreated into romantic "claims to originality and transcendence," claims that (despite being influenced by Wordsworth's feeling for nature in parts of *Childe Harold's Pilgrimage*, the poem that made him famous) Byron was sceptical about.[48]

In many ways it is the irreverence and downright bawdiness bordering on obscenity that made *Don Juan* so revolutionary a publication in its time. It is not surprising that a conservative journal like *The British Critic* should notice in the first two cantos not only their tendency to excite the passions, but also how the stanzas showed "the readiest means and method of their indulgence." Yet it was Wordsworth himself, no doubt wounded by Byron's personal attacks, who became so offended that he wanted the Tory *Quarterly Review* to attack the "damnable tendency" of the poem:

> What avails it to hunt down Shelley, whom few read, and leave Byron untouched? I am persuaded that *Don Juan* will do more harm to the English character, than anything of our time. . . .[49]

There is a deep irony about this situation. Although by 1819 Wordsworth was a famous poet in Britain, Byron was, after

Napoleon, "the most famous man in the world."[50] This was partly because the adventures of the capricious outlaws of his best-selling poems came to be confused with the real-life sexual scandals of Byron's own life in the minds of the European reading public who had made him a literary "superstar." But his vast popularity also shows that the poetic language he used was so accessible to readers that, ironically, "Byron may fulfil more closely than Wordsworth the prescriptions of the preface to *Lyrical Ballads*."[51]

At the same time, if Byron rather than Wordsworth had become the more successful poet as "a man speaking to men" in their real language, just how many women were either speaking to, in their poetry? To say it would have been "a good many" in Byron's case is probably true. But the more important fact for us to notice is that while male romantic poets were in their various ways drawing attention to the need for revolutionary change, Mary Wollstonecraft's assertion in *A Vindication of the Rights of Woman* (1792) that the "most salutary effects tending to improve mankind might be expected from a REVOLUTION in female manners,"[52] was also making a strong impact on many readers.[53] The reverberations of that particular revolutionary demand from the romantic period are still being felt around the world today and no doubt will be for a long time to come.

### Notes

1. Quoted by Aidan Day, *Romanticism* (London & New York: Routledge, 1996) 84.
2. Marilyn Butler, *Romantics, Rebels, and Reactionaries: English Literature and Its Background 1760–1830* (Oxford: Oxford Univ. Press, 1981) 1.
3. Day, *Romanticism*, 84.
4. Ibid.
5. Frank Darvall, *Popular Disturbances and Public Order in Regency England* (Oxford: Oxford Univ. Press, 1934) 306.
6. *The Complete Works of William Hazlitt*, ed. P. P. Howe, 21 vols. (London & Toronto: J. M. Dent, 1930–34) IV:161.
7. *The Prelude*, Book Ten, "Residence in France and French Revolution," ll. 824–29.
8. Ibid., ll. 837–39.
9. Ibid., ll. 906–07.
10. See Chapter 7 of Nicholas Roe's *Wordsworth and Coleridge: The Radical Years* (Oxford: Clarendon Press, 1988).
11. *Preface* (1800), in Wordsworth and Coleridge, *Lyrical Ballads 1798,*

ed. W. J. B. Owen, 2d ed. (Oxford: Oxford Univ. Press, 1983) 153.

12. Ibid., 154–55.

13. Butler, *Burke, Paine, Godwin*, 224.

14. *Lyrical Ballads*, 105.

15. William Shakespeare, *As You Like It*, II.1. ll. 16–17.

16. See Day, *Romanticism*, 10–12.

17. "The Female Vagrant," ll. 37–38., in *Lyrical Ballads*, ed. Owen, 42. All subsequent references are to this edition.

18. Roe, *Wordsworth and Coleridge*, 128.

19. *Preface, Lyrical Ballads*, 156.

20. Ibid., 156–57.

21. For an informative discussion of the fascination eighteenth-century literature and drama had for the theme of arbitrary power, see James Boulton, "Arbitrary Power: An Eighteenth-Century Obsession," in *Studies in Burke and His Time*, IX, No. 3 (Spring 1986).

22. Mary Shelley, quoted in Maurice Hindle, *Mary Shelley, Frankenstein* (London & New York: Penguin Books, 1994) 127.

23. Percy Bysshe Shelley, *Alastor, or the Spirit of Solitude*, ll. 150–54, 176–79, in *Romanticism: An Anthology*, ed. Duncan Wu (Oxford: Blackwell, 1994) 839.

24. Richard Holmes, *Shelley: The Pursuit* (London: Quartet Books, 1974) 301.

25. See Day, *Romanticism*, 160–61.

26. Ibid., 161.

27. Percy Bysshe Shelley, "Ode to the West Wind," ll. 13–14, in Wu, *Romanticism*, 871.

28. Ibid., ll. 61–70.

29. From Andrew Motion's excellent biography, *Keats* (London: Faber & Faber, 1997) xix.

30. Quoted in Nicholas Roe, *John Keats and the Culture of Dissent* (Oxford: Clarendon Press, 1997) 12.

31. Roe, *John Keats*, 14.

32. See Motion, *Keats*, 225, on this and on the inspiration Shakespeare had for Keats, *passim*.

33. See Wu, *Romanticism*, 1007.

34. Quoted by Roe, *Keats*, 15, n39.

35. "To Autumn," in Wu, *Romanticism*, 1063.

36. Roe, *Keats*, 256.

37. Ibid., 257–60.

38. See Holmes, *Shelley*, 530.

39. No relation to Leigh Hunt.

40. See E. P. Thompson, *The Making of the English Working Class* (Harmondsworth: Penguin Books, 1975) 746–47.

41. Roe, *Keats*, 260.

42. See Wu, *Romanticism*, 1015. Keats is here rejecting the rationalism of Godwin, as was Wordsworth in the first quote from the preface of *Lyrical Ballads* given above.

43. The words of Keats's mentor and friend Charles Cowden Clarke, quoted in Motion, *Keats*, xxiii.

44. From a letter to Countess Blessington, quoted in *Romantic Writings*, ed. Stephen Bygrave (Milton Keynes: The Open University, 1998) 178.

45. Jerome McGann, *The Romantic Ideology: A Critical Investigation* (Chicago: Univ. of Chicago Press, 1985) 138.

46. *Don Juan*, I, ll. 1633–36.

47. Bygrave, *Romantic Writings*, 162.

48. Ibid.

49. See ibid., 165, 164.

50. Ibid., 172.

51. Ibid., 181.

52. Mary Wollstonecraft, *A Vindication of the Rights of Woman* (Harmondsworth: Penguin Books, 1982) 317.

53. See Anne K. Mellor, *Romanticism and Gender* (New York & London: Routledge, 1992) 39.

# ROMANTICISM AND REVOLUTION
## The Vision of Jules Michelet
### *Arthur Mitzman*

*Portrait of Jules Michelet*

European romanticism, appearing in the context of movements of liberation at the end of the *ancien régime*, embodies that problematic tension of spirit and nature, reason and unreason, which Horkheimer and Adorno described in *Dialektik der Aufklärung* [Dialectic of Enlightenment]. But romanticism also constitutes an aesthetic and intellectual response to this dialectic; that is, it questions the double-edged process of rationalization in the economic, political, social, and intellectual spheres of existence that defines modernity.[1]

The English romantics protested simultaneously against the scarring of the natural and cultural landscapes by the industrial revolution and against the desiccated utilitarianism that accompanied it;

the German romantics, against the bureaucratic *Kleinstaaterei* held in place by the Napoleonic invasion and against the unimaginative rationalism that characterized both the old and the new oppressors; the French romantics against the utilitarian, materialist values, the atomization, and the social injustice of the new bourgeois society.

In all of these cases, the obvious obsolescence of the old regime and the fragility and lack of authority of the new one unleashed aspirations in the artist and intellectual realms—aspirations alternately egoistic and altruistic—for another order of things. Sometimes these aspirations were cast in the ideological mold of a patriotic idealism (associated with the heroism of national revolutions), sometimes in that of a demonic exaltation of the self, sometimes in that of a mystical community of humanity with nature, and sometimes one of these was mixed with another. Common to all these ideological molds was a dialectical conflict between two underlying mentalities, both of them provoked by the cataclysmic social and political changes of the period: on the one hand, a utopian yearning rooted in the transgressional impulse, the rejection of the laws and principles of both the old and the new moral orders; on the other, a nostalgic longing for a rapidly disappearing, premodern world. This world could be that of the pre-absolutist aristocracy, simultaneously individualistic and proud of its caste honor. Or it could be that of the popular culture, epitomized in *Des Knaben Wunderhorn*, in Rabelais, in the grotesque, the carnivalesque, and the charivari. But in either case, this nostalgia coexisted uneasily with the transgressional impulse, sometimes fusing with it, sometimes rejecting it.

If we restrict our focus to French and German romanticisms, we are struck by certain fundamental differences between the courses of these movements. To begin with, while German romanticism may be said to begin either in the 1770s with *Sturm und Drang* or with the group around the brothers Schlegel two decades later, both points of departure precede by decades the proliferation of a French romantic movement in the 1820s. Even if we were to consider Chateaubriand's *Génie du Christianisme* as the French starting point instead of as part of a fragmentary preromanticism, it would still be a quarter of a century after the decade of the *Sturm und Drang* poets. Moreover, the early German romantics—again whether we look at the 1770s or the 1790s—were rebels and cultural revolutionaries. Many of those in the 1790s were sympathetic to the French Revolution. The turn to a conservative, Catholic, and nationalist romanticism comes only after the French occupation, and it is against this Catholic idealization of the Middle Ages and the feudal order that Goethe sets off his Weimar classicism and liberalism.

At roughly the same time that German romanticism has identified itself definitively with political reaction and is about to transform itself into an ossified Biedermeier, in the early 1820s the young Victor Hugo, with similarly reactionary political perspectives, sets up the first romantic *cénacles* in Paris. His evolution in the next thirty years, however, as well as that of French romanticism in general, is the reverse of that in Germany. Around 1830, Hugo and French romanticism become liberal, and in the 1840s we see a radicalization into social romanticism in the works of Hugo, George Sand, Eugène Sue, and Michelet.

The difference in the decades of their appearance and the reversed trajectories are both explicable in terms of the different weight and significance of the enlightenment tradition in the two countries. German romanticism appears much earlier than French for two reasons. The weaker implantation of the enlightenment in Germany, reflecting the weakness of the German third estate, its alliance with an antinational, French-oriented court system, and its incapacity to confront the aching problem of national disunity explain the fact that the early resistance to the bureaucratic state system of the old regime was permeated by an antirational, antienlightenment cultural nationalism rather than by the effort, characteristic of the French revolutionaries, to replace Catholic absolutism with a religion of reason. Moreover, the very weight and centrality of enlightenment thought in the French eighteenth century gave to the mentality of rationalism and the classical standards that were based on it a stability and momentum in the literate middle classes that they lacked in Germany. This momentum, plus the onset of a quarter of a century of revolutionary turmoil in 1789, insured that any fundamental innovation in the arts would be excluded in France for decades. Only in the placid climate of the Restoration, under the protection of a restored and bitterly antienlightenment aristocratic elite, could the French romantic movement take root.

The reverse trajectory was similarly conditioned by the relation between enlightenment and the cultural radicalism of romanticism.

On the one hand, in Germany, the bond with enlightenment and with the French revolutionary tradition was definitively undermined by the French occupation, which confirmed and continued the pre-revolutionary resentment of French cultural domination in the court societies of the *ancien régime*. Whatever potentialities there may have been for some kind of "progressive" integration of mystical-nationalist and revolutionary elements in early romanticism, such integration became impossible with the antirational rejection of everything enlightened and everything French.

In France, on the other hand, romanticism, after its initial reactionary phase, had a highly ambivalent relationship to the enlightenment tradition. That tradition was rejected insofar as it produced a sterile, utilitarian society in which passion and intuition were suppressed. But to the extent that it inspired the French Revolution, and to the extent that the French Revolution was seen as a model of emancipation and of resistance to objectified rationalism, the enlightenment tradition was not altogether rejected. In fact, the continued vitality of the French revolutionary tradition during the heyday of French romanticism, exemplified in the coincidence of the breakthrough of romantic drama in the year of the July Revolution and in the important role of French social romanticism in preparing elite mentalities for 1848, strongly suggests an interdependence of romanticism and the French revolutionary tradition in the first half of the nineteenth century.

The interweaving of French revolutionary and social romantic mentalities is nowhere more evident than in two works by France's most important nineteenth-century historian, Jules Michelet. Michelet's early work, influenced by the philosophical ideas of Victor Cousin, was more in the liberal than the romantic tradition, but he openly embraced social romanticism after 1840, partly in reaction to the increasing conservatism of French liberalism. This left-populist turn is evident in his *Le Peuple*, which anticipated in 1846 the renewed national *fraternité* of the February days, and in his six-volume *Histoire de la Révolution Française*, written in the tumultuous years between 1846 and 1853 to provide his compatriots with a social romantic interpretation of the Revolution.

French social romanticism can be defined as the semireligious quest for harmony in social existence, in nature, and in the cosmos, of dissenting writers and ideologists during the 1840s. As such, it pulled together diverse efforts to write the common people into society, politics, religion, and history. These efforts were the work of ex-Saint-Simonians, of Christian Socialists, of popular romantic novelists, and of left liberal men of letters.[2] They expressed the urgency of the moment in the idiom of the age. The urgency was for the broadest possible coalition against the prevailing system, an alliance of disenfranchised popular elements with critical intellectuals and with those left-liberal and republican elements excluded by the various governments of the July Monarchy's Party of Resistance.[3] The prevailing romantic idiom lent itself easily to the need for oppositional consensus: in the poetry of Lamartine and Chateaubriand, it was an idiom of cosmic harmony; in Hugo's *Notre Dame de Paris* and in the various romantic borrowings from the theater of farce and melodrama, it reflected the popular culture; and in the *feuilletons* of George Sand and Eugène Sue, it took on the radical contours of early socialism. Lamennais had already set a broad Christian Socialist framework for the social romantics of the 1840s, to which Michelet's *Le Peuple* gave an unmistakable left-nationalist echo.

All of these intellectual forces represented a challenge not only to the ideological presuppositions of the July Monarchy about the necessary relation between ruler and ruled but to broader assumptions about the hierarchical relations between mankind and nature, spirit and matter, the king and his subjects, men and women, fathers and children, masters and workmen, and elite culture and popular culture. These assumptions linked the governing bourgeois elites of the nineteenth century to old regime attitudes. For in contrast to the quest of radical forces for a leveling of political barriers between high and low and, concomitantly, for the integration of the popular into the elite culture, the attitudes of the governing elites continued the mixture of fear, contempt, and moralizing pedagogy toward the common people that, before 1789, had characterized the antipopular mentality of church and State.[4]

In opposition to this mentality, Michelet's *Le Peuple* pleads for the unity of the French people in the revolutionary ideals of fraternity and social justice, for the destruction of the barriers separating peasant from townsman, educated from uneducated, industrial worker from factory owner, artisan from master, the poor from the idle rich, and the embattled shopkeeper from everyone else. Its initial section, "*Servage et Haine*," discusses in these terms the alienation and oppression of virtually all these groups in the society of his time; the second part outlines the instinctual, natural basis for liberation from societal estrangement; the third part discusses the social and political bases of this liberation: the social community of the nation.

Thus, a theory of human nature underlies the new community; it is summarized toward the end of the second part, where Michelet argues that the truth of the common people, its *"plus haute puissance,"* its *"grande âme,"* lies in *"l'homme de génie."* (186) This creative genius, incarnation of the popular spirit, is androgyne, embodying the "two sexes of the spirit," popular instinct, and cultivated reflection. He adds that it is female as well as male, child-like as well as adult, savage as well as civilized, popular as well as aristocratic.

It is from the standpoint of this union of natural instinct and reflection that he condemns most of the institutions of Western civilization—religious, philosophical, political, and economic—for their rejection of the natural, for their machine-like and antipopular character. "Machinism" had been in 1843 Michelet's principal accusation against the Jesuits. Here the charge is expanded. The church, though its doctrine of election seems democratic, is actually aristocratic by the complexity of its doctrines and the small number of men capable of understanding them. Worst of all, the church condemned natural instinct since the Fall as in principle corrupt and postulated as the condition for salvation the abstract formulas of a metaphysical science. (172)

Michelet's main attack on machinism presupposes that, in addition to all the moral and material torments of the modern world order, there is a psychological one: mankind has become extremely sensitive to the deprivations imposed by nature and society. So much the more painful is it, he argues, that in the modern world collective, mechanical, vastly impersonal systems roll on in their enormity: "immense, majestic, indifferent, without any awareness that their little wheels, moving so painfully, are living men." (143)

Supplementing this philippic against machinism is a thumbnail history of the relation between human thought—philosophy and religion—and the realm of animal nature, from ancient India to modern times. Michelet reverses an earlier abhorrence of Indian culture's celebration of nature; India is here represented, because of its belief that animals contain sleeping or enchanted human souls, as the hearth of the tradition of universal fraternity, exemplified in its gifts of pity and its infinite fertility. Contrariwise, Greco-Roman antiquity was doomed by its prideful contempt for nature, its exclusive and self-centered concern for art:

> Everything that appeared base and ignoble disappeared from sight; the animals perished as well as the slaves. Relieved of both, the Roman Empire entered the majesty of the desert. Always expending and never replenishing itself, the earth became, among so many monuments that covered it, a garden of marble. There were still cities but no more fields; circuses, triumphal arches, but no more huts, no more plowmen. Magnificent roads still awaited voyagers who no longer used them; sumptuous aqueducts continued to carry rivers to silent cities, and quenched the thirst of no one.

Christianity put an enormous distance between man and his animal nature, which it abominated and identified with Satan. Michelet knew that the devil was a very real part of the medieval mental world, since popes, emperors, bishops, and monks all swore they had seen him and the churches sculpted him into their façades as horned beasts; through the church's identification of the devil with nature, the common people were supposed to fear both. Nonetheless, Michelet was aware of the discrepancy between what the Christianized peasantry was supposed to think about nature and what they expressed in their festival rituals and folklore—such as the legend of Geneviève de Brabant, saved in the forest by a wild doe—and he hypothesized that the peasants resisted Christianity's contempt for nature. What he called *le génie populaire* carried out, he thought, a timid "rehabilitation of nature . . . and the earth regained its fertility." In church festivals open to the popular culture, like those of the Christmas season, the donkey took a privileged position.[5]

It should be evident from all this that, like most social romantic positions, Michelet's had powerful religious overtones. In fact, the socialism of the period, from the Saint-Simonians of 1830 to the democratic socialists of 1848, usually considered itself a replacement of Christianity; moreover, the Saint-Simonians had anticipated Michelet's desire to rehabilitate the body scorned by Christianity.[6] The desire to replace Christianity by the exalted creed of the modern Revolution is the motive inspiring Michelet's *Histoire de la Révolution Française*. If

Michelet initially focused on the "classical" side of this creed (*la justice*), he quickly added to it a social aspect, which he integrated to the "religious" revolution through the concept of fraternity.

For Michelet, the roots of religious and political questions were so intertwined that for all practical purposes they should be considered as one, both in past and present. If the old regime monarchy shared with the Catholic church that represented its moral order the principle of arbitrary grace, the Revolution that overthrew the old regime relied ethically on the contrary principle of justice, which made it in Michelet's eyes necessarily anti-Christian; it was nonetheless as profoundly religious as the system it replaced. In fact, anyone reading hurriedly the first ten pages of Michelet's introduction to his book on the Revolution might think he had stumbled by mistake into a theological treatise: there seem to be as many references to grace and damnation as to justice and revolution, and the only names he will read are those of Adam, Jesus Christ, God, Saint Paul, and Papinian.

This is somewhat misleading, since Michelet was by then a convinced anti-Christian. Moreover, he became increasingly critical, as his book progressed, of most of the revolutionaries. Partly this was because so many of them, educated under the old regime, were unclear about the fundamental difference opposing their cause to that of the Christian faith, and compromised themselves and the Revolution in seeking a rapprochement with Catholicism. Partly, however, it was also because, in the course of his six years of work on the Revolution, a new revolution had broken out and Michelet, after the bitterness caused by the civil war between rich and poor in June 1848, became radicalized. This is not to say that he was transformed into an advocate of violent revolution, but rather that his social romantic idealism became more militant. Thus he continued to infuse his lectures with the values of revolutionary fraternity and, as the conservative party of order obtained ever more authority over the frightened middle classes, his amphitheater became a rallying point for idealistic students still devoted to the Revolution. By March 1851, the head of the Collège de France, on instructions from the ministry, could organize a majority of Michelet's colleagues to vote for his suspension. A year later, after the Bonapartist seizure of power, Michelet was dismissed from his teaching as well as his archival functions. The later parts of his history of the Revolution, dealing with the Terror and the popular movements of the year before Thermidor, reveal a shift in focus away from what he came to call the classic or the political revolution, toward what he viewed as an embryonic religious and social revolution.

He had anticipated the new social religion in book 3, written in 1847 and dealing with the rural federations of 1790. The federations stemmed from a spontaneous movement of fraternity among the hamlets, towns, and provinces of the French countryside. Michelet described in them never-to-be-forgotten scenes of emotional reconciliation between social classes and regions as well as folkloric ritual: rural banquets that local people described as a *Pays de Cockaigne* kind of abundance and kilometer-long serpentine farandoles. It was an unplanned movement of national fraternity he was narrating, rooted in the rural popular culture.[7] The religious points of departure of his vision were unmistakable:

> Everybody is in motion and all march forth as in the time of the crusades. Whither are they all marching thus in groups of cities, villages, and provinces? What Jerusalem attracts thus a whole nation, attracting it not abroad, but uniting it, concentrating it within itself? . . . It is one more potent than that of Judea, it is the Jerusalem of hearts, the holy unity of Fraternity, the great living city, made of men. It was built in less than a year and since then it has been called *patrie*.[8]

As Michelet had to admit, this early effort at establishing a popular religion of the revolution was swallowed up and forgotten in the domestic and foreign threats that followed soon after the national festival of federation in Paris on July 14, 1790.

Michelet's courses in the Collège de France during the Second Republic were intended to lay the intellectual foundations for a resurrection of this "new religion." After the suspension of his course he focused for a year on writing popular legends for the left-wing *feuilleton* press, but when it became clear that the coup d'état of December 2, 1851, had ended, at least for some years, the republican project, he reconciled himself to completing his history of the first French Revolution. This he did between July 1852 and October 1853 in Nantes, where he had gone to live after the loss of his chair, because Paris had become too expensive.

His subject now was the Terror, a long agony for a man who yearned for national unity and social harmony. He saw the roots of the Terror in the atmosphere of war and civil war, but he also saw the exploitation of this atmosphere by Robespierre and his group to eliminate popular as well as aristocratic opposition; he feared the tendency of "the Incorruptible" to reproduce the authoritarian features of the old priesthood and even to attempt a rapprochement with the Catholic faith. Above all, he lamented the failure of the Jacobins to understand the need that so often surfaced between 1792 and 1794 for a new religious and social revolution, one that would transcend the political institutions created on the individualizing basis of liberty and equality.

> Could the political revolution persist without becoming a
> social and religious revolution? The classical revolution of
> Rousseau and Robespierre, will it live in safety without taking
> into account the other, the romantic revolution, which roars,
> confused, outside the walls, like a voice of the ocean?[9]

Michelet wrote of "an infinity of living forces" that were the hidden life-blood of the republic, and that were suppressed by the Jacobin dictatorship. Partly these forces were in the Convention. In contrast to the *laissez-faire* liberalism of the Constituent Assembly, the Convention inaugurated the "great era of social fraternity"—he praised its humanitarian measures for family assistance, orphanages, and so forth. Other important seedbeds of the new religion were the Cordeliers club and the Commune of Paris. The personnel of these two overlapped, and both were bled to death by the purges of Robespierre.

Earlier in his history, Michelet had singled out the Cordeliers club as the source of a rebirth of the Joachimite *évangile éternel*. He saw the Cordeliers as the incarnation of the spirit of the federations, the herald of " the social and religious age of the Revolution."

Neither the Girondins nor the Jacobins, Michelet asserted, were capable of transcending the political, "classical" revolution, which could only survive if supported by "the religious revolution, the social revolution. . . its power and its depth." Even the most advanced Jacobins, such as Saint-Just, were afraid to touch what Michelet saw as the three central issues of the Revolution: religion, education, and property. The Revolution, he wrote, "had to show that its negation of an arbitrary religion of favors for the elect contained the affirmation of the religion of equal justice for all . . . that the negation of privileged property contained the affirmation of nonprivileged property, extended to all." But on both counts, the Revolution failed: "It closed the Church for a moment and didn't create the temple. It let property change hands but left it as a monopoly; the privileged were reborn as . . . speculators manipulating the assignats and the national domains." The only alternative to the certain death of the Revolution was a reconstitution of "the relation of man to God and of man to nature, religion, property . . . on a new and strong dogma."[10]

It was precisely the advocates of such a reconstitution in the Commune, the Cordeliers club and in the radical section of Gravilliers, which represented the artisan heart of Paris, who fell victim to the Robespierrist juggernaut. The Cordeliers club, much more open to dissent and to the common people than the Jacobin club, was a mass of warring factions, a "living anarchy" according to Michelet. Opposed to the left-wing demagogue Hébert, but helpless against him, was the Rhineland revolutionary, Anarchasis Cloots, who, in identifying God with the human race, anticipated what Paul Bénichou has called the "romantic heresy."[11] For a while in 1793, Cloots's ideas strongly influenced the head of the Commune, Chaumette, whose administration implemented a host of humanitarian measures for the poor, the aged, and the young, as well as an enlightened program of protection of libraries and museums. Both Cloots and Chaumette fell under the blade of the Terror. But their message was heard in the Gravilliers district, where it blended with the preaching of the ex-priest Jacques Roux, an early communist advocate of a complete division of all property. Roux too was martyred for his views by the Terror, and the final result was that Robespierre's men, who had castrated the Cordeliers club and butchered the leadership of the Gravilliers section, took over key positions in those local groups as well as in the Commune, thus eliminating any possibility of a further development of the religious and social revolution that Michelet yearned for.

Michelet's last chapters on the Terror and Thermidor were written between January and June 1853. He was painfully conscious of the sardonic echoes between past and present: if the coup of December 2 was not exactly Thermidor, it was as much the death blow of the Second Republic and of social romanticism as the Terror and

Thermidor were that of the first revolutionary vision of fraternity, a vision he believed in so profoundly that he became breathless and physically ill as he described its demise. His reflections on the symmetry of the natural and political worlds as he was about to begin the description of this fatal apocalypse nonetheless point to a stubborn belief in the regenerative power of nature, a certain residue of the romantic revolution that, surviving its execution, would guide Michelet and other republicans through the dark years of the Second Empire:

> I plunge with my subject into night and winter. The stubborn storm winds that have pounded my windows for the last two months on these hills of Nantes, accompany with their voice, sometimes serious, sometimes harrowing, my *Dies Irae* of '93. . . . Many things that remained misunderstood have appeared clearly in the revelation of these voices of the ocean. . . . That these winter threats, all these semblances of death, were in no way death but, to the contrary, life, the profound renewal. From the destructive powers, from the violent metamorphoses in which you thought it crushed, emerges the eternal irony of nature, buoyant and smiling.[12]

It is hardly accidental that, in the wake of the tumultuous 1960s, there was a new wave of interest in Michelet, popular culture, and the social romantics.[13] The countercultural movements of three decades ago posed the same kind of challenge to the dominant technological rationality of our time—embodied in military-industrial complexes on either side of the Iron Curtain—as the social romantics had posed to the intellectual and social power structures of the July Monarchy. In the nineteenth and twentieth centuries, the hegemonic powers used philosophy, science, and the educational system to obtain obedience to the "imperatives" of modern society's moral order. In Orléanist France these included the *monarchie censitaire*, the *juste milieu*, and a system of exploitation based on liberal individualism; in the twentieth-century West they have meant corporate liberalism, the Cold War, and bloody crusades against the ideological enemy (Korea, Vietnam); and in the twentieth-century East, Marxist-Leninism, the Cold War—and bloody crusades against the ideological enemy (Hungary, Czechoslovakia, Afghanistan). In both centuries, rebels against these modernist fatalities decried the violence done to human nature in particular and to the natural world in general in the name of what the *philosophie d'état* decreed was the true, the good, and the beautiful. Their intellectual response—whose nineteenth-century version this essay has explored—took the form of a revalorization of the popular culture, a new ethic of fraternity, a festive, often carnivalesque rejection of the official morality, and a denial that an ethical ontology could be derived from the suppression or ignoring of physical nature.

Some of this was no doubt hokum—even the social romantics rarely knew what rural popular culture was really all about, and novelists who paid eloquent homage to the common people in their writings often dealt disdainfully with their evil-smelling, illiterate reality. Nor should we have any illusions about resuscitating the mortal remains of the sixties counterculture. Dead is dead. Yet the movements of the nineteenth and the twentieth centuries, as part of a transgressional impulse, an antinomian reflex that is as essential to the human spirit as the currents of rationalization to which it is a reaction, have an important place in the history of Western culture.[14]

As this apocalyptic century lurches to its close, some further thoughts about the manifestations of this recurrent antinomianism are in order. To begin with, it is worth recalling that the two waves of transgressional fervor I have mentioned were preceded by another, that overlaps the later Middle Ages and the early modern era: the Christian antinomianism that stretches from Joachim to Thomas Müntzer and Rabelais and more or less ends with the mystical communism of Winstanley. This first transgressional cycle, source of the *évangile éternel* later incorporated in social romanticism, was in reaction to the breakup of the medieval world order and marked the transition to the world of the Renaissance, the Counter-Reformation, and royal and religious absolutism.

The second transgresssional wave represented by European romanticism at the end of the absolutist *ancien régime* has been discussed at the beginning of this essay: Michelet's social romantic celebration of the people, the nation, and the French Revolution has been my main focus. That Michelet juxtaposed nature and the revolutionary national community against the "machinism" of both capitalist production and the establishment liberalism of his time has to be understood in its romantic revolutionary context, and not as a portent of the sinister, pseudoromantic, reactionary ideologies of a half-century later. The epoch that gave birth to European romanticism was ended by the universal defeats of the revolutions of 1848.

It is possible that the most recent cycle of antinomian revolt, the youth revolt of the 1960s, heralded a transitional period comparable to that which gave birth to European romanticism. Its character is complex, its precipitants multiple. In Europe and North America, the 1960s marked the end of the postwar recovery of economic vitality and confidence; it also signaled the transition from a productivist to a consumerist social order and, bleakly, for the young, from a social order in which the increasingly large proportion of university-educated youth could be confident of their material existence to one in which their numbers guaranteed for a large proportion of them either social decline or membership in an underemployed intellectual proletariat. More particularly, in France, it signaled the adolescence and young adulthood of the first generation to experience the rapid changes in social and economic life brought about by the French industrial revolution, which only really set in and transformed personal existence after 1945. Most importantly, it revealed the limits of the twin ideologies that had been driving Western culture since the onset of the industrial and national revolutions: the Promethean ideology of productivity and the Faustian ideology of power. In Algeria and Vietnam, the sixties saw the end of the Western capacity to dominate the Third World. They also saw the beginning of the ecological crisis that made clear the dangers of a Prometheus unbound.

And Michelet? To begin with, the social romantic group he aligned with in the forties—Sand, Leroux, Sue, and others—represented a fusion of the value of heroic idealism associated with the national revolution and the notion of mystical community with nature. In the years leading up to 1848, Michelet's thinking was guided by patriotic idealism as well as by a version of the ideology of mystical community, his *évangile éternel*. The latter was based on a transfigured notion of nature as divine, harmonious, beneficent, and nurturing, and it was this "romantic heresy" that had become the indispensable foundation of his political engagement.

Cousin, Guizot, and their associates, however, were centrally imbedded in the power structure of the July Monarchy, which viewed itself, in the historiographical vision of Augustin Thierry, as the end of history.[15]

In the tradition of absolutism's *offensive moralisatrice* against peasant immorality, the establishment thinkers drew sharp boundaries between mind and body, between male and female, between the high culture of the elites and the popular culture of the masses, between the capacities of the wealthy and educated few and those of the impoverished and illiterate common people. Since they were convinced they had found the solution to the breakup of the *ancien régime*, they viewed all who opposed them, whether on the issue of church-state relations or on that of political and social justice, as muddleheaded troublemakers. But for those who, like Michelet, remained unconvinced by their position, the antinomian, transgressional romantic option—which in science, in history, in culture generally, sought harmony between all the high/low antitheses assumed by the liberal civilizers—remained open.

And now? We have recently heard powerful echoes of Thierry's annunciation of the end of history. And that is not the only similarity between the contemporary scene and the ideological self-celebration of the July Monarchy. After several decades of postwar welfare states, Europe east and west has slipped into a neoliberalism and an egoistic individualism rather similar to that against which the social romantics of the July Monarchy protested in the name of human fraternity. These similarities, however, are accompanied by vast differences. Postrevolutionary France witnessed the restructuring of society based on the rationalist and productivist values of the national and industrial revolutions of 1750–1870; our own era, with its stagnating multinational economies, its mounting structural unemployment, and its looming ecological disasters, probably signifies the decomposition of that restructured society. Indeed, the need to break out of the exclusive concern with linear material progress and rationalization to a renewed understanding of the cyclical character of much of our world and of the links between the social and the natural orders has been stressed repeatedly even by the leaders of contemporary world industrial society.

Under these circumstance, an analytic examination of the doctrines both of the social romantics and of their 1960s counterparts, with the aim of sifting out what may be usable and salutary from what really was contingent nonsense, could save us from future confusions: the antinomian angel of cosmic harmony, now apparently dormant in the dust of history, is not likely to remain there forever.

## Notes

1. For an interesting examination of romanticism in these terms, see Michael Löwy and Robert Sayre, *Révolte et Mélancolie, Le Romantisme à Contre-courant de la Modernité* (Paris: Payot, 1992).

2. Roger Picard, *Le Romantisme Social* (New York & Paris: Brentano's, 1944); David Owen Evans, *Le Socialisme Romantique: Pierre Leroux et ses Contemporains,* preface by Edouard Dolléans (Paris: M. Rivière, 1948); David Owen Evans, *Social Romanticism in France 1830–1848* (Oxford: Clarendon Press, 1951); Fr. and J. Fourastié, *Les Ecrivains Témoins du Peuple* (Paris: J'ai Lu, 1964); *L'Esprit Républicain: Colloque d'Orléans, 4 et 5 Septembre 1970,* présenté par Jacques Viard (Paris: Klincksieck, 1972) [contributions on the social romantics by Viallaneix, Lacassagne, Salomon, Savidan, and Sabiani]; *Romantisme,* No. 9 (1975), *Le Peuple;* Sarane Alexandrian, *Le Socialisme Romantique* (Paris: Seuil, 1979); *1848, les Utopismes Sociaux: Utopie et Action à la Veille des Journées de Février,* preface by Maurice Agulhon (Paris: SEDES/CDU, 1981); Geneviève Bollème, *Le Peuple par Ecrit,* preface by Jacques le Goff (Paris: Seuil, 1986); Gérard Fritz, *L'Idée de Peuple en France du XVIIe au XIXe Siècle* (Strasbourg: Presses Universitaires de Strasbourg, 1988); Alain Pessin, *Le Mythe du Peuple et la Société Française du XIXe Siècle* (Paris: Presses Universitaires de France, 1992).

3. This term designates the loose coalition of opponents within the parliaments and governments of the July Monarchy of any democratization of the political or cultural order. The group favoring such democratization was referred to as the Party of Movement.

4. A. Mitzman, "The Civilizing Offensive: Mentalities, High Culture, and Individual Psyches," *Journal of Social History* 20/4 (1987) 663–687. The identification of the popular strata with social danger appeared in the classic study by H.-A. Frégier, *Des Classes Dangereuses de la Population dans les Grandes Villes et des Moyens de les Rendre Meilleures* (Brussels: J.-B. Baillière, 1840) [the title page notes that the author was "chef de bureau à la préfecture de la Seine," and that his monograph was "récompensé en 1838 par l'Institut de France (Académie des Sciences morales et politiques)"; in other words, by the official intellectual establishment of the July Monarchy]. Frégier's title was echoed in 1958 by Louis Chevalier's brilliant *Classes Laborieuses et Classes Dangereuses à Paris pendant la Première Moitié du XIXe Siècle* (Paris: Plon, 1958; Hachette, 1984). Unfortunately, Chevalier's work has convinced an entire generation of scholars that there was no important difference between the establishment's top-down view of the common people and that of its social romantic opponents, an argument opposed in this study.

5. In *La Sorcière* (1862), Michelet went much further and argued that, because of the Christian relegation of nature to the domain of Satan, the popular religion of the Middle Ages developed, through witchcraft, a

means of retaining the older view of the relation between man and the natural world. Max Milner has argued that other romantics—Sand, Esquiros, Leroux, Hugo—preceded Michelet in connecting the myth of Satan to the defense by the popular culture of its traditional values: "La Signification Politique de Satan," in *Romantisme et Politique 1815–1851: Colloque de l'Ecole Normale Supérieure de Saint-Cloud* [1966] (Paris: A. Colin, 1969) 160; also Milner, *Le Diable dans la Littérature Française de Cazotte à Baudelaire 1772–1861*, 2 vols. (Paris: J. Corti, 1960).

6. *Doctrine de Saint-Simon. Exposition—2e Année, 7e Séance* (Paris, 1830) 92–93. (Reference supplied by Sophie Leterrier.)

7. Mona Ozouf, *La Fête Révolutionnaire, 1789–1799* (Paris: Gallimard, 1976) 49–55.

8. Jules Michelet, *Histoire de la Révolution Française*, 2 vols. (Paris: Gallimard, 1952) 1:306; translated by Charles Cocks as *History of the French Revolution* (Chicago: Univ. of Chicago Press, 1967) 324f.

9. Michelet, *Histoire de la Révolution Française*, 2:408.

10. Ibid., 622–23.

11. In *Le Temps des Prophètes*.

12. Michelet, *Histoire de la Révolution Française*, 2:696. Michelet indicates in the autobiographical introduction to *L'Oiseau*, written in September 1855, the itinerary that led him from the celebration of nature, and in particular of the link between man and the animal world in *Le Peuple*, to his works on natural history. Michelet, *L'Oiseau*, édition critique par Edward Kaplan in *Oeuvres Complètes*, tome XVII (Paris: Flammarion, 1986) 62.

13. In particular, Michelet's *L'Etudiant, Le Peuple*, and *La Sorcière*, centrally important for his social romantic views of nature, witchcraft and popular culture, the student world and the common people, were all reprinted between 1966 and 1974.

14. See Peter Stallybrass and Allon White, *The Politics and Poetics of Transgression* (Ithaca: Cornell Univ. Press, 1986), for an illuminating analysis of Bakhtin's concept of the carnivalesque in terms of "the imaginary repertoire of transgressive desire" (6–26).

15. Lionel Gossman, "Thierry and Liberal Historiography," in *Between History and Literature* (Cambridge, MA: Harvard Univ. Press, 1990) 145.

# RUINS AND FOUNDATION STONES
## The Paris Commune and the Destruction
## of the Vendôme Column
### *Christopher Winks*

*Illustration by Guy Girard*

Among the gallery of character profiles with which Jules Vallès populates *L'Insurgé* [The Insurgent], his novelized memoir of the background, development, and destruction of the 1871 Paris Commune, the self-educated cobbler Edouard Rouiller voices one of the central desires that animated this revolutionary moment. Holding court in a dive, the hard-drinking philosopher constantly returns to his favorite theme:

> "Ain't but two questions! Number one: the interests of Cap'tal! . . . Number two: autonomy! You oughta know about

that one, Vingtras, having gone to school and all, huh? It comes from the Greek, according to what the graduates say! They know where it comes from, but they don't know where it leads!"

Laughter as he chugged down his glass!

"Gimme a little explanation of this here autonomy now, lemme hear it, okay?" he said after wiping off his beard.

Everybody awaited the answer.

Amidst the silence, he repeated:

"Me, I'm for autonomy anywhere—in the neighborhoods, the streets, the houses. . . ."

"What about the wine cellars?"

"Oh yeah, that. . . ."[1]

Subsequently, Vallès reveals that Rouiller, beneath his clownish exterior, is a serious, thoughtful individual who has gained sufficient respect among his comrades to earn a position on the Commune's Committee of Public Instruction. In fact, he has taken the time to formulate an educational document that, in Vallès's words, "overturns, in its wisdom, all the catechisms of the Academies and Grand Councils." (336) His preoccupation with autonomy should therefore be viewed less as the *idée fixe* of an eccentric than as the articulation of a social need at a moment in history when, according to an eyewitness, Villiers de l'Isle-Adam, "a whole population is discussing serious matters, and for the first time workers can be heard exchanging their views on problems which up until now have been broached only by philosophers."[2] This socialization of intellectual property is both a movement of demystification in Marx's sense ("All social life is essentially practical. All mysteries which lead theory to mysticism find their rational solution in human practice and in the comprehension of this practice."[3]) and of self-institution. In short, the concept finds a place for itself, that "somewhere" unknown to Rouiller's graduates, to which it might lead. Rouiller understands that autonomy, more than a word with an attached etymology, is a way of life that unfolds in and through social space—"the neighborhoods, the streets, the houses," and—why not?—the wine cellars. In order to be established in a particular somewhere, autonomy has to be imagined as existing in a universal anywhere.

The practical assertion of autonomy creates a fissure, a fault line of demarcation between the contending forces in society. When Marx summed up the meaning of the Commune with the aphorism, "Paris all truth, Versailles all lie,"[4] he was not indulging in narrow moralism. Rather, he was emphasizing the defining action of revolutions; by resisting the Thiers government's attempts to disarm the Paris National Guard detachments, thereby forcing the regime and its hangers-on to flee to the former home of royalty at Versailles, the Parisians exposed the republican pretensions of Thiers, Favre, Simon, et al. to be mere rhetorical fig leaves. The old Versailles-Paris antagonism was this time played out in a new guise and a new language of combat, but it was no less emblematic of a fundamental division between rulers and ruled. The nature of the "truth" articulated in the Commune's activities was incompatible with any artificially imposed unanimity of purpose or conception. In many respects, as Marx remarked in an earlier Parisian context, the content went beyond the phrase. But if in turn "the great social measure of the Commune was its own working existence,"[5] it is possible to specify certain aspects of that existence as crystallizations of the Commune's truth and, by extension, the social lie against which the Communards took up arms. To a certain extent, revolutionary moments stage themselves quite consciously, and in many details of its festive *mise en scène*, the Commune deployed itself in an empty space, cleared of the forces of a suspect Order, and filled by a philosophizing (in Villiers' sense), poeticizing (as in Isidore Ducasse's "Poetry should have as its goal, practical truth"), acting (in both the dramatic and productive sense), autonomizing crowd, moving freely through space and time instead of being moved by exterior forces and interests. The destruction of the Vendôme Column on May 16, 1871, encapsulated all these qualities.

Marx himself indicated the historical importance of this action: immediately preceding his famous statement about the Commune's "working existence" he wrote: "to broadly mark the new era of history it was conscious of initiating . . . the Commune pulled down that colossal system of martial glory, the Vendôme Column."[6] Revolutions are as much struggles over meaning (symbolic and semantic alike) as over the allocation of social wealth. New eras begin with a qualitative leap, the kind of irrevocable decision from which "any retreat is impossible" (Marx). Vallès recounts the moment in the first hours after the proclamation of the Commune when it became clear that the cash boxes in the municipality's possession would have to be jimmied open and raided to pay the National Guard's regular wages:

The abyss had been dug once and for all as if with a gravedigger's spade. This lock-picking involved the Committee as much as the execution of the generals had. The whole crowd of those with four sous, the "honest folk" of all classes and countries, would hurl curses, bombs, and soldiers at this hall of looters. (320–21)

Acts such as these transgress the reigning symbolic (bourgeois) order; if property is theft (something to which many Communards, as followers of Proudhon, would have enthusiastically subscribed), then robbing the thieves for the public benefit is an act of social responsibility. (One of the first decrees of the Commune was the cancellation of back rents for the prior three quarters.) Reversing the accepted terms and conditions of political discourse was to characterize the Commune's thought and action; even if the "dangerous classes" displayed a thorough grasp of politics and the "public good," the "better classes" could react only with impotent rage and, ultimately, barbarity. A popular song of the Commune, after enumerating the solidarity and mutual respect of its participants, climaxed in the refrain, "If that's the rabble, okay then—I'm one of them." Destroying the Vendôme Column, to the Versaillais a sacrilegious act of vandalism, thus became a creative act.

Mikhail Bakunin asserted, "the urge to destroy is also a creative urge," but the rhetorical weight of this statement properly falls on its second half. The question revolves around what exactly is to be created atop the ruins. Baron Haussmann's explicitly counterrevolutionary urbanism, which razed entire sections of Paris and displaced their inhabitants to the periphery, was rightly derided by Marx as "vandalism . . . razing historic Paris to make place for the Paris of the sightseer."[7] The negative creations of this self-styled "artist in demolition," the wide boulevards for which Paris would eventually gain fame (precisely among tourists) were intended, as Walter Benjamin pointed out,

> to secure the city against civil war . . . Haussmann seeks to prevent barricades in two ways. The breadth of the streets is intended to make their creation impossible, and new thoroughfares are to open the shortest route between the barracks and the working-class districts. Contemporaries christen the enterprise "strategic embellishment."[8]

Haussmann's urge to create was also a destructive urge, an expansion of physical space that served to restrict social circulation, to massify the crowd, and to enhance the reciprocal isolation of individuals. Space became an imposition upon people rather than an extension and reflection of their conscious activity. Mirroring the social hierarchy, center and periphery were clearly staked out.

The Commune's festive atmosphere can be attributed as much to the exhilaration of the forcibly marginalized Parisians moving to retake the urban center as to any tradition of revolutionary festivals carried over from the Great French Revolution. Recapturing this space necessarily entailed its physical transformation, to the extent of turning evidences of the enemy's presence into absences, "positive holes," as the Situationist International termed them. The Situationists, in fact, succinctly enumerated this anticreation's attributes: "attacking on the spot the petrified signs of the dominant organization of life, understanding social space in political terms, refusing to accept the innocence of any monument."[9]

In the case of the Vendôme Column, its destruction was not only a moment in the liberation of urban space, but an intervention into the official order's historical time. First built in 1805, the column was fashioned from melted-down Russian and Austrian cannons captured in the Napoleonic Wars; a statue of Napoleon crowned the summit. In subsequent years, the authorities altered the column in several ways, depending upon the prevailing political winds (for example, the statue of Napoleon was removed during the Restoration and melted down to provide raw material for another monument; and even after it had been replaced with a new statue, Louis Napoleon ordered it recostumed in a new frock coat during his reign). Proof that it is only when monuments (and the official history they represent) are wrested from the control of their guardians that the latter endow it with sacred and inviolable status. Even before the Commune, there had been talk in republican circles of getting rid of the column; Gustave Courbet remarked *inter alia* that "it got in the way of the traffic."[10] As if to emphasize this point, the official admission tickets to the demolition ceremony read: "let (the bearer) pass and circulate freely."[11]

Two and a half weeks after the Commune had been proclaimed, the official newspaper published a decree (authored by Félix Pyat, a one-time melodramatist turned histrionic Jacobin) calling for the column to be pulled down:

The Paris Commune,

Considering that the Imperial Column in the Place Vendôme is a monument of barbarism, a symbol of brute force and false glory, an affirmation of militarism, a denial of international law, a permanent insult directed at the conquered by their conquerors, a perpetual attack upon one of the three great principles of the French republic,

decrees:

The column in the Place Vendôme shall be abolished.[12]

Monuments commemorate specific events or individuals. Therefore, demolishing them requires a preliminary undermining of their ideological foundations, which the object materializes. As the declaration makes clear, the column is a real symbol not of its superficial occasion, the Napoleonic conquests, but an ever-renewed "permanent" "perpetual" reminder of a state of affairs and affairs of state that deny what republican life (the goal of the 1789 Revolution) should affirm and affirm what should be denied. The column is an untenable contradiction erected in the very heart of Paris, a sign of a history constructed by the victors as a physical and metaphorical means of excluding the defeated, as illustrated in G. Barthélemy's poem (published in *Le Prolétaire*, May 10, 1871): "Every time we walk by this monument in this wealthy district, citizen workers, we avert our gaze, accusing history."[13] History is contained in a space filled with the inert weight of homogeneous, alienated time. To look at its monuments is to become their accomplice, to turn to stone.

Invariably, the alienated gaze travels upward when confronted with a monument, in an involuntary gesture of reverence. Kristin Ross has counterposed what she calls the "general 'horizontal' effect of the Commune"[14] to the ruling society's "verticality." Under the impact of antihierarchical leveling, idols like Napoleon are literally dragged down to earth and shattered. Fraternity cannot tolerate obedience. Neither can power tolerate dialogue held on an equal footing. When Marx, in the concluding sentence of *The 18th Brumaire of Louis Napoleon*, anticipated the Vendôme Column's demise—"But when the emperor's mantle finally falls on the shoulders of Louis Bonaparte, the bronze statue of Napoleon will come crashing down from the top of the Vendôme Column"[15]—he was speaking in purely metaphorical terms, as if the contradictions accumulated by successive moments of imperial rule would ultimately become so untenable as to strip its monuments of whatever aura still clung to them. By one of those fortunate "accidents" of world history—which, paraphrasing Marx, militate against its mystical unfolding—the Communards "stormed heaven" (Marx) to dethrone the statue from its quasicelestial abode. The ceremony of destruction was a theatricalization, with all requisite pomp and panoply, of what Marx saw as essential for modern revolutions, "break[ing] the modern state power"[16] in the effigy of its founder, Napoleon.

In his memoirs, the Communard Louis Barron likens the collapse of the column to a "stage decor," as if its fall rang down the curtain on a long-running albeit unpopular show. State power's grandeur is a mere façade: "This colossal symbol of the Grand Army—how it was fragile, empty, miserable! It seemed to have been eaten out from the middle by a multitude of rats, like France itself, like its old tarnished glory, and we were surprised not to see any (rats) run out along the drainpipes."[17]

Against this image of an exhausted, hollow historical ruin, rotting away from within, Rouiller's counterproposal for the column site testifies to a desire for a monument that would instruct and would therefore have to be read horizontally and meditated upon: "(He) asks that a pedestal be erected in its place, bearing the following inscription: 'Twice Bonaparte ruled over France and thrice he delivered Paris to the foreign invader.'"[18] The past becomes part of the present, and those living in the here-and-now can literally walk amidst the ruins on a basis of equality, dominating through *praxis* a no-longer-fossilized history. "A sailor who had picked up a paving stone," writes Henri Lefebvre,

> wanted to chuck it at Napoleon I's head, but was prevented from doing so. From atop the rubble, Citizen Henri Festriné then said a few words. "Citizens," he said, "we have seen this column fall, along with the man who now lies on the excrement that was meant to receive him. . . . He who crushed the Republic beneath his heel is now prostrate at the people's feet."[19]

In the moment of its demise, the statue is restored to human form, as if the Commune were performing an exorcism; the image no longer represents anything but itself. An artist's rendition of the column's fall (reproduced in Stewart Edwards's history of the Commune) shows it breaking into three pieces in mid-air, although Barron and another eyewitness, Maxime Vuillaume, claim that it hit the ground in one piece. Allegorically speaking, however, the three pieces of the column can be said to represent the Republican triad Liberty-Equality-Fraternity, now liberated from the totalitarian unanimity of the sculpture. Various photographs taken before and after the crucial moment show that the column's removal had the salutary effect of emancipating the heavens from the phallic incursion of the architectonically maladroit monument.

In short, the creative destruction of the column exemplified "the awareness that they are about to make the continuum of history explode (which) is characteristic of the revolutionary classes at the moment of their action."[20] The Commune expressed this lived transcendence in a mixture of solemnity and festive joyousness, well summed up by Villiers in his declaration, "Paris is fighting and singing."[21] "Time filled with the presence of the Now" in Benjamin's sense is a time out of time. Although Marx lamented that "time was not allowed to the Commune,"[22] he was speaking in terms of a limited chronological time, from the perspective of the outside observer. Like others after him, he forgot "that for those who really lived it, the fulfillment was *already there*."[23] Lefebvre estimates that 20,000 people crowded the area near the square to watch the spectacle, waiting almost three hours for its consummation, entertained by brass bands playing "La Marseillaise" and (in a touch of black humor) a song called "Le Chant du Départ." And this at a time when the Versaillais were at the outskirts of Paris, when the Commune itself had undergone a serious split between the partisans of a "Committee of Public Safety" and those who saw forebodings of dictatorship in the lack of accountability of such an institution.

But as Villiers pointed out, "No more effective weapon could ever be found than the laughter of the people ringing out joyfully in the midst of the gloomy crowd like a shaft of lightning in a terrible storm." And further: "Let him laugh heartily, the giant loved by Rabelais and feared by Robespierre!"[24] In first-hand accounts of the column's fall, a distinct trace of what Walter Benjamin identified as the *culte de la blague* emerges. Barron speaks of rats and Vuillaume describes "Caesar['s] laurel-wreathed head" as having "rolled like a pumpkin into the gutter."[25] Many of the Blanquist orators and journalists used the *blague* to good effect—Vallès sketches vignettes of the shrill-voiced orator Ducasse threatening recalcitrant bartenders with the guillotine "when the time comes" and Raoul Rigault, later to become the Commune's chief of police, singing "Rock-a-bye-baby" to his revolver. The unknown sailor who unsuccessfully attempted to smash the statue of Napoleon's head with a brick was a *blagueur* of the first order. However, this seemingly irresistible temptation to provoke has its serious side, originating in an indefinable something "in the air" that Mikhail Bakhtin discerned as intrinsic to "popular-festive forms":

> The birth of the new, of the greater and better, is as indispensable and as inevitable as the death of the old. The one is transferred to the other, the better turns the worse into ridicule and kills it. . . . The whole of the people and of the world is triumphantly gay and fearless. This whole speaks in all carnival images; it reigns in the very atmosphere of this feast, making everyone participate in this awareness.[26]

"I feel a profound drunkenness," says Jules Vallès,

> lost in this multitude which hurls into my ears everything it thinks about me. . . . It seems that it's no longer my own, this heart that so many ugly wounds have flayed, and that it is the crowd's very soul that is filling and swelling my heart. Oh, if only death would take me now, if only a bullet would kill me in this fulfillment of resurrection! I would die today at the height of my revenge—and who knows what the struggle will make of me tomorrow? (324–25)

Vallès, a declassed bohemian, journalist and agitator, friend of Baudelaire, Courbet, Blanqui, a member of what he once considered as "the generation of the (post-1848) defeat" discovers that he is both subject and object of the revolutionary moment. He is both in and of the crowd, all the while remaining wholly himself, fulfilling what Baudelaire saw as the passion and profession of the painter of modern life. He does not seek to cushion himself against the shocks of everyday life, preferring to go forth to meet them. If he has a fear, it is not that of getting too close to things but of becoming once again separate from them and their new-found carnivalesque aspects. For this brief moment, Vallès is living a dream, and he tries to reflect the discontinuous pace of events in the style of his memoir, with its rapid-fire sketches of personages briefly surfacing from the agitational wave, its gaps in chronology, and its antiliterary, antirhetorical style.

Watching the crowd as it surged onto the Place Vendôme, an English observer, Colonel Stanley, noted that "the excitement was so intense that people moved about as if in a dream."[27] Compare Baudelaire: "As for me, I shall be quite satisfied to leave/ A world where action is never sister of the dream";[28] and Marx: "The reform of consciousness consists only therein, that one wakes the world . . . out of its dream of itself."[29] But what if this awakening consisted in entering another dream, one dreamt with open eyes? Would it not tend to efface the boundaries between action and dream and join them in sisterly unity? Benjamin, at once skeptical and optimistic about the possibilities of the collective dream, saw in the work of Charles Fourier the outline of a world where "All places are cultivated by human beings, made useful and beautiful by them; all, however, stand like a roadside inn, open to everyone."[30] In the rubble strewn about the newly cleared space of the Place Vendôme, the crowd begins to cultivate a *topos*, in an atmosphere that can rightfully and without exaggeration be termed poetic.

Strolling through a Paris ruined by Haussmann's urban renewal, Baudelaire lamented: "Paris changes. . . . But nothing in my melancholy/ Has stirred! new palaces, scaffoldings, blocks,/ Old districts — all becomes allegory for me/ And my cherished memories are heavier than rocks."[31]

In a nonrevolutionary situation, the isolated *flâneur* feels the weight of time, along with a subjective distance from the sanctioned destruction of the city, of which the ruins are emblems. Old and new alike collapse into allegory, becoming signs of something for which the poet has no words. Memories, the stuff of individual and collective history, become so much *impedimenta*. What is unbearable can be borne only through the poetic gesture, itself, however, insufficiently equipped to alter the poet's melancholic state. Writing at the time of the Commune, Arthur Rimbaud countered the weight of memory through his poem "Workers," who rebel against the tawdriness of their enforced exile in the *banlieues*: "No! We will spend no summers in this grasping land, where we will forever be nothing but orphans betrothed. This hardened arm will drag along no more 'sweet memories.'"[32] By de-allegorizing the urban whole and selectively re-allegorizing that which illuminates their particular condition, Rimbaud's workers take a step that is denied to Baudelaire. Rimbaud's poetry directly socializes Baudelaire's: the workers are able, as much as Baudelaire, to drink from melancholy's cup but they supplant Baudelaire's fleeting awareness of history with the knowledge that their condition is produced by their own "hardened arms," and that it is accordingly in their power to refuse it and to resolve to create another kind of life outside the parameters of the poem.

The destroyers of the Vendôme Column were well acquainted with the allegorical significance of monuments. Their poetic reverie as they walked and posed amidst the ruins corroborates and subverts Benjamin's aphorism, "Allegory is in the realm of thought what ruins are in the realm of things,"[33] as well as his reference to "the strewn implements with which allegory has so disfigured and mauled the material world that only fragments remain as the object of its contemplation."[34] In situating Baudelaire's allegorical problematic in the realm of *praxis*, the Communards carried out a reversal of perspective analogous to Marx's project of standing the Hegelian dialectic on its feet. The violation of an allegorical representation of a man (and a society) that "disfigured and mauled the material world" and its resulting reduction to ruins amounted to a salutary fragmentation, the contemplation of which was filled with constructive potential. In this light, it is worth mentioning an incident in Louise Michel's memoirs:

> I remember a student who didn't agree with our ideas
> (although he agreed even less with the other side's) who
> came to shoot with us [during the Commune]. . . . He had a
> volume of Baudelaire in his pocket, and we read a few pages
> with great pleasure—when we had time to read. What fate
> held for him I don't know, but we tested our luck together.[35]

Could "Le Cygne" have been among those pages?

Rimbaud's "Villes I"[36] unveils some of the possibilities of this oneiric actuality. A delirious *mélange* of extravagant architecture and mythic figures, the city and its topography soar, plummet, and sound in perpetual motion: "The ideas of peoples sound from thickly clustering bell towers. Unknown music vibrates in towering castles of

bone. All legend evolves, and excitement rushes through the streets."
What anchors this poem is its conclusion: "What strong arms, what
shining hour will bring me back this country, the source of my
repose, moving the least of my movements?" In Paul Schmidt's translation, the "strong arms" have an ambiguous connotation insofar as
they could belong to a lover, thereby grounding the poet's vision
exclusively in erotic experience. However, the original French "*bons
bras*," with their overtones of physical strength and solidity, are
unmistakably those of a worker. No longer condemned to drag
around falsely "sweet" memories, the arms of the worker are now
engaged in forging a world where the imagination and the individual
are sovereign. The poet's memory is therefore a happy one, born
from an imaginative improvisation on actual conditions in a "shining
hour" where time is filled with the presence of the Now. Most importantly, this memory is social and dialogic in nature. It certainly counts
for something that the poet should be able to write of his dream, and
that it should determine "the least of [his] movements," but it can only
flourish again through another's purposive activity.

In this poem, Rimbaud subverts the consolatory pretensions of
the poetic phantasmagoria. It was a dream (the poet says), I saw
these things, and yet I know it can all return in real life, because the
freedom with which they passed before my eyes and into my consciousness demands a practical prolongation. If Baudelaire had con-
tented himself with living inside the phantasmagoria that Marx saw
as characteristic of the rising bourgeois society and describing its lin-
eaments, Rimbaud—and the Communards—sought to dominate it
and exorcise it. "Just as the Communist Manifesto ends the epoch of
the professional conspirator, the Commune puts an end to the phantasmagoria that dominates the freedom of the proletariat."[37] And this
*coup de grâce* can be conceptualized as a linguistic demarcation; in
the name of the *agora*, the phantasms are driven away. A favorite
nineteenth-century hallucination was the statue rising from its
pedestal and striding or galloping off into the nocturnal city. By shat-
tering the statue of Napoleon and excoriating it as though effigy and
emperor were one, the Communards in effect drove a stake through
its heart. An antagonistic observer of the Commune, Catulle Mendès,
understood the significance of this action, to the point of resuscitating the phantasmagoria in his own mind as a strange source of self-
consolation:

Don't think that demolishing the Vendôme Column is just toppling over a bronze column with an emperor's statue on top; it's unearthing your fathers in order to slap the fleshless cheeks of their skeletons and to say to them, "You were wrong to be brave, to be proud, to be grand!"[38]

Significantly, he equates demolition with disinterment: pulling down is cognate with hauling up, and storming heaven is a violation of the earth. At the proletarian Last Judgment, the skeletons do not rise and put on flesh; rather, their disobedient sons resurrect them for the dust-heap. If "humanity will be prey to the anxiety of myth for so long as the phantasmagoria has a place in it,"[39] those who have grown accustomed to and even celebrated or promoted such mythic unease are struck with the terror that they themselves have sown when the workings of the phantasmagoria are brought to light and revealed as—in the end—mere mechanism. And this terror must itself be rendered phantasmagoric, whence the demonization of the Communards in Versaillais rhetoric. However, once deprived of its symbolic foundations, phantasmagoric consciousness can only articulate itself in the perpetration of bloodstained horror and atrocities on a massive scale.

Inevitably, the Commune's exorcism of historical phantasmagoria had consequences for the revolutionary tradition to which it was heir. The myths of the Great French Revolution produced an anxiety of repetition among many Communards who dreamed of a newly incarnate Jacobinism complete with a Terror, a Committee of Public Safety, and the sectarian zeal for incorruptibility that allegedly animated their predecessors. To a definite degree, every revolutionary movement returns to and reinvests the ideas of the past; the very creation of an entity known as "Commune" was a self-conscious renewal of the 1793 Paris Commune, which created a situation of "dual power" *vis-à-vis* the central government. But there is a difference between the sort of "world-historical necromancy" that served "to recover the spirit of the revolution, rather than to set its ghost walking again"[40] and "the tradition of the dead generations [that] weighs like a nightmare on the minds of the living."[41] The Commune engaged in a constant self-interrogation of its own ideological bases; individuals like Vallès criticized revolutionary mythology with as much fervor as they did the bourgeoisie:

How terrifying the sectarians are! Draftees or vets, sextons of
the Convention, or demsocs of the Church. . . . I hate
Robespierre the deist, and believe it's pointless to ape Marat,
suspicion's galley-slave, the Terror's hysteric, the neurotic of a
bloody era . . . defrocked people only change their cult, and
even on heresy's terrain, they still preserve memories of
religion. (345, 347)

Nothing was more phantasmagoric than the engine of the guillotine,
with its assembly lines of victims, and no myth was more powerful
among revolutionaries than the Jacobin illusion. The April 6 burning
of the guillotine in the 11th arrondissement "for the purification of
our Arrondissement and the consecration of our new freedom,"[42]
before the statue of Voltaire (who appreciatively applauds the spectacle in a contemporary caricature), should therefore be seen as a
complement to the demolition of the Vendôme Column, a moment in
the dispelling of illusions required for the flowering of what Marx
called the poetry of the future. To brand the guillotine, originally created as a "humane" method for the capital punishment of royalists,
as "a servile instrument of monarchist domination"[43] is an assault on
royalist or republican kings alike, and symbolically outlines the possibility of a system of nonretributive justice.

This said, the Commune proved itself excessively indulgent
toward such strategic monuments as the Bank of France, which, as
Stewart Edwards points out, could if nothing else have been used as a
bargaining counter, and failed notably to resurrect the tradition of the
revolutionary march on Versailles, which had a profound impact in
1789 when the women of Paris confronted the royal establishment face
to face. There are moments when targets must be chosen not to supplant but to counterpoint the festive ceremonies of demystification.

And whereas the Vendôme Column's fall proved itself to be
strategically necessary in view of the outrage it provoked among the
Versaillais and their cohorts, the destruction of the guillotine was an
almost outmoded measure. For the preferred technique for state suppression of mass uprisings had long been and continued to be the
fusillade, defined by Gustave Flaubert as "the only way to silence the
Parisians."[44] When the Versaillais finally invaded Paris, two months
after the proclamation of the Commune, the Parisians had to answer
this destruction-in-the-name-of-order with their own phantasmagoria

of resistance: "The leaping flames erected fantastical architectural shapes in the dark night—blazing arches, domes, ghostly buildings."[45] Here, the act of destruction creates an imaginary city, through whose portals the Parisians enter into a company of other heroic peoples who have preferred immolation to capitulation to the invader. "Ah," exclaims Vallès, "I didn't surrender, I didn't become an arsonist without embracing the entire past with my gaze, without searching for ancestors!" (388) The destruction of the Vendôme Column is repeated on a larger scale, this time in the literal heat of passion instead of the solemnity of ritual. "Oh yes! I understand the fury of the bourgeois," says a National Guardsman. "In the torchlight, they've seen the invincible weapon relit, the tool that can't be broken." (389) While most of the fires set by the Communards were measures of deterrence against the army, the incendiaries demonstrated definite iconoclastic tendencies. Many of the Communards were prepared to strike the Versaillais in the heart of what they cherished most—buildings and monuments. Vallès relates a confrontation with a band of fighters determined to blow up the Panthéon, that mausoleum of deified "great men of France" in whose crypts Saint-Just once dreamt of installing the eighteenth century:

> "You're not the one to be defending these monuments," Totole said to me. "Monuments, for Vingtras—oh dear me! He's the one who doesn't give a damn about temples of glory and boxes for great men! Right, citizen? Come on now and let's do in that whole world over there!"
> I took great pains to hold Totole back and explain to him that even though I didn't like monuments, I wasn't asking that they be used to kill half of Paris. (391)

In the end, the Panthéon was not destroyed. But in what Edwards calls the "final revolutionary potlatch," many other monuments shared the Vendôme Column's fate, albeit by means of the "tool that can't be broken" instead of ropes and pulleys. Responding to the burning of the Tuileries Palace, Benoit Malon proclaimed: "It is allowed to these people, avant-garde of the new world, that knows how to fight and how to die so well, to burn the palace of kings."[46] Fear vanishes in an epic moment of laughter, inspired by the perceived discrepancy between humanity's pretensions to eternity and the short life span of the individual. To live long enough to tread on kings and their works is to have lived well: "My rancor is dead. I have had my day." (431)

Ultimately, the fires of the Commune reveal as artificial Benjamin's distinction between "destruction of the historical record—which alone makes revolutionary consciousness possible—and destruction in remembrance of this record."[47] Vallès, for one, wrote out a permit for the destruction of a granary—"More ground grain'll get cooked up than would have nourished me through all my years of famine"—while resisting the destruction of the Panthéon. Which of these acts is a permissible destruction? The Vendôme Column was an instance of the "historical record"—should it then have been allowed to remain intact as a reminder of past oppression while "remembrance" expressed its destructive impulses elsewhere? As long as human memory exists, oppression can never be wholly forgotten nor its existence as part of an historical fabric. Since "it is common knowledge that in the end everyone is going to die,"[48] what mattered for the Communards was the manner of their departure, and if that entailed, for better or worse, that they should immolate aspects of an alienated past, then, as Marx understood well, "while tearing to pieces the living body of the proletariat, its rulers must no longer expect to return triumphantly into the intact architecture of their abodes."[49] Rimbaud's act of poetic incendiarism, "Parisian Orgy,"[50] hurls invective like bombs against the "repopulation" of Paris by the Versaillais. With the same courage exhibited by Louise Michel when she declared that among all those she encountered in the streets of Paris during the resistance, she was the only one calling for fire, the poet places himself in the forefront of the counterattack. A typical *blagueur*, he "invites" the Versaillais into the topography of Paris, whose architecture he enumerates in ironic detail, gradually modulating into a scream of disgust whose echoes are reflected in the language's guttural twists and expectorations. Paying tribute to the "sorrowful city . . . now struck dumb," Rimbaud recognizes that, in losing past and future to the cowardly invaders, Paris is a "city the dismal Past can only bless." Whereas the flames of resistance are "stars of fire," the past and its representatives cannot create anything; they can only rape and plunder. In a powerful quatrain, Rimbaud perceives quite clearly that the Versaillais restoration is a restoration of the phantasmagoria:

Society, all is restored: orgies, the old
Groans choke the lupanars once more,
Maddened gaslight on blood-stained walls
Lights the blue dark with a sinister glare!

Significantly, among the first priorities of the victorious government, once sufficient blood had been spilled, the mock trials concluded, and the deportations accomplished, was the reconstruction of the ruined monuments in the same style as before, particularly the Vendôme Column. In her memoir of the Commune, Louise Michel tersely remarked that "the Vendôme Column was destroyed but the fragments conserved, so that it was later rebuilt in order that youth should stand before this hideous bronze and eternally hypnotize itself with the cult of war and despotism."[51] It is as if even the ruins must be demolished in order to forestall the reconstruction of the old order. The symbolic order had to take precedence over political consolidation; in the eyes of the rulers, rebels must not only be defeated, they must be persuaded of the complete and utter futility of their actions. Hence the construction of another memorial, intended ostensibly as a gesture of atonement for the violent repression but actually to serve as a warning for the working class of Montmartre—the Basilica du Sacré-Cœur. Appropriately painted the color of the White Terror, this sacred heart of a heartless world, crushing in its ugliness, received its retaliation in a song that emerged after the Commune: "Versaillais, Versaillais, you have shot away the heart of a revolution . . . but the spirit of the insurgents remains in Paris still."

Indeed, Louise Michel also noted that

upon my return from Caledonia, I could salute [the ruins of
the Hôtel de Ville]; the Taxation Bureau, the Tuileries still
bore witness to our desire to die unvanquished; only today
[1898] have the ruins of the Taxation Bureau been carried off
by those working on the Exposition.[52]

While the phantasmagoric display of commodity abundance may enjoy temporary ascendancy over the ruins of insurrection, it can never wholly put an end to the faculty of memory, unconquerable when it is self-consciously deployed against the social-historical panorama. "The storm has christened you supreme poetry," declared

Rimbaud, as if to say that anyone who truly wished to practice the poetic art in Paris would inevitably encounter the Communards' accomplishments. "One returns from such exalted experiences as one would awake from a dream, but the memory remains of a brief moment of ecstasy, an illusion of fraternity."[53] Perhaps Rimbaud's celebrated desire to bring about a "disorganizing [of] all the senses" expressed in his May 13, 1871, letter to Georges Izambard,[54] was as much an attempt, inspired by the Commune's "objective poetry," to enter into that "brief moment of ecstasy" from his suburban existence in Charleville, as it was reflective of a vatic impulse.

Buildings and monuments can inspire leaps of memory and association, but they are not the stuff of which memory is made. That belongs to lived moments: a word, an encounter, a glance. Louise Michel tells the story of a young woman who arrived to help the fighters on the Commune's last barricade at Rue de-la-Fontaine-au-Roi, at the moment when the ammunition was almost gone. Despite their warnings, she stayed with them. The barricade exploded in a hail of gunfire:

> To the nurse of the last barricade and the final hour, [the poet] J.-B. Clément dedicated, long afterwards, the "Song of the Cherries." Nobody saw her again.

> *I will always love the season of cherries*
> *From that time, I preserve in my heart*
> *An open space.*
> *And even if Lady Fortune should give herself to me*
> *She could not calm my sorrows.*
> *I will always love the season of cherries*
> *And the memory I preserve in my heart.*[55]

What remains after the death of a young girl are the blossoming cherry trees, each year dying in winter and bearing fruit as they awaken into spring. Monuments and allegories fade beside the "open space," a reminiscence of the social space that once belonged to the Communards. Perhaps revolt, like the trees, will bloom again. But that which has been lost can never fully be recovered. Happiness, which Saint-Just had once rashly sought to legislate, had emerged spontaneously in the laughter Villiers heard in the streets, the songs of the concerts, the grandeur of the popular festivals, and the enthusiasm and kindness that Louis Barron found in daily intercourse. But as Jules Vallès knew, the Commune was made by those "who, the victims of social injustice, took up arms against an ill-made world and formed, under the flag of the Commune, the great federation of sorrows" (dedicatory note to *L'Insurgé*). Underlying the joy and hope of this brief moment in history was a consuming rage at existing conditions. "This suppressed rage—*la rogne*—was the emotion which a half century of barricade fights had nurtured in Parisian professional conspirators."[56] Vallès speaks of avenging his impoverished youth through his participation in the Commune. Rage and its attendant sorrow can only be transcended if they are federated, channeled toward social transformation and metamorphosed into the "free and passionate work" that Charles Fourier saw in the construction of street barricades. Once repressed in the Versailles hecatomb, this rage would simmer slowly in the social cauldron, overflowing in such acts as the anarchist bombings at the end of the century and culturally in the project of linguistic demolition undertaken by Stéphane Mallarmé, who once declared "Destruction was my Beatrice," and whom Guy Debord described as "the guide for a few others in rather perilous explorations."[57]

Shortly after the inception of the Commune, J.-B. Clément affirmed:

> They can kill us, if they wish, they can rip down our posters and remove all traces from the walls, but the principles that have been affirmed will still exist, and whatever is done, whatever is said, they are monuments that the Versaillais cannot destroy either by strokes of the pen or shots of the cannon.[58]

And because "every image of the past that is not recognized by the present as one of its own concerns threatens to disappear irretrievably,"[59] these monuments of and to the spirit have to be reconceptualized anew in the present historical conjuncture. Otherwise, they become ossified revolutionary phantasmagoria, places of pilgrimage like the Mur des Fédérés in Père-Lachaise cemetery. The image of the Vendôme Column collapsing into rubble on a pile of dirt retains its power to inspire not only because its reconstructed version continues to occupy the Place Vendôme but because the Parisian powers-that-were-are-and-will-be have never really pardoned the insurrectional moment it epitomized, nor indeed those revolts which followed it, notably the May 1968 uprising (where one leaflet assured, "No, Nicolas, the Commune isn't dead"). In 1989, Guy Debord declared:

> I believe that [Paris] was ravaged a little before all the others because its ever-renewed revolutions had so worried and shocked the world, and because they had unfortunately always failed. . . . Whoever sees the banks of the Seine sees our grief: nothing is found there now except the bustling columns of an anthill of motorized slaves.[60]

Yet the season of the cherries may yet return, even if for the time being "*Paris n'est plus dans Paris.*" Against Haussmann's spiritual descendants in the various urban-renewal programs organized by modern municipal administrations, the question of social space continues to be posed. Those who study the Commune will better understand such contemporary struggles as the fight to preserve the community gardens in New York City against government encroachment, the 1992 Los Angeles uprising, and the on-going efforts in Puerto Rico against the construction of a monument to the hapless explorer and colonizer, Christopher Columbus, where the allegorical dimension of history has been actively engaged. All of these movements trace possible pathways toward Rouiller's self-instituting "autonomy," along with a few suggestions of where it might lead.

### Notes

1. Jules Vallès, *L'Insurgé*, 333–34 (my translation); all subsequent references incorporated into the body of the text.
2. Villiers de l'Isle-Adam, in *Le Tribun du Peuple*, May 10, 1871; quoted in Stewart Edwards, *The Paris Commune 1871*, 283.
3. Karl Marx, "Theses on Feuerbach," in *Early Writings*, 423.
4. Karl Marx, *The Civil War in France*, in *The First International and After*, 220.
5. Ibid., 217.
6. Ibid., 217.
7. Ibid., 230.
8. Walter Benjamin, *Paris, Capital of the Nineteenth Century*, in *Reflections*, 160.

9. Guy Debord, Attila Kotányi, Raoul Vaneigem, "Theses on the Commune," in Ken Knabb, *Situationist International Anthology*, 315.

10. Edwards, *Paris Commune*, 301.

11. Reproduced in Stewart Edwards, *The Communards of Paris, 1871*, 141.

12. Reprinted in Eugene Schulkind, *The Paris Commune of 1871: The View from the Left*, 159.

13. Reprinted in Edwards, *Paris Commune*, 303.

14. Kristin Ross, *The Emergence of Social Space: Rimbaud and the Paris Commune*, 4.

15. Marx, *The Eighteenth Brumaire of Louis Napoleon*, in *Surveys from Exile*, 249.

16. Marx, *The Civil War in France*, 211.

17. Louis Barron, *Sous le Drapeau Rouge*, 167; in Ross, *Emergence*, 7.

18. Edouard Rouiller, in *The May 16 Minutes of Sessions of the Club in the Church of Saint-Ambroise*, reprinted in Edwards, *Communards*, 104.

19. Henri Lefebvre, *La Proclamation de la Commune*, 425; my translation.

20. Benjamin, "Theses on the Philosophy of History," in *Illuminations*, 261.

21. Villiers de l'Isle-Adam, in Edwards, *Communards*, 140.

22. Marx, *The Civil War in France*, 219.

23. Debord, Kotányi, Vaneigem, "Theses," 316.

24. Villiers de l'Isle-Adam, in Edwards, *Communards*, 142.

25. Maxime Vuillaume, *Mes Cahiers Rouges au Temps de la Commune*, quoted in Edwards, *Communards*, 148.

26. Mikhail Bakhtin, *Rabelais and His World*, 256.

27. Quoted in Edwards, *Paris Commune*, 303.

28. Charles Baudelaire, "Le Reniement de Saint-Pierre," quoted in Susan Buck-Morss, *The Dialectics of Seeing*, 196.

29. Quoted in ibid., 281.

30. Benjamin, *Passagen-Werk*, quoted in Buck-Morss, *Dialectics*, 276.

31. Baudelaire, "Le Cygne," in *Les Fleurs du Mal*, 269; my translation.

32. Arthur Rimbaud, "Worker," in *Complete Works*, 227. I have restored a prose lineation while keeping Paul Schmidt's translation.

33. Benjamin, *Trauerspiel-Study I*, 354, in Buck-Morss, *Dialectics*, 165.

34. Benjamin, *Passagen-Werk V*, 441, in Buck-Morss, *Dialectics*, 187–88.

35. Louise Michel, *Memoirs*, 66.

36. Rimbaud, *Works*, 231–232.

37. Benjamin, *Paris, Capital of the Nineteenth Century*, 160.

38. Catulle Mendès, *Les 73 Journées de la Commune*, 149–150, in Ross, *Emergence*, 6.

39. Benjamin, *Passagen-Werk V*, 1256, in Buck-Morss, *Dialectics*, 107.

40. Marx, *The 18th Brumaire of Louis Napoleon*, 148.

41. Ibid., 146.

42. Proclamation reprinted in Edwards, *Communards,* 150.
43. Ibid.
44. Gustave Flaubert, "Dictionnaire des Idées Reçues," in *Bouvard et Pécuchet,* 384.
45. Prosper-Olivier Lissagaray, *Les Huit Journées de Mai,* 102, in Edwards, *Communards,* 168.
46. In Edwards, *Paris Commune,* 327.
47. Buck-Morss, *Dialectics,* 316–17.
48. Guy Debord, *Panegyric,* 69.
49. Marx, *The Civil War in France,* 228.
50. Rimbaud, *Works,* 59–60.
51. Louise Michel, *La Commune,* 257–58; my translation.
52. Ibid., 322.
53. Louis Barron, *Drapeau Rouge,* 112, in Edwards, *Communards,* 142.
54. Rimbaud, *Works,* 100–101.
55. Michel, *Commune,* 320.
56. Benjamin, *Charles Baudelaire: A Lyric Poet in the End of High Capitalism,* 15.
57. Debord, *Panegyric,* 17.
58. *Le Cri du Peuple,* April 23, 1871 in Edwards, *Paris Commune,* 275.
59. Benjamin, "Theses," 255.
60. Debord, *Panegyric,* 44, 45.

### Bibliography

Bakhtin, Mikhail. *Rabelais and His World.* Trans. by Helene Iswolsky. Cambridge: MIT Press, 1968.

Baudelaire, Charles. *Les Fleurs du Mal.* Trans. by Richard Howard. Boston: David R. Godine, 1983.

Benjamin, Walter. *Charles Baudelaire: A Lyric Poet in the Era of High Capitalism.* Trans. by Harry Zohn. London: New Left Books, 1973.

Benjamin, Walter. *Illuminations.* Ed. by Hannah Arendt; trans. by Harry Zohn. New York: Schocken Books, 1977.

Benjamin, Walter. *Reflections.* Ed. by Peter Demetz; trans. by Edmund Jephcott. New York: Harcourt Brace Jovanovich, 1979.

Buck-Morss, Susan. *The Dialectics of Seeing: Walter Benjamin and the Arcades Project.* Cambridge: MIT Press, 1990.

Debord, Guy. *Panegyric.* Trans. by James Brook. London & New York: Verso, 1991.

Edwards, Stewart. *The Paris Commune 1871.* New York: Quadrangle Books, 1973.

Edwards, Stewart, ed. *The Communards of Paris, 1871.* Ithaca: Cornell University Press, 1981.

Flaubert, Gustave. *Bouvard et Pécuchet.* Paris: Garnier-Flammarion, 1966.

Knabb, Ken, ed. and trans. *Situationist International Anthology.*

Berkeley: Bureau of Public Secrets, 1981.

Lefebvre, Henri. *La Proclamation de la Commune*. Paris: Editions Gallimard, 1965.

Marx, Karl. *Early Writings*. Harmondsworth: Penguin Books, 1977.

Marx, Karl. *The First International and After (Political Writings, Volume III)*. Ed. by David Fernbach. New York: Vintage Books, 1974.

Marx, Karl. *Surveys from Exile (Political Writings, Volume II)*. Ed. by David Fernbach. New York: Vintage Books, 1974.

Michel, Louise. *La Commune*. Paris: Editions Stock, 1971.

Michel, Louise. *The Red Virgin: Memoirs of Louise Michel*. Ed. and trans. by Bullitt Lowry and Elizabeth Ellington Gunter. University: Univ. of Alabama Press, 1981.

Rimbaud, Arthur. *Complete Works*. Trans. by Paul Schmidt. New York: Harper & Row, 1976.

Rimbaud, Arthur. *Oeuvres*. Edition de Suzanne Bernard. Paris: Editions Garnier Frères, 1960.

Ross, Kristin. *The Emergence of Social Space: Rimbaud and the Paris Commune*. Minneapolis: Univ. of Minnesota Press, 1988.

Schulkind, Eugene, ed. *The Paris Commune of 1871: The View from the Left*. New York: Grove Press, 1974.

Seigel, Jerrold. *Bohemian Paris: Culture, Politics, and the Boundaries of Bourgeois Life 1830–1930*. New York: Penguin Books, 1987.

Vallès, Jules. *L'Insurgé*. Paris: Editions Gallimard, 1964.

# WILLIAM MORRIS
## The Politics of Romance
### *Miguel Abensour*

*Portrait of Jane Morris* (Astarte Syriaca *(1877) by Dante Gabriel Rossetti,*
© *Manchester City Art Galleries)*

W hat is it that makes *News from Nowhere* an exceptional work in the history of utopias? How is it that the same critics who denounce the repressive character of the utopian form, nonetheless argue that in writing *News from Nowhere*, William Morris invented an exception to the rule and created a newfound space for utopia? A first answer to this question consists in putting forward the libertarian dimension of the Morrissian utopia. For anarchist critics such as Max Nettlau and George Woodcock, Morris succeeded in writing such an authentically libertarian utopia that doubts may be raised as to the necessarily authoritarian destiny of utopianism. With Morris, utopia would be a magical atmosphere of freedom; the society of the future would be wreathed in an aura of peace. Yet is it sufficient to recognize the libertarian tone of *News from Nowhere*? By emphasizing the themes or choices that demonstrate the antiauthoritarian tendencies of the author, do we not run the risk of turning Morris's utopia into a gem of literary anarchism?

The problematic is indeed poorly construed when we claim to account for the uniqueness of Morris's "utopian romance" by way of the themes or the doctrine that the utopian story illustrates. I would like to suggest that it is more appropriate to focus on the form of the story and, beyond this, on the form of the utopia itself. This conversion of the gaze is all the more easily undertaken if the reader abandons the very idea of mastering and appropriating a text.[1] It is enough to first let oneself be seduced by Morris's vision of a time of rest and friendship, to welcome this promise of happiness and the pleasure it provokes, to be lured, and to unhesitatingly succumb to its movement—the invitation to the voyage. And once the moment of separation has come, it is enough to ride up the course of time; that is, the course of the reading that seeks its magic. Rather than rushing to extract theses that supposedly explain the utopian text, it is more worthwhile to heed the charm of the utopia and the presence of this charm, to take on the adventure of a reading that may reproduce along its very course, and right up to the separation that comes with closing the book, something of the utopian adventure itself. If we accept to be taken in by the ordeal of the utopian journey, if we freely embark on the "voyage," we are oriented to the junction chosen by Morris, where his aesthetic experience and the different forms of his political engagement cohere. Let us imagine for a moment what a utopia would have been like if it were written by Charles Baudelaire or Gérard de Nerval, a utopia fostered by the interest these two poets shared for the utopian illuminations of the nineteenth century. . . .

Beyond this poetic quality, *News from Nowhere* belongs to what I have called the new utopian spirit: the remarkable constellation that arose in the wake of the three great "changes of course" effected by Claude Henry Saint-Simon, Charles Fourier, and Robert Owen at the beginning of the nineteenth century.[2] This new utopian spirit is characterized by the integration of the revolutionary criticisms of utopia—for example, Marx's and Proudhon's (though not only theirs)—without for all that spelling the end of utopia. To the contrary, the integration of the radical critique of utopia redirected it on channels that gave it the foresight to resist the dialectic of emancipation—the reversal of emancipation into its opposite. However, in Morris's case the new orientation results in the very transformation of utopia—thus his originality—to the point that in the same *oeuvre* the resumption of classical utopianism and its transcendence are juxtaposed. Morrissian utopia substitutes the inherited form of utopia with a utopia that, for lack of a better word, we may call experimental, in the sense that the structure of the narration involves putting utopia to the test, to the point that utopia itself is affected by an irremediable fragility. This self-testing of utopia awakens yet again Morris's poetic talent, and propels him to transpose the quest of the medieval "romance" in his vision of the society of the future. As will be seen, the quality of "utopian romance" in *News from Nowhere* indicates that the reemergence of Morris's early romanticism in the revolutionary phase of his later years was of a kind to bring about a new romantic utopianism.

If we keep these three dimensions in mind—the libertarian tone, the new utopian spirit, the metamorphosis of "romance"—it becomes clear that, for Morris, the question was not simply to go from romanticism to revolution, but also to invent a juncture between romantic rebellion and the new revolutionary demand.

In what way did this juncture result in an innovation of the form of modern socialist utopia? This is none other than the question of the transformation of function strikingly announced by Walter Benjamin:

> It is not spiritual renewal as Fascists proclaim, that is
> desirable: technical innovations are suggested. . . . I should
> like to content myself here with a reference to the decisive
> difference between the mere supplying of a productive
> apparatus and its transformation. And I should like to preface
> my discussion . . . with the proposition that to supply a
> productive apparatus without—to the utmost extent
> possible—changing it would still be a highly censurable
> course even if the material with which it is supplied seemed
> to be of a revolutionary nature.[3]

## The New Utopian Spirit and Technical Innovation

When reading *News from Nowhere* we may find several indications of technical innovation. First of all, the way the book first appeared is worth considering. Morris had *News from Nowhere* published as a serial in a revolutionary socialist periodical, *The Commonweal*, from January to October 1890. The decision to have his utopia published in this way already implies a transformation of "the instrument of production" in its relation to distribution and the practice of writing itself. Above all, it aims at revising the distinction between author and reader in the way suggested by Benjamin: "For the reader is at all times ready to become a writer, that is, a describer, but also a prescriber."[4] We need only compare this mode of publication with the traditional kind—the closed medium of the book—to realize that the presentation of utopia over a ten-month period establishes, and aims at establishing, a different relation with readers. According to Benjamin, the description of the author as producer must extend as far as the press. While we should avoid any optimistic illusions as to the possibility of a dialogical community, we can nonetheless see that this mode of publication—undertaken in a milieu highly concerned with descriptions of socialism—is designed to solicit responses, to open a forum for the negative or positive reactions of readers during the very process of composition, *in statu nascendi*. A relation of exchange is thus engaged in the publication process itself: from beginning to end alterations, distinctions, amendings, and changes of course remain possible. In a certain sense, the reader is invited to participate in the act of writing utopia. As Benjamin shows, the press is the fundamental basis from which one can judge whether the separation of author and reader has been truly challenged.

Morris's decision to have his book published by a radical press indicates his overall effort to struggle against the ambivalence of utopian writing as a form of anticommunication that is simultaneously an invitation to break that very closure. The means to overcome this ambivalence is to transform utopian writing into a necessarily partial and provisional moment of revolutionary practice within a specific group; in this case, the Socialist League and the readers of *The Commonweal*. The moment of revolutionary practice belongs as such to the recipients no less than to the producer, since the recipients are encouraged to propose their own utopia, to inscribe written utopia elsewhere than on paper, to criticize it and take a step beyond the written word. This form of publication aims at reducing the coercion specific to written utopia. By virtue of its periodic, instantaneous, ephemeral, and unstable character, the open form endows utopia and its recipients with a freedom resembling that of speech. Written utopia is no longer a closed totality that one must take or leave, but is instead a sort of lateral play in relation to classical political activity that by and through the intervals it opens, draws more and more players into active participation.

This transformation is all the more real given that the writing and the publication of the utopian *oeuvre* is inscribed in a theoretical and political whole—the radical journal—that oversteps utopian writing itself and whose own demands do not fail to come into play, making their mark on the orientation of utopia at the moment it is still being written. This was also the method chosen by Joseph Déjacque for *L'Humanisphère*, first published in *Le Libertaire* from 1858 to 1861. Not only is the relation more open but, more importantly, this mode of publication seeks to counter the dogmatism of classical utopianism. Utopia does not aim at creating or informing the movement; it is an integral part of the movement, a utopian variation within a common experience. A new type of reception is thus targeted. A book first aims for the milieu of specialized critics: men of letters, reviewers, philosophers, famous writers, etc., and beyond this, if we consider *Voyage en Icarie* or *Looking Backward*, for instance, the goal is to transcend ideological differences and the division of classes and to reach the greater public. With Morris, to the contrary, the first and most important milieu to be addressed is the extremely limited circle of radical readers of a theoretically and politically engaged journal. This new type of reception corresponds to a new type of utopian production. Morris does not write outside of the social movement to bring it a "new awareness"; he does not bring the good news of a socialist system, nor does he write a book-sized "new Jerusalem" that he intends to impose on a grateful world. E. P. Thompson rightly insists on the spontaneity of *News from Nowhere*; and this spontaneity is specifically what distinguishes Morris's utopia from the grand-scale tactics of the kind that tempted Cabet, who threw himself into writing *Voyage en Icarie* in order to found a socialist school.[5]

Indeed, Morris intervenes from within the movement as a member participating in an active and specific way. It is in the thick of the debates and oppositions of various socialist groups that he offers his personal vision of a communist society and the path likely to attaining it. One of the great merits of Thompson's critical study is to have withdrawn Morris's utopia from literary history in order to return it to the history of socialism. Moreover, *News from Nowhere* effects a definitive rupture with utopian socialism's monological principle by its open and pluridimensional character; it is composed so as to allow for an exchange to ensue between producer and recipient. Or rather, the story of utopia itself contains an invitation for readers to respectively formulate and communicate their own vision of communism. The open quality of *News from Nowhere* is itself indicative of this dialogical goal. One may for example consider "a brisk conversational discussion" between six different political tendencies on the question of knowing what may happen "the day after the revolution." Far from the narrator mounting on a podium in order to impose the truth of his perspective, he expresses a wish: "If only I could one day see this new life." The subjectivity of the narrator's desire rebounds and draws the desire of the recipients, inviting them to in turn envision the new life at the moment they are reading about it, thereby establishing a two-way movement of feelings and desires. From the outset, Morris situates his text on the side of one of the foundational principles of the new utopian spirit announced by Déjacque:

> Happiness makes me sigh, and I evoke this ideal. If you find this ideal desirable, then do as I do and admire it. If you notice imperfections, then correct them. If the ideal as such does not please you, then create another one. My ideal is not exclusive—if yours should strike me as more perfect, I would willingly abandon my own for it.[6]

This basis for technical innovation involves the rejection of the utopia-model and its replacement by the utopia-*simulacrum*. Yet if one recalls the use of the *via obliqua* by Thomas More, the father of classical utopianism, one must perhaps clarify what forms the basis of the opposition. The technical innovation of the apparatus of production and publication indeed involves a radical mutation in the very form of utopia.

For those like Morris who deliberately and intellectually adhere to the theory of Marxian history—a theory that specifically claims the right of historical innovation and carries within it the prescience of a radically new future, inconceivable and heterogeneous—the alternative becomes: either to entirely renounce the form of classical utopianism (juridico-political model-building) or to invent and propose, on the basis of a historical expectation, a new form of utopianism inspired by sources other than those of the classical model and one that, above all, displaces its intervention to another region of society. In a certain sense, one can first measure Morris's technical innovation negatively. In the first place, a slide to juridical regulation is revealed as impossible. And by contrast to Cabet's or Bellamy's utopias, which respectively gave rise to "Icarian communism" and "nationalism," one cannot extract from *News from Nowhere* any doctrine or any specific socialist system. An even more significant characteristic that indicates a deliberate rupture with the monological principle of utopian socialism is the criticism, nearly unanimous in the press, that Morris failed to offer any educational method. And classical Marxist criticism, which is up to a certain point favorable of Morris, does not for all that emphasize any less the weakness of the Morrissian *oeuvre* from an educational perspective.[7]

However, far from being a weakness or an omission, as the Marxist educationalists would have it, the absence of educational method highlights precisely what is new about *News from Nowhere*. The power of Morris's utopia stems from there being no ideal or plan for the moral education of humanity and, furthermore, from the impossibility of there being one. The rupture with utopian model-building implies a radically antipedagogical effect to the extent that any model necessarily contains an educational method and vice versa. No imaginary description of a new mode of social repression of impulse inspires or haunts the author of *News from Nowhere*. Morris's originality comes from his utopia being situated elsewhere, on another terrain. For this reason it is at once difficult and sterile to feign systematizing the Morrissian utopia in the form of a reasoned list of "solutions" that answer the great questions treated in classical utopias. Such an attempt can only have a provisional meaning; in the case of *News from Nowhere* it is only of interest if it leads the critic who undertakes it to discover its illegitimacy by his very failure and, consequently, to also discover the extent to which Morris's utopia indicates an original tendency characterized by ordeals and exploration, over and against all solutions.

Morris's utopia first distinguishes itself by a dramatic structure that is developed on two levels—between the characters of the narrative, and between the characters and the narrator—consisting of scenes concerned much less with proposing solutions as with depicting *in vivo* another way of life, a more desirable life that breaks with the bourgeois idea of happiness as much as with the utilitarian descriptions within socialism. The passing of time, rendered all the more striking by the three-day ride up the river, intensifies the dramatic structure. Few have truly taken into consideration the subtitle that Morris himself chose for his novel: *News from Nowhere; or, An Epoch of Rest, Being Some Chapters from a Utopian Romance.*

The great idea and the great innovation of Morris is to have introduced in socialist literature an often neglected and sometimes condemned quality: the utopian marvelous. To borrow an expression dear to Fourier, who also on occasion made use of the utopian marvelous, Morris presented utopia in "the romantic style." *News from Nowhere* plays out the utopian marvelous just as the "romances" that Morris so admired are steeped in the medieval world of chivalry, its initiations, and its ordeals during the quest for the Holy Grail. It is only in the greatest and most emphatically dreamlike utopias that the marvelous emerges. And yet, as Pierre Mabille so rightly emphasizes, the marvelous calls for utopia just as utopia calls for the marvelous:

> The marvelous expresses the need to bypass empirical limits, imposed by our structure, to attain a greater beauty, a greater power, a greater pleasure, a greater duration. The marvelous wants to bypass the limits of space and of time, it wants to destroy all barriers, it is the struggle of freedom against everything which reduces, destroys, and mutilates; it is a tension, that is to say, something different from routine mechanical work, an impassioned and poetic tension . . . it is the strange lucidity of the delirium, the light of the dream and the green light of passion; it burns above the masses at the time of revolt. But the marvelous is less the extreme tension of being than the juncture of desire with external reality. The marvelous is, at a specific moment, the troubling instant in which the world give us its assent.[8]

This is the moment that *News from Nowhere* grasps, the epiphany that transforms England into an island of happiness. But this moment is fragile and necessarily ephemeral, for as a soon as it is achieved, the threat of separation surges on the horizon, as if in anticipation of the fading of the time of rest at nightfall, the protagonists of *News from Nowhere* were preparing for the experience of new tensions. E. Guyot correctly perceives the magical quality, the dreamlike climate that animates the landscape and the river as much as the strange beings of *News from Nowhere*.[9] One cannot consider Morris's utopia a socialist parable based on the *Critique of the Gotha Program*, designed to illustrate the Marxian theory of the two stages of history, without totally misreading the text.

In a fundamental way, "romance" is the matrix of the Morrissian utopia. The "utopian romance" resembles the "fantasy novels" that express the unsettling and strange marvelousness of countries situated outside familiar space and time. Soliciting the reader's desires, provoking his pleasure, playing with his fantasies—this is what connects "utopian romance" to "fantasy novels." Wonderland and Nowhere are neighboring countries, and it is easy for Morris's imagination to step from one to the other or even to bring them together and form a composite image. In the "utopian romance" the dialectic of the real and the imaginary calls out to an unknown future; it unfolds as a promise of a new, strange, and fascinating happiness, like the portent of a change of scenery that takes on the mottled appearances of a continuous temptation. The figure of the woman, personified by Ellen in *News from Nowhere*, receives a privileged role. This recourse to the utopian marvelous intensifies the ambition of Morrissian utopia to awaken and energize desires so that they might rush toward their liberation, by contrast to those utopias that are an imaginary projection of a new mode of social repression of impulses. In his utopian writing, Morris plays the marvelous against the closure of juridico-political model-building. Through the quest and the practice of the marvelous, Morris's utopia is akin to the romantic utopianism of Novalis, Hölderlin, and Déjacque in ways that have as yet to be explored. It is the affinity of Morrissian utopia with what André Reszler calls "the anarchist aesthetic," with a tradition distinct from the bourgeois sensibility of the nineteenth century, and whose political radicalism is coterminous with changes in aesthetic form, that one sees the strong rapport of Morris's work with the libertarian spirit. Peter Kropotkin tried to formulate this aesthetic starting with the writing of Proudhon, Wagner, Tolstoy, Belinsky, Chernyshevsky, Ruskin, and Morris; it may be defined as the cult of the unknown—a Dionysian religion of the marvelous and revolutionary fantasy.[10]

Throughout his life Morris attempted to break open the doors to the unknown, to the "nowhere"—not in an "afterworld," but on the surface of this very earth. The medieval marvelous, the pre-Raphaelite marvelous, news from nowhere, and the reign of freedom are leitmotifs in the development of Morris's thought. If Morris's work covers a variety of fields—the great sagas, the interest in ethnological writings, the fantasy novels—there is nonetheless a common theme to his diverse experiments: the cult of the unknown, the sudden change of course that leads to an "otherwhere." And rather than emphasizing the weakness of Morris's romanticism in relation to the tradition of realism, as Marxist critics have done, it is more insightful to see how beyond all doctrine Morris, like Bakunin, deplored the everyday absence of "the love for fantasy, for extraordinary and unbelievable adventures, undertakings that open our eyes to an unlimited horizon for which no-one can predict the outcome."[11]

The intervention of Morrissian utopia in the social sphere harks back to the experiments of Fourier and the Saint-Simonians in the region of passions: it is action on the movement of passion, what Georges Bataille calls affective formation. If history has leveled everything to the point of atrophying desire and of narrowing it to the limits of "man" such as he has been shaped over centuries of oppression (history for the Fourierists is the procrustean bed of desire), utopia has as its goal to undo the work of history, to disentangle all the cords, to reactivate beyond historical sedimentation a new being-in-the-world grounded in the play of multiple energetic and violent passions. Fourier invents a flamboyant vision of the primitive Eden: "Men had none of that pastoral simplicity that never existed anywhere but in the writings of poets. They were proud, sensual, slaves to their fantasies; the women and children acted likewise."[12] Throughout his life Morris would explore a major leitmotif of nineteenth-century revolutionary thought: the theme of "the barbarians." This theme was enriched by Morris's ethnological conversations with Edward Carpenter and the latter's stigmatization of civilization, which scandalized the Fabians who were convinced of swimming with the stream of history. It is in this context that Morris's time of rest becomes intelligible as a highly original utopian hypothesis on the "hazy realm of non-history," the moment of forgetfulness that alone clears the way for a new history, an amazing history beyond everything it has heretofore told or produced.

With the time of rest, we do not achieve a superior phase of history, we no longer inherit the past, we no longer work to undo the stigmata of capitalist society—we forget, we emigrate elsewhere. In short, we leave history, we put an end to the pattern. We make a new body, a new sensibility, a new understanding. And without casting any light on the hypothesis of a time of rest, the critic is condemned to miss what is new about *News from Nowhere*. He can only see an improved Arcadia, or he will condemn the forgetfulness or semiforgetfulness of economic and political problems and evoke the weakness or the gratuity of Morrissian utopia. But there is in fact only a semiforgetfulness, for the time of rest stems from a communist society that has already attained a state of saturation; that is, from a society that has met all its fundamental needs. Thus the extraordinary liberation of unprecedented possibilities and thus the quest for new ways of playing out the ontological affirmation of passion. This is in fact what best signals the rupture with Marxian teleology. For Marx, the veritable reign of freedom can flower only by being rooted in the reign of necessity, and necessity as such constitutes the closure of the Marxian projection. By contrast, Morris is oriented in a completely different direction: the reign of freedom instead develops starting only with itself, a "concretely positive" movement. To better understand what is at stake in this adventure, one may compare Morris's time of rest—the great holiday from historical time, the vacation of humanity, the temporal bracketing from which a new way of existing may emerge—to Nietzsche's poetic imperative:

> This condition—unhistorical, anti-historical through and through—is the womb not only of the unjust but of every just deed too; and no painter will paint his picture, no general achieve his victory, no people attain its freedom without having first desired and striven for it in an unhistorical condition.[13]

And Nietzsche points out the essential condition for this freedom:

> In the case of the smallest or of the greatest happiness, however, it is always the same things that makes happiness happiness: the ability to forget or, expressed in more scholarly fashion, the capacity to feel *outside of history*. He who cannot sink down on the threshold of the moment and forget all the

past, who cannot stand balanced like a goddess of victory without growing dizzy and afraid, will never know what happiness is—worse, he will never do anything to make others happy.[14]

The great Nietzschean theme of forgetfulness is present in Morrissian utopia in the form of a severance from the historical continuum. A very complex play is established between the morphological projection of communism taken from Marx and the time of rest, the springboard for the leap into the unknown. The question is not to again valorize utopia against science but—and this new approach is what epitomizes Morris's originality—to base a new utopia on expectation. A very subtle dialectic of forgetfulness and memory—the memory of nostalgia and not that of heritage—is apparent in the roles people act out at different moments in *News from Nowhere*, and it unfolds throughout the hidden and most profound structure of the novel. The ride up the river with Ellen (Ellen-Diotima) signals a return to the origins at the same time that it provokes the ordeal of forgetfulness. The question arises whether the narrator will shed his old skin, forget all the past events and the glum repetition of history. If on the one hand the narrator has the role of reintroducing history to this nowhere land, on the other the inhabitants of *News from Nowhere*, and especially Ellen, triumph over history by submitting it to the ordeal of nonhistory.

There is another angle of approach that may cast some light on what is meant by the time of rest. Morris thinks the future society not so much in terms of the subversion of the State than as the subversion of bourgeois society as a whole. This again points to the difference between Morrissian utopia and utopian model-building. Key to this distinction is the question of work. In the eyes of nearly all the great historical utopians, work is at best one of the essential conditions of humanity, at worst its fundamental condition. The goal of utopia is to propose a new organization and regulation of work without putting work itself into question and without envisioning the subversion of work—one of the major taboos of civilization in the Fourierist sense. The classical utopias are, as such, strictly dependent on the model of production.

By contrast, the time of rest expresses a will to exit from the realm of work. By applying to the sphere of work the radical criticism characteristic of his *oeuvre*, Morris reveals the content of his critique and, more specifically, he points out a radical discrepancy in utopian thinking: a utopia that embodies the criticism of work necessarily withdraws from the utopian model that can offer only variations in a closed circle, and it rediscovers the dynamic of play and festivity in the horizon that it opens as much as in the movement that propels it forward. Bataille, in his study of erotism, can be seen as carrying out a similar critique of instrumental production:

> There is in nature and there subsists in man a movement
> which always exceeds the bounds, that can never be anything
> but partially reduced to order. . . . In the domain of our life
> excess manifests itself insofar as violence wins over reason.
> Work demands the sort of conduct where effort is in a
> constant relation with productive efficiency. It demands
> rational behavior where the wild impulses worked out on
> feast days and usually in games are frowned upon.[15]

When interpreting a utopia the fundamental question is to know whether or not this rational basis of human life is challenged. The "carnivalesque" inspiration best illustrates the tendency of certain utopias to transgress this dominant limit. Through this transgression, utopia necessarily increases and multiplies its hold over affective formations. By its tendency to immediately withdraw passion from the imperative of production and the reign of utility, utopia orients affective formations in a radically different direction; it sets out to realize a new principle of reality whose desire and foretaste can be communicated and presented only by means of a *simulacrum*. The difference concerns not only the effect produced but also the now transformed object: utopia becomes an extreme disruption of everyday life, a new a way of living, a presentation of new surroundings, at once the product and the instrument of new modes of behavior— a poetry of the future.

According to Morris's vision, the originality of the society of the future will specifically consist in discovering or in rediscovering happiness in multiplicity, in the glimmer of daily life: "They will discover, or rediscover rather, that the true secret of happiness lies in taking a genuine interest in all the details of daily life and in elevating them to art."[16] In such a utopia technical innovation is expressed by the imaginary construction of situations, in the manner related by Guy Debord in "Report on the Construction of Situations":

> that is to say, the concrete construction of ambiances of life and their transformation into a superior passional quality. We must develop a methodical intervention based on the complex factors of two components in perpetual interaction: the material environment of life and the comportments it gives rise to and which radically transform it.[17]

By virtue of its rupture with juridico-political model-building, by virtue of its refusal of an educational method—and especially *qua* doctrinal system—by virtue of its generalized will to subversion that extends all the way to the realm of work, and by virtue of the call to awaken the passions, such a form of utopia is almost automatically driven toward a radical opening and merits the title of "the open work." Its constitutive principle is the exchange of fantasy, and utopia becomes the stage for this exchange, for a dialogue of passions. This function of utopia is all the more crucial when one considers that it corresponds to the function Morris attributes to the work of art in general: to arouse the pleasure of the spectator, to increase his capacity of happiness, his faculty of desiring and dreaming, and maybe even awaken the impulse to make the beautiful pass over to reality—in short, the function of art like the function of utopia is to be a promise of happiness. Utopia thus practiced bears a new poetry of humanity's relation to the world, a new poetry of human relations, "the call of each freedom to all the others" in the words of Merleau-Ponty.[18] For Morris, the function of utopia is grounded in the function of art, and "the end proposed by a work of art is always to please the person whose senses are to be made conscious of it. It was done *for* someone who was to be made happier by it."[19]

## Technical Innovation and the Critique of Culture

This technical innovation of the form of utopia deserves our attention, for throughout his life Morris would incessantly tackle the problem of changing the function and form of production in modern society—and this problem was behind all those fields in which he excelled: furniture, the minor arts, the decorative arts, painting, architecture, printing. To understand exactly what Morris means by technical innovation, it is also important to abandon the traditional image of him as an aesthete, a partisan of the religion of art, or, rather, a prophet who envisioned the redemption of modern society through beauty. Morris's undertakings are incorrectly associated with this completely unacceptable image. In all of Morris's writings on art, a theme insistently returns: the dependence of art on a situation and a historical system that overtakes and contains it. This thesis results in the deliberate, lucid, and consistent abandoning of the traditional concepts proper to classical art criticism, such as those of inspiration, genius, and creation. Indeed, for Morris the dependence of art forbids the separation of aesthetic criticism and social and political criticism.

Confronted with the crisis of art that arose in Europe especially around 1850—resulting, among other things, from the rise of unprecedented techniques of reproduction and the institution of new relations with the public—rather than reactively avoiding it and professing "art for art's sake," Morris chooses to instead focus all the more on social issues, in the wake of Ruskin at first and more independently later on.[20] Ruskin indeed provided the *élan* by teaching what in Morris's eyes amounted to a great discovery, that "the art of any epoch must of necessity be the expression of its social life."[21] Refusing to consider art an autonomous region separate from society, Morris refuses to even interpret the crisis that plagues art from an idealist perspective. The crisis of modern culture cannot be simplistically understood as a spiritual crisis or a crisis in values: it signals a far more deeply embedded historical crisis. Nor should Morris's struggle be confused with a struggle for beauty or a struggle to save art in a world in crisis. The fascist slogan *"fiat ars pereat mundus"* is the antithesis of Morris's vision. Time and time again, he went out of his way to remind audiences too exclusively preoccupied with art that the issue is not to cultivate art in colonies or on "artists' islands" in the margins of bourgeois society, nor to launch a new crusade for beauty and transform the "soul." Morris's plea is a plea not for beauty as such, but for life, for a more beautiful life—one that is enriched, more sensual, more intense.[22] Against those tempted to analyze the crisis of culture as the result of a lack of creative individuals or even of geniuses, Morris outlines a theory of an "artistic subject" that prohibits the belief that a clarion call for strong artistic personalities is likely to bring about a renaissance.[23]

Morris does not separate art from the system of production contemporaneous with artistic activity, and that is why the crisis of culture strikes him as being extremely profound, if not irreversible. He belongs to the century when Hegel began his course on aesthetics with the famous phrase: "Art is for us a thing of the past," thus indicating that art is no longer capable of satisfying our needs for the Absolute and that from here on all its truth and life belongs to the world, and to real work in the world. Morris is moreover very conscious of the enormous process behind the remolding of artistic forms, a process central to modernity and inextricable from the withering away of art. To judge the fate of art and culture, Morris adopts a concept that breaks with the usual perspective for aesthetic judgment: that of production.

*Art and Its Producers* is the title of one of his lectures, delivered in 1888 at Liverpool. Considering art from the point of view of production, Morris posits the existence of a relationship of dependence between artistic production and the general productive system of a society. For Morris there is a dependence between art and materials; between art and the individual or the collective mechanism of production; between art and the division of work; and, above all, between art and the social situation in which the mass of producers are maintained. Therefore the issue is not to ask what the political perspective of artistic production is regarding the relations of production as whole—whether the perspective is reactionary by encouraging these relations or revolutionary by challenging them or helping to bring about their transformation—but to ask the perhaps more modest but necessarily primary question: what is the place of artistic production in the relations of production? This question submits the products of artistic activity to a direct social analysis.[24] To answer it Morris juxtaposes the place of art in the Middle Ages and its place in the nineteenth century, considering them from the perspective of production as much as from the point of view of consumption. The conclusion is clear-cut: in modern society, art has become a separate activity, specialized and even esoteric, accessible only to a small cultivated "elite" that encloses art in museums and in culture; it is practiced in a coterie or limited to an ornamental function. By way of contrast, the tendency of art in the Middle Ages was unitary: produced by the collectives that functioned as "guilds," art tended to penetrate and shape the whole of social life.

For Morris the point of arguing the contrast is not to advocate a return to the Middle Ages but solely to appreciate a historical description of a generalized communication between art and society. Unlike certain trends in modern art, Morris thought and took on the task of thinking through the withering away of art in modern society. His struggle for socialism is strictly allied to this thinking and to the phenomenon that corresponds to the disappearance of art *qua* place of exchange between members of a society. Seen in this light, Morris's historical critique is not far removed from Jean-François Lyotard's:

> In a society reputed archaic . . . communication takes place not according to the criteria given by Freud and Marx—the criteria of practical transformation and of verbalization—but by forms—plastic, architectural—and by rhythms that allow for a kind of "communication" at the level of the individual unconscious. This is the art-society; it was the mode of existence of art during millennia.[25]

In modern society where the integrating function of art has disappeared, art no longer has a place, the poet is stripped of any prophetic function.

By going from poetry to utopia, Morris attempted to recover the function of *vates*. On this journey, by tirelessly devoting himself to all the obligations required of daily propaganda and the political practice of a small circle of revolutionaries, he came to know what Benjamin calls the experience of poverty. It is by scandalizing friends who blamed Morris for sacrificing his poetic vocation to purportedly lesser goals, that the man who could have been the poet laureate of his generation transformed himself into a revolutionary. Little did it matter: convinced of the withering away of art in the modern world, Morris knew just how "poor" he had to be to start from scratch and clear the way for a new opening. Indeed, Morris never renounced his function of *vates;* rather, he obeyed the new demands that come with such a role in modernity. The passage to active utopia was his way of instituting a new communication between the poet and the public, of breaking the wall of silence by inventing a new "art-utopia," where the place of nowhere functions as a device for communication at the level of the individual unconscious, to borrow Lyotard's expression.

Morris—whose teachings inspired those who searched for a renewal of forms (Van de Velde, Walter Gropius, Hannes Meyer)—thereby mapped out the fundamental perspective of modern art: its dissolution *qua* socialized activity and its integration in a network of activities that are freer and vaster—a counterstructure that aims to transcend the division between art and technique, between art and everyday life. Unlike the opposite trend that would triumph with the rise of fascism and the aesthetic cult of war, Morris is not attracted to the search and absolute valorization of beauty in a world turned ugly; he instead opens the way for technical innovations.

For Morris the essential technical innovation—the one that draws other technical innovations in its wake and that allows for judgment on the progressive or revolutionary character of a work—consists in the abolition of the separation between producer and consumer, a relation that is itself a result of the modern system of production. The task is to reactivate the function of communication that once belonged to art, to enlarge it, to transform the apparatus of production to the point where the roles of producer and consumer become interchangeable—to construct works that would be a call for the transgression and destruction of the frontier between consumers and producers, a call for consumers to themselves become producers.[26] It is through Morris's engagement as an artist, through his innovations in architecture and the decorative arts, that the aporias of a reform of art conducted from above, separately from society, were revealed to him. For Morris, the division of work is situated at the heart of the crisis of modernity, and it is against the division of work (appraised by Prince Albert, during the great exhibit of 1851, as "the real principle of the division of work that we may call the motor of civilization") that he unleashed his theoretical and practical attacks. It is the revelation of the irreversible withering away of art in a world transformed root and branch by the division of labor that led Morris, through a progressive displacement, to go beyond aesthetic criticism in speech and deed, to demand a unitary critique of modern civilization, and to join the socialist movement. For Morris, the primary historical task consists of transforming the system of production by working for the abolition of the division of work, "the great intangible machine of commercial tyranny, which oppresses the lives of all of us."[27]

Does this verdict imply that artists must abandon all artistic production to become radical activists while awaiting "the great night of revolt"? In other words, does the experience of poverty necessarily entail renouncing all artistic activity? Not entirely: if it is true that the artist has to reorient his energy toward propaganda, in the strongest sense of the term—that is, as a necessary part of a great historical movement that demands the participation of artists—Morris does not for all that conclude that a total renunciation is necessary, as if it were even desirable for artistic talent to be sacrificed on the altar of the revolution. Pomposity, masochism, ostentatiousness are likewise alien to him. In truth, his position is richer and more complex. He proposes a dialectic of technical innovation and revolutionary practice. The point is to find the technical innovations that tend toward revolution and socialism. Art must renounce its "sacred" character, its exceptional quality, and cohere with the practical movement of unitary critique destined to foster the historical appearance of a new form of activity; and, conversely, the work of the revolution, of propaganda—"part of a great whole" in the words of Morris—must not be limited to the revolutionary process and become a new *deus ex machina* but should on the contrary throw itself into the entirety of productive activities and work here and now for their transformation.

Once we recognize Morris's original position in relation to the crisis of modern culture, as well as his innovative work for a renewal of forms—whose crowning achievement is the foundation of the Bauhaus in 1919 by Walter Gropius—we are better equipped for understanding the type of pursuit that structures the new utopian spirit.[28] Reintegrated in the context of a general will for technical innovation, Morris's transformation of utopia takes on a new fullness. It plays a leading role in the overall movement for the renewal of forms within modernity and encourages us to focus our attention on how, as a specifically modern movement, the function of utopia is transformed.

Benjamin insists that whoever wants to act on the conditions of production must not only concentrate on changing the products but must also discover new means of production. In short, the products of the innovator must possess an "organizing function," and Benjamin concludes with some essential propositions concerning such revised products:

> Their political tendency alone is not enough. . . . Now it is
> true that opinions matter greatly, but the best are of no use if

they make nothing useful out of those who have them. The best political tendency is wrong if it does not demonstrate the attitude with which it is to be followed. And this attitude the writer can only demonstrate in his particular activity: that is, in writing. A political tendency is the necessary, never the sufficient condition of the organizing function of a work.[29]

In our context, this means that it is not enough to analyze the new utopian spirit starting with the political tendency, the doctrine—in Morris's case the Marxist theory of the future. Above all, the new utopian spirit must be interpreted starting with the function it attributes to utopia and with the new form that it attains. This perspective also has the merit of keeping away the useless quarrels of appropriation between Fabians, Marxists, and anarchists or, rather, it answers these quarrels specifically by leaving the sterile framework in which they take place.

It is all the more legitimate to examine Morris's work in this "technical" perspective given that his theoretical, political, and even utopian texts contain a preliminary theorizing on utopia and the dream. Without here going into detail, suffice it to say that Morris poses the question of the function of utopia in society within a problematic that involves three terms: utopia, truth, and *praxis*. While fully taking into consideration historical practice and its accomplishment in class society—i.e., revolutionary practice—Morris retrieves utopia from the scientific projection with which it is too often confused: he dissociates utopia from truth, from the "truth of history" understood as the existence of a unique meaning to history that utopia, as it were, would have the function of illustrating. Unlike the utopianism of the Saint-Simonians or Cabet, utopia is not thought by Morris as being the authority whose function is to impose truth on *praxis*. Indeed, according to Morris there is more truth in an even modest stage of *praxis* than in the most achieved and the most harmonious utopia.

And even if the morphological projection, taken from the Marxian theory of the communist movement, constitutes the ground for Morrissian utopia, the latter is far from being thereby limited. To the contrary, Morris's utopianism distinguishes itself from the Marxian foundation by soaring above it and intervening elsewhere differently. Utopia withdraws from the concept to become a mediating image open to "the truth of desire." For Morris, we cannot know the future, we cannot with any authority predict what "solutions" socialism would bring about; as it happens, socialism would not bring about any solutions, it would turn bourgeois civilization as a whole on its head:

> To attempt to answer such questions fully or authoritatively
> would be attempting the impossibility of constructing a
> scheme of a new society out of the materials of the old,
> before we knew which of those materials would disappear
> and which would endure through the evolution which is
> leading us to the great change.[30]

Yet this admission, specified and nuanced time and time again, rather than signing utopia's death warrant and designating its end, as the positivist tendency within Marxism had done, instead opens and discloses the dream, the utopia, the vision that asks to be clarified, to its veritable dimension: the education of desire. Therefore to integrate Morris's utopia in a scientific projection, or even to see his utopia as an illustration of the scientific truths of Marxism in the form of a parable, constitutes exactly the interpretative countersense of *News from Nowhere*—one which is all the more wrongheaded inasmuch that it totally misses what is new about Morris and reveals only the uneasiness of critics before a newness that they may sometimes sense but which they then promptly and energetically distort. Marxian criticism indeed fosters contradictory ambitions: it wants to take on the modernity of Morrissian utopia but without for all that breaking with positivism. This is why it takes refuge in the loophole that consists in reducing utopia to a scientific projection or even in unabashedly designating *News from Nowhere* a "scientific utopia."

The education of desire is the "organizing function" of Morrissian utopia. This formula may cause some confusion: the point is not for utopia (unlike the tradition that calls for the "moral education of humanity") to assign "true" or "just" goals to desire but rather to educate desire, to stimulate it, to awaken it—not to assign it a goal but to open a path for it: "Only this remains to be said that socialism does not recognize any finality in the progress and aspirations of humanity; and that we clearly understand that the furthest we can now conceive of is only a stage of the great journey of evolution that joins the future and the past to the present."[31] Desire must be taught to desire, to desire better, to desire more, and above all to desire otherwise; it must learn to shatter the dead weight, to alleviate the weakness of appetence, to liberate the firebirds of desire, to give free rein to the impulse of adventure.

"A feeling of adventure" shapes one of the more hidden themes of *News from Nowhere*. It is just as implicit in the upsurge of a new humanity toward an unknown future society, as during the ride up the river when the narrator experiences the ordeal of a strange recollection and rebirth. The time of rest is the beginning of desire's conversion, its qualitative transfiguration, as if beyond the renunciation of the principle of renunciation, the time of rest fosters the liberation of desire from the tendency of greed, the frenzy of pleasure, and from every form of plenitude that remains dependent on the predatory model, such as it may be glimpsed in the bourgeois concept of nature. For Theodor Adorno "fullness is inseparable from craving," "there is no hope without quenching of the desire."[32] It is in this suspension of time, on the mottled surface of the river, facing this fluid mirror, that humanity recognizes again the beauty of appearance by abandoning itself to the ephemeral quality of water. The time of rest is one of the more original channels followed by Morrissian utopia to undo the dialectic of socialism, to ward off its effects, and to open by this rhythm an unexplored realm to desire—beyond need and beyond work. The time of rest withdraws desire from reified forms of satisfaction and pushes it to take its flight above all repetition, toward a veritable "otherwhere." According to the old Hammond, this complex relationship of utopia with desire is inscribed in the structure of utopia itself and in the origin of revolution: "Looking back now, we can see that the great motive-power of the change was a longing for freedom and equality, akin if you please to the unreasonable passion of the lover."[33]

The bringing into play of the "dialectical images" constitutive of utopia occurs in a very subtle way in Morris's *oeuvre*.[34] To simplify, a first approach may be seen in the relation that links the dream to the medieval romance: the dialectical image turns toward the past from where a voice rises that calls on the present (*A Dream of John Ball*). From another approach the relations of romance and utopia are deployed: the dialectical image orientates itself toward the future which in turn acts on the present (*News from Nowhere, A Utopian Romance*). However this is indeed a simplification, for in truth the temporal dimensions incessantly interpenetrate and are exchanged, so that the farthest future awakens and reactivates the most distant past, "the elements coming from a primitive history, this is to say, from a society without classes."

The newest future is nourished at the deepest and freshest source of humanity "the childhood of the world," and at the ontogenetic level one of the inhabitants of *News from Nowhere* evokes the connection between childhood, play, and the imagination: "it is the child-like part of us that produces works of imagination."[35]

Finally, there is a highly nuanced dialectic of forgetfulness and memory that subtly constructs the relations between the protagonists; it functions as a set of communicating vessels between a consciousness weighed down by history and a consciousness that by imagining the suffering of the past, attempts to break the envelope of forgetfulness.

## The Open Work and Experimental Utopia

Once the function of Morrissian utopia has been recognized, once its contribution to the renewal of forms has been valorized and the nature of its dialectical imagery has been affirmed, the prerequisites have been met for opening critical pathways that may lead to the height of their object—the new utopian spirit—without straying from the adventure at hand.

*News from Nowhere* first comes across as an essentially mixed work. It is a romance, a political tract, a literary composition, the memoirs of a revolutionary, a text of educational propaganda for a radical review, a dream, a historical projection, a political debate, a parody, a *simulacrum*. As a work that easily conforms to different uses, one can interpret it as one pleases; and this is indeed the clearest indication of its modernity. It is the composite character of Morris's utopia that makes it eminently modern as an "open work," in Umberto Eco's sense. For Eco, "in fact, the form of the work of art gains its aesthetic validity precisely in proportion to the number of different perspectives from which it can be viewed and understood."[36] Conversely, classical utopia dangerously resembles what Eco opposes to the work of art: the traffic sign. Indeed, by virtue of its monologism classical utopianism tends to function as a traffic sign placed on the road of the future: this way and not another, this goal and not another. Also the ironic dimension present in many utopian texts—if it is not itself constitutive of utopian play (obviously, the very term *utopia* comes from a game on words)—should be considered, for it divides the utopian text in such a way that it can never coincide with itself. It is precisely this authoritarian pedagogical character, this monologism, that the young Marx had already stigmatized, who juxtaposed it with the *new tendency*, writing "that we do not anticipate the world dogmatically . . . we first try to discover the new world from a critique of the old one. . . . Thus we do not confront the world dogmatically with a new principle, proclaiming: Here is the truth. Here kneel before it!"[37]

Moreover—and this is where the relation to the renewal of forms becomes clear—Morris's utopia is open in a less metaphorical and in a more concrete way. Following Umberto Eco's analysis, the author offers the critic an "incomplete work" that is "quite like the pieces of a Mecano; the critic is given the impression that the author is disinterested as to their ultimate end."[38]

One indeed observes a certain correlation between the poetics of the open work and the specificity of the new utopian spirit; or, more exactly, one can even say that the new utopian spirit is germane to the poetics of the open work. It conceives and practices utopia as an open work in three related ways.

First, both the new utopian spirit and the open work encourage the interpreter to engage in acts of conscious freedom. Utopia does not aim to turn those who receive it into disciples whose activity is determined in advance by the very organization of the work instilled; it aims instead to inspire a new historical *praxis* that, by breaking with the repression of written utopia, makes utopia appear as a *simulacrum*. To the exact extent that it is a break with any form of modeling, Morris's utopia is unfinished and incomplete, and moreover it is a play on this incompleteness.

Second, if a serious consideration on the nature of the relation of interpretation to art founds the poetics of the open work, a valorization of *praxis* as the principle and motor of historical invention founds the new utopian spirit. The *praxis* of the new utopian spirit receives the essential role that the open work attributes to the interpreter who, according to Eco's poetics, does not perform a secondary work, a derived performance, but on the contrary engages in an act of interpretation that is as constitutive of the work as the writing of the work itself.

Third, utopia *qua* open work breaks with the vision of a well-ordered hierarchical world in which the stable hierarchy of beings and of laws must be reflected in the strict order of significations. There is here a correlation between the order of content and the very structure of communication. Thus Cabet has a way of informing that strictly corresponds to the authoritarian government and extreme regulation of Icaria. In Icaria, where the Icarians finally had the good fortune of finding a dictator who sincerely wanted their freedom and their prosperity, the same closure is manifest both in the form of communication and in the actual vision. The case of Cabet merits all the more to be considered given that he endowed his utopia with a "romantic aspect" borrowed from Rousseau's *Nouvelle Héloïse*, chiefly because of his desire "to be read by women." But unlike *News from Nowhere*, *Voyage en Icarie* subordinates the romantic aspect to the signified: the only goal for Cabet is to describe in a pleasant way an unequivocal social and political system. Morris, on the contrary, practices a way of informing that is in harmony with the extreme form of freedom that makes up the essence of his romantic utopia.

Moreover, it is for this reason important to examine in detail the often neglected differential structure of *News from Nowhere*. This difference is based on the contrast between the classical utopian form of presentation (the didactic and systematic form of the discussions with the old Hammond) and the dramatic form of presentation (the ride up the river that emphasizes the indeterminacy of communication and that allows for the reader's freedom of interpretation). The aspect that is in the "romantic style" in fact becomes progressively more pronounced. It is no longer there for the presentation of a system and subordinated to the signified; instead, it becomes an experimental *oeuvre*. The experience of the narrator during his voyage in utopia is transformed into the reader's own experience. This mutation and this innovation appear in the very structure of the utopian book, either in the form of an ironic commentary on Hammond and his didacticism or in the direct form of an explicit call for direct experience. A number of means strengthen this experimental situation and help establish a new relation of inwardness, or even of inherence, between the narrator and his experience of the new society. The point is to withdraw utopian experience from the classical situation of the narrator whose exterior position throughout the imaginary voyage makes the new society appear two-dimensionally, like a painting held before his eyes.

Thus the opening of the Morrissian utopia and its orientation toward radical freedom comes from its resolutely experimental character. If *News from Nowhere* is so attractive to libertarian thought and to the quest for an emancipated society, it is because through the mode of communication chosen by Morris, a rupture is effected with two forms of systematization: (1) a rupture with the systematization of classical utopia which, as a system of ideas, tends to introduce a new principle of order and organization that extends to the totality of reality by way of the sovereignty of an instituting consciousness; (2) a rupture with the systematization of Marxism, since Morris's experimental utopia specifically has as its goal the exploration of what is situated beyond the reign of necessity, what stands beyond the dialectical grasp, or, more exactly, Morris's experimental utopia aims for the transcendent *topos* where dialectical thought is confronted by the ordeal of its limits. If we may borrow a rather inelegant barbarism from Cabet, for Morris the goal is to "utopianize" Marx, but not only that. Morris transplants, so to speak, his own hypothesis on the leap from the reign of necessity to the reign of freedom, as if the discontinuity implied by the idea of a leap could not in itself be sufficient. According to Morris's vision, the passage from prehistory to a truly human history requires, over and above the leap, an even more radical discontinuity, but one that is also more patient: a suspension of historical continuity, an unresolved time apart, a bracketing that, through the gap it establishes, allows for the emergence of a new apprenticeship, a new being-in-the-world, and a new living-together. In this sense, utopia itself, the reign of freedom under the banner of a time of rest—a rest considered as a rhythmic stopping-point and not as the culmination of a voyage or an odyssey—shapes the irreducible experience that exceeds the constraints of the system. Furthermore, Morrissian utopia has a philosophical meaning by virtue of the stakes at hand and the innovation it brings about: indeed, it manifests from within the utopian tradition— and against it—the same specifically modern innovation as the "experimental philosophies" that arose in the form of nonphilosophy in the wake of the completion of the Hegelian system.[39]

Let us return to the text to see the relation between things said and things lived, and to better understand how the emphasis on experience comes about.

From the outset it is made clear to the visiting stranger that it would be pointless to describe the content of the country to be visited and that it is better that he patiently discover it on his own: "I can tell that you *are* a stranger, and must come from a place very unlike England. But also it is clear that it won't do to overdose you with information about this place, and that you had best suck it in little by little."[40] When the visitor inquires about the phalansteries and the form of community life, Hammond answers that only experience can allow one to better understand the arrangements of the new society: "I need not say much about all this, as you are going up the river with Dick, and will find out for yourself by experience how these matters are managed."[41]

Experience is emphasized over words a second time when Hammond himself (despite his inclination to present and explain everything) warns the visitor-questioner against his desire for knowledge by suggesting that the complexity of the new life is such that the meaning of anything said cannot adequately communicate the savor of the new world.

> "Neighbor," he said, "although we have simplified our lives a great deal from what they were, and have got rid of many conventionalities and many sham wants, which used to give our forefathers much trouble, yet our life is too complex for me to tell you in detail by means of words how it is arranged; you must find that out by living amongst us. It is true I can better tell you what we don't do, than what we do."[42]

Finally, the primacy of lived utopia is conveyed during the voyage up the river, when a woman, Clara, is careful to remind her lover that it is necessary not to confuse the two levels—didactic presentation and experience—and that, consequently, it is better to leave the narrator in his ignorance and not answer his questions, so that he may experience the newness on his own: "'Do the women work at it in silk dresses?' said I, smiling. Dick was going to answer me soberly; but Clara put her hand over his mouth, and said, 'No, no Dick; not too much information for him, or I shall think that you are your old kinsman again. Let him find out for himself.'"[43] Let him find out for himself! With this utterance the principle of communication intrinsic to *News from Nowhere* is declared; and because this principle also applies to the *praxis* of humanity in history, the scope of utopia and its function within historical action is defined as well. The care with which Clara preserves the discovery of the new is all the more significant in light of the erotic desire that suddenly emerges during the narrator's journey. For is not the desire to see the new society often compared to the passion that comes from being in love?

The inner structure of Morrissian utopia encourages this experimentation. It encompasses two phases of life (things said in relation to old age, things lived in relation to youth) and their associated spaces of communication: a didactic and theoretical communication (which is in truth not without a certain discomfort when, at times, the visitor recognizes the old Hammond as being his duplicate), and a playful, utopian, and fantastic communication that resembles the encounter with Ellen in the quest for the Holy Grail. Before joining the search, the narrator has a moment of hesitation. He indeed prefers to stay by the side of the old man, who bears all the memory of the old world, rather than confront the new world itself:

> And also I rather felt as if the old man, with his knowledge of past times, and even a kind of invested sympathy for them caused by his active hatred of them, was as it were a blanket for me against the cold of this very new world, where I was, so to say, stripped bare of every habitual thought and way of acting; and I did not want to leave him too soon.[44]

Experimental utopia is always bound to the river. The river functions as a focal point of very complex relationships between the experience of the journey—which is not any journey but the ride up to the source—with the dream and sleep. Little by little, the visitor experiences a new time and a new space. Furthermore, as yet another indication of the priority accorded to experience, experimental utopia frames and subordinates the classical utopia that consists of narratives or of an exchange of questions and answers. From chapters II to VIII, the visitor experiences, so to speak, a "horizontal" contact with the new society after a morning bath that punctuates the entrance into the new world. When meeting the old Hammond, the curator of the British Museum, the visitor is absorbed into experimental utopia by a series of small events that bring about the disturbing experience of the old and the familiar becoming indissolubly confused. It is in chapters IX through XVII (classical utopia) that the visitor gains a historical awareness of the new society by the narrative of the revolution; in short, a vertical dimension that will bestow greater substance to the process of discovery. Once the interview with Hammond is concluded, experimental utopia begins anew and takes on a greater intensity, culminating with the ride up the river and the appearance of Ellen, that "strange and fierce beauty."

If we consider the privilege Morris grants experience, we can see how the profound rhythm of *News from Nowhere* unfolds in the permanent and mobile tension between integration—the progressive belonging to a new society, the place of a new home—and the menace of separation that silently looms in the background over this fragile serenity. It suddenly tears the serenity apart like lightning and gathers momentum the more the feeling of recognition and return becomes imminent. The greatness of *News from Nowhere* as a modern utopia results from the dialectical image being simultaneously present as the golden age, the reactivating of the classless society, and as hell, the reactivating of suffering—as if the suffering of past generations, the shadow of injustice, stood at the gates of the homeland, barring the path that leads back home.[45] Different phases punctuate this adventure between the poles of return and separation. Experimental utopia takes place entirely between a morning bath that gives one access to the new society and the final bath that signifies the fall back into the old world. This morning bath is a bath of initiation, the baptism of socialism, and it is inevitably reminiscent of Feuerbach's remarks on water, where he attempts to give an explanation of baptism:

> Water is the readiest means of making friends with Nature.
> The bath is a sort of chemical process in which our
> individuality is resolved into the objective life of Nature. The
> man rising from the water is a new, a regenerate man. . . .
> Water, as a universal element of life, reminds us of our origin
> from Nature, an origin which we have in common with plants
> and animals. In Baptism we bow to the power of a pure
> Nature-force; water is the element of natural equality and
> freedom, the mirror of the golden age.[46]

The final bath that marks the exclusion from the new world is immediately followed by the strange uneasiness that precedes separation, the breaking of intersubjectivity. Suddenly the gazes no longer meet. "A pang shot through me, as of some disaster long expected and suddenly realized." As soon as the charm is broken, the specter of suffering that had never ceased to haunt the ride up the river like a remote dissonance suddenly arises to confirm the fall back to the past, as if the threat of incompleteness loomed overhead from the outset:

> I came upon a figure strongly contrasting with the joyous, beautiful people I had left behind in the church. It was a man who looked old, but whom I knew from habit, now half-forgotten, was really not much more than fifty. . . . Inexpressibly shocked, I hurried past him . . . but suddenly I saw as it were a black cloud rolling along to meet me, like a nightmare of my childish days; and for a while I was conscious of nothing else than being in the dark.[47]

This clashing tension is all the more accentuated given that the narrator, by changing clothes, goes from the status of visitor to the status of "neighbor"; that is, he becomes a member of the new society. While in the utopia of Sébastian Mercier, *L'An 2240*, the visitor from the past changes clothes immediately in order to not stand out and be in a position of discovering the new world, in Morris's utopia the visitor keeps the clothing of the old world during the whole first part of the experimental utopia, all the way up to the interviews with the old Hammond (chapters II to XIX); he is even beseeched by his hosts not to change his clothes. Thus the situation of being an outsider is reinforced, the visitor can see the new society only from without. It is only at the end of his conversation with the sedentary and old Hammond, and only once he knows the history of the revolution that led to the new society, that the visitor is invited to "shed his skin." The visitor is therefore dressed in the beautiful clothes of the new society at the very moment that his critical distance fades away: the society of nowhere becomes internalized through a new relation of inherence that can now be subjectively understood. Thanks to Hammond's narrative, a bridge (however ephemeral and fragile it may be) has been thrown between the visitor and the new world. The clothes act as a symbol for the internalization of history that allows consciousness to communicate with the new. The more the visitor is immersed in the sensuous fabric of the new society, the more he is introduced to this split between the happiness of recognition and the pain of renewed distance. Hence the conflict between the old and the new emerges in the visitor at the same time that the ordeal of initiation begins. This is mixed with the painful sensation of recollection, for beyond the new the question is indeed that of recovering a second childhood.

The encounter with Ellen and the shock of recognition further complicates this dimension. The ordeal of initiation intertwines with the possibility of forgetting: can the visitor really forget the prehistory of the old world, can he put aside this "terror of an impending collapse" that always threatened him and prevented his attaining the contemplation of works of art, that deprived him of living the new life or of living in a new way, that separated him from this other form of time where there is no longer really history, where the event has taken on a new status? Such is the nerve-shattering question that Ellen-Diotima never ceases to ask him in trying to heal the wounds of the past. Such is the lived drama of the second experimental sequence, which ends with failure and the fall back into the old world. Conversely, thanks to the visitor, Ellen gains a new awareness of the past, thereby attaining an unprecedented consciousness of the new society, one that worries about the future, sensing in the vaporous realm of nonhistory the potential menace of the hidden dimension of history.

For not having been able to overcome the vague terror that inhabited him, the fall that the visitor feared comes about. The model of the quest for the Holy Grail wins over the myth of Ulysses returning to his native island.

Aside from confronting us with the impossibility of a return to the origin, or of a resurgence of the originary, the ride up the river results in accentuating even more the structure of utopia. The reader is not forced to accumulate a quantitative knowledge on the different society, but is instead invited to observe an object in perpetual transformation, as fluctuating and diverse as the course of the river, where the qualitative is emphasized more than anything else. One can say of *News from Nowhere* what Umberto Eco says of the modern work of art: "The work of art is not an object whose well-founded beauty may be contemplated. It is a mystery that is to be discovered, a duty to be accomplished, a stimulant for the imagination."

A mystery to discover or, better yet, an enigma to maintain, to affront, to pluralize, to share, to exchange, to live and think in common. As soon as communism is no longer construed as the finally resolved enigma of history that "knows itself as such," the nature of emancipated society is again posed in the form of a question; against all thought of identity or unique meaning it recovers its enigmatic character. Emancipation becomes the object of a pluralistic experience of questioning, a self-questioning of the social being. Faced with this insoluble character of history, and by the force of circumstances, utopia thinks itself and realizes itself under the banner of questioning. It is in this sense that Morris, as a modern utopian, best makes utopia a libertarian work: by bringing together the infinite freedom at the heart of modernity with the orientation of utopia toward the infinite, toward this passage that transcends limits, outside the system. Such is the movement intrinsic to utopia that, in its excess, can steer it away from all ideologies of control.

This libertarian element is first manifest at the level of writing. For, faced with the duality of the Morrissian corpus (the socialist lectures and the utopian texts), it is appropriate to favor the properly utopian texts, to give them priority over the theoretical essays. To paraphrase Merleau-Ponty, thought cannot be defined solely by what it has mastered, one must also take into account what it attempts to think at its farthest limits. Utopian writing, the oblique path that is foundational by definition, aims to maximize the lateral implications; it thus opens a specific path to this unthought and unsaid of theoretical texts, as if utopia fulfills an insufficiency of the theoretical text through its dual movement of construction and obliteration. Inasmuch as it focuses on letting excess flourish, utopia lends itself to a philosophical interpretation.

The libertarian element is also present at the level of the utopian vision itself. As E. P. Thompson and Raymond Williams have correctly pointed out, Morris is a great political writer by virtue of the quality of his socialism. And intrinsic to this quality we find his thinking of utopia. The greatness of Morris is to have invented a new utopia: the utopia of ambiguity. By having dared to think and practice utopia from within the "vague terror of an impending collapse," Morris also developed a utopia that, while understanding how to maintain the meaning of suffering—the time that leads to emancipation is neither a homogenous nor an empty time—does not for all that close itself again in the illusion of reconciliation. As such, Morris makes the fragility of utopia, the place of an endless experimentation and incompleteness, the essential quality of a yet-to-be-explored form of modern utopia.

One may be taken aback by the emphasis on literary expression and by the way in which I have sought to valorize Morris's libertarian and romantic inspiration. But whoever accepts Leo Strauss's teachings regarding the interpretation of works of political philosophy (and thus regarding the interpretation of utopian works, since they are based on political philosophy more than on any other perspective) would be surprised by this surprise. Indeed, the Straussian teaching concerning Plato's dialogues—we can understand Plato's teachings such as he understood them himself only if we first know what a Platonic dialogue is—holds true for utopia as well. We can apprehend the libertarian and romantic quality of Morrissian utopia only if we first question the form of Morrissian utopia. This affirmed dependence of "substance" on "form," far from being based on a classical literary approach, aims instead to recover the political significance of the literary question, inasmuch as it is a form of communication. I say political significance, for communication *qua oeuvre* contains within itself a living-together and is in its form already the highest living-together. This is why, according to Leo Strauss, the literary question is inseparable from the political question:

> The study of the literary question is therefore an important
> part of the study of society. Furthermore, the quest for truth is
> necessarily, if not in every respect, a common quest, a quest
> taking place through communication. The study of the literary
> question is therefore an important part of what philosophy is.
> The literary question properly understood is the question of
> the relation of society and philosophy.[48]

If we go back to the question I raised concerning the libertarian and romantic character and how to judge Morrissian utopia, one can therefore answer that it is through a meticulous attention to all the details of the *oeuvre*, and to the form of communication chosen, that one can best apprehend the antiauthoritarian character of the society envisioned and the quality of Morrissian politics. For the utopian text is already a working out of a new relationship to the Other, the experience of a new being with others—utopia-art as a stage for the unconscious exchange of the elements of childhood that lie dormant in each of us.

Finally, by having stood at the closure of classical utopia and the closure of Marxism, Morris proposed—in the romantic mode—a new function for modern utopia: the struggle against the dialectic of socialism. Called on and provoked by this movement of emancipation that by an inner logic turns into its opposite and produces a new form of barbarism, alerted by the so-called necessity of progress, the task of modern utopia is to engage in order to deconstruct these visible or hidden centers that are at the origin of the reversal and transformation of humankind and of the domination of nature. Whereas the dialectic of socialism culminates by its inner logic in an Other that reproduces the Same, utopia, on the contrary, is the guardian of alterity by its orientation toward the no-place, by the forever incommensurable distance that the space of nowhere excavates. It is moreover in this sense that the predominance of water in the Morrissian utopia takes on a meaning distinct from Feuerbach's analysis. Indeed, to borrow Adorno's distinction, beyond the transformation of nature in and by work, water is the milieu on earth that makes one heed the difference between *praxis* and happiness. It is the element consubstantial to the promise of happiness, beyond the hold of work.[49]

Here we may return to the words that have guided us all along in our essay, and that designate water as the place of no-place where negative utopia can experience the chance of undoing the strings—which are not irremediably tied—of the dialectic of emancipation. It is this chance that Adorno strives to seize in *Minima Moralia*, where he distinguishes the dialectic of emancipation from the dialectic of socialism:

> On water. . . . The conception of unfettered activity, of
> uninterrupted procreation, of chubby insatiability, of freedom
> as frantic bustle, feeds on the bourgeois concept of nature
> that has always served solely to proclaim social violence as
> unchangeable, as a piece of healthy eternity. It was in this,
> and not in their alleged leveling-down, that the positive
> blue-prints of socialism, resisted by Marx, were rooted in
> barbarism. It is not man's lapse into luxurious indolence that
> is to be feared, but the savage spread of the social sphere
> under the mask of universal nature, the collective as a blind
> fury of activity. . . . If we imagine emancipated society as
> emancipation from precisely such totality, then pathways of
> escape come into view that have little in common with

increased production and its human reflections. . . . Enjoyment itself would be affected, just as its present framework is inseparable from operating, planning, having one's way, subjugating. Doing nothing like an animal, lying on water and looking peacefully at the sky, "being, nothing else, without any further definition and fulfillment," might take the place of process, act, satisfaction, and so truly keep the promise of dialectical logic that it would culminate in its origin. None of the abstract concepts comes closer to fulfilled utopia than that of eternal peace. Spectators on the sidelines of progress like Maupassant and Sternheim have helped this intention to find expression, timidly, in the only way that its fragility permits.[50]

*Translated by Max Blechman*

### Notes

1. As Claude Lefort suggests. See his *Le Travail de l'Oeuvre, Machiavel* (Paris: Gallimard, 1972) 306–309.
2. M. Abensour, "L'Histoire de l'Utopie et le Destin de sa Critique," *Textures* 6–7 (1973) and 8–9 (1974).
3. W. Benjamin, "The Author as Producer," in *Reflections* (New York: Harcourt Brace Jovanovich, 1978) 228.
4. Benjamin, "The Author as Producer," 224.
5. E. P. Thompson, *William Morris, Romantic Revolutionary* (London: Lawrence & Wishart, 1955) 759.
6. J. Déjacque, *L'Humanisphère* (Paris: Editions Champ Libre, 1971) 91.
7. W. Morris, *Nouvelles de Nulle Part*, intro. by Paul Meir (Paris: Editions Sociales, 1961) 68.
8. P. Mabille, *Le Merveilleux* (Paris: Editions des Quatre Vents, 1946) 68–69.
9. E. Guyot, *Le Socialisme et l'Evolution de l'Angleterre Contemporaine* (Paris: F. Alean, 1913) 409.
10. A. Reszler, "L'Esthétique Anarchiste," *Diogène* 78 (1972) 55–56.
11. Cited by Reszler, "L'Esthétique Anarchiste," 205.
12. Ch. Fourier, *Oeuvres* (Paris: Editions Anthropos, 1966) I:56.
13. F. Nietzsche, "On the Uses and Disadvantages of History for Life," in *Untimely Meditations* (Cambridge & New York: Cambridge Univ. Press, 1997) 64.
14. Ibid., 62. Translation modified.
15. G. Bataille, *Erotism, Death, and Sensuality* (San Francisco: City Lights Books, 1986) 40–41.
16. W. Morris, *The Aims of Art*, in *The Collected Works* (Princeton: Princeton Univ. Press, 1996) 23:94.

17. G. Debord, "Report on the Construction of Situations," in Ken Knabb, ed. and trans., *Situationist International Anthology* (Berkeley: Bureau of Public Secrets, 1981) 22.

18. "Un Inédit de Merleau-Ponty," *Revue de Métaphysique et de Morale* 4 (1962) 407.

19. Morris, *Aims of Art*, 23:82.

20. W. Benjamin, "The Work of Art in the Age of Mechanical Reproduction," in *Illuminations* (New York: Schocken Books, 1968) 217–252.

21. W. Morris, *The Revival of Architecture*, in *Collected Works*, 22:323.

22. Morris, *Aims of Art*, 23:96. Also *Art and Its Producers*, in *Collected Works*, 22:352.

23. Morris, *Art and Its Producers*, 22:346.

24. On this problematic, see W. Benjamin, "The Author as Producer," 222–223.

25. J.-F. Lyotard, "Notes sur la Fonction Critique de l'Art," *Revue d'Esthétique* 3–4 (1970) 402–403.

26. W. Morris, "Useful Work versus Useless Toil," in *Collected Works*, 23:118.

27. Morris, *Art and Its Producers*, 22:352–353.

28. N. Pevsner, *Pioneers of Modern Design: From William Morris to Walter Gropius* (London: Penguin Books, 1960).

29. Benjamin, "The Author as Producer," 233.

30. W. Morris, "Useful Work versus Useless Toil," in *Collected Works*, 23:118.

31. Letter to G. Bainton, April 2, 1888, in *Letters of William Morris*, ed. Ph. Henderson (London: Longmans, Green, 1950) 284.

32. T. Adorno, *Negative Dialectics* (New York: Continuum, 1996) 378.

33. W. Morris, *News from Nowhere*, in *Collected Works*, 16:104–105.

34. W. Benjamin, "Paris, Capital of the Nineteenth Century," in *Reflections*, 148.

35. W. Morris, *News from Nowhere*, 16:102.

36. U. Eco, *The Open Work* (London: Hutchinson, 1989) 3.

37. Marx, letter to Arnold Ruge, September 1843, in *The Letters of Karl Marx*, ed. and trans. S. Padover (Englewood Cliffs, NJ: Prentice-Hall, 1979) 30, 32.

38. Eco, *The Open Work*, 19.

39. K. Löwith, "L'Achèvement de la Philosophie Classique par Hegel et sa Dissolution par Marx et Kierkegaard," *Recherches Philosophiques* IV (1934–35) 232–235.

40. Morris, *News from Nowhere*, 16:11.

41. Ibid., 16:65.

42. Ibid., 16:79.

43. Ibid., 16:143.

44. Ibid., 16:103.

45. On W. Benjamin's critique of the dialectical image and the necessary ambiguity of the dialectical image, see T. Adorno's letter in *Correspondance* (Paris: Aubier, 1980) 2:171–174.

46. L. Feuerbach, *The Essence of Christianity* (New York: Prometheus Books, 1989) 276.

47. *Letters of Karl Marx.*

48. L. Strauss, *The City and Man* (Chicago: Univ. of Chicago Press, 1978) 52.

49. T. Adorno, *Aesthetic Theory* (London: Routledge, 1970) 17.

50. T. Adorno, *Minima Moralia* (London: Verso, 1978) 155–156. Translation modified.

# THE MOUNTAIN OF TRUTH
## *Martin Green*

Der Krieg *by Eugen Hoffmann,* Die Aktion *18 (May 10, 1919)*

At the end of the nineteenth century, intellectual Europe became preoccupied with the problem of its own unhappiness, malaise, or—to use Freud's word—*Unbehagen*. The favorites of this rich and powerful civilization—the economically and educationally privileged, the most intelligent and imaginative—felt themselves to be unhappier than more "primitive" peoples. The people who most felt the crisis were the Germans—the inhabitants of Germany, but also the speakers of German all over Europe—who were moving faster than other peoples to grasp the glittering prizes of progress. The industrial power of Germany and the size of its cities had been growing for some time, and the dismay and the dislike of both industrialism and city life grew apace. In 1800, twenty-two million people lived in what later became Germany; in 1900, fifty-six million, and every second one lived in a place different from where he was born, and probably in a city. By 1910, Germany contained as many big cities as all the rest of Europe.[1]

Max Weber spoke of an iron cage or framework, which closed around a society when it entered the modern world.[2] He was referring primarily to impersonal phenomena (such as bureaucracy), but his biographer, Arthur Mitzman, has applied the phrase to Weber's personal problems. Sigmund Freud, in *Civilization and Its Discontents* [*Unbehagen*], said "it is impossible to overlook the extent to which civilization is built upon a renunciation of instinct."

> Human life in common is only made possible when a majority comes together which is stronger than any separate individual and which remains united against all separate individuals. The power of this community is then set up as "right" in opposition to the power of the individual . . . [and this] constitutes the decisive step of civilization.[3]

Many of the best European minds from 1900 on were devoted to understanding this problem and to "solving" it. Both Freud and Weber were intellectually conservative, and their moral enthusiasms were subdued to a prime loyalty to "objectivity" and "scientific neutrality." But other people were trying to solve the problem of civilization and unhappiness more practically and enthusiastically, by *living* a new life together—by withdrawing from the cities and the professions and the "objective" ways of thought—by risking their own lives. These people thought of Freud and Weber as enemies, and Weber and Freud thought of them as dangerous fools. But as we look back on that period—so like our 1960s—we can see the two groups as complementary; both must engage our interest and perhaps compete for our loyalty.

Understanding the enthusiasts requires an extra effort on our part, for they have been largely consigned to the dustbins of intellectual history—it was a risk they knew they ran—and they now look flimsy beside the serried volumes of Freud and Weber. But at the same time it was different. The anarchist Kropotkin, a spokesman for these enthusiasts, said in his 1880 pamphlet *Spirit of Revolt:*

There are periods of human society when revolution becomes an imperative necessity, when it proclaims itself as inevitable . . . the need for a new life becomes apparent. The code of established morality, that which governs the greater number of people in their daily life, no longer seems sufficient . . . those who long for the triumph of justice . . . perceive the necessity of a revolutionary whirlwind which will sweep away all this rottenness, revive sluggish hearts with its breath. . . . Weary of these wars, weary of the miseries which they cause, society rushes to seek a new organization.[4]

And, as Roger Baldwin noted about Kropotkin, this change was not merely political but included "all social relations—marriage, education, the treatment of crime, the function of law, the basis of morality."[5] Kropotkin was one of the people who came to Ascona in the period from 1900 to 1920.

In the late nineteenth century, Ascona was a small mountain village of about one thousand inhabitants. In the mid-twentieth century it became (as it remains) a popular holiday resort, offering golf, tennis, nightclubs, waterskiing. But between these periods it was, briefly, something very different; it became the semiofficial meeting place for all Europe's spiritual rebels.

Where is it? On the Swiss shore of the north end of Lago Maggiore, which separates Switzerland from Italy, on the very edge of the Alps. The delta of the Maggia River projects into the blue waters of Lago Maggiore, in roughly rectangular form, and helps create a rougher rectangle of bay to its south. Along the southern curve of that bay runs the Swiss-Italian border; Ascona is sheltered in the inner northern corner. The town of Locarno (Ascona is only a village, at least in our period) stands on the flat land of the delta, but Ascona is at the base of the foothills of the Alps. Monescia, the Mountain of Truth, is the first of those foothills; it was and is a stiff climb up from the little square and the tall-towered church to the sanitarium the intellectual immigrants built on the hilltop. Behind Monescia (which is three hundred meters high) the hills loom higher and higher, rising rapidly toward the true Alps. Baladrume (associated with pre-Christian fertility rites) is followed by Corona dei Pinci (1293 meters) and that by Gridone (2188 meters).

The first immigrants settled on the top of Monescia, either in the sanitarium or in ramshackle cabins they built with their own hands.

Visitors often stayed in inns or furnished rooms in the village, or they rented one of the houses, or they slept outdoors. Gradually, as more solid citizens arrived, they had villas built for them, almost always somewhere between the town and the hilltop, and so somewhere on the lower slopes of Monescia. And they walked the landscape, so totally unlike the industrialized cities of northern Europe. Along the footpaths they found many shrines to the Madonna, tended by the local people. More were dedicated to her than to the saints or Christ himself, a fact the immigrants found—gladly found—indicative of a pagan cult of Woman among these supposedly Christian peasants. There was, for instance, a Madonna della Fontana on the northern face of Monescia, which was a place of pilgrimage for the local population, and about which political feminists were to write.

Ascona's moment of glory was not unrelated to its beautiful Alpine setting. Certain places, often set in mountains, are, like certain people, so remarkable in their beauty that they transcend ordinary categories and suggest to us that our ordinary expectations of life have been too tame. For Indian culture, the Himalayas have been the traditional locus of all efforts at sanctity and spiritual struggle. In Europe men built a more secular and rationalist civilization than ever existed in India, but the Alps have served something of the purpose of the Himalayas. Romantic writers—Wordsworth, Byron, Shelley, Rousseau—found in the Alps what Hindu poets found in the Himalayas. And around the year 1000 CE Christian monks, like the Benedictines of Talloires, retreated from the world into those mountains in expectation of the millennium. Ascona, nine hundred years later, was the locus of a different "religion," in some ways quite opposite, since it was erotic and sun-worshipping, not ascetic and cross-worshipping. The idea of God the Father was replaced by God the Mother, the divinity of Nature and Woman. But seen in its activity of rebellion, this was a world-renouncing religion, too.

One way to approach our subject is through Gerhart Hauptmann's once famous novel *Der Ketaer von Soana* [The Heretic of Soana]. This narrates the story of a young Catholic priest in the Swiss mountain parish of Soana (very like Ascona) who leaves Christ for Eros. He encounters and succumbs to paganism in the form of a beautiful girl who has been brought up outside our Christian religion and civilization because she is the child of a "guilty" love affair. When we first see the ex-priest he is a goatherd, now wearing a goatskin instead of a soutane and looking like a Donatello statue, except that he still wears glasses.

This novel was published in 1918 and had great international success. By 1925 it had sold 140,000 copies, and was translated into every literary language. It formed part of that literary propaganda for eroticism which was so prevalent at that moment; in English literature one can point to Maugham's story "Rain" and Lawrence's stories like "Sun" as parts of the same project. In an earlier version, Hauptmann's novel was entitled *Die Syrische Gottin* [The Syrian Goddess], one of the titles of Magna Mater, the Great Mother, then current. Lawrence spoke of Syria Dea in *Women in Love*, his 1920 novel, which echoes the idea of Ascona. Otto Gross, the Asconan psychiatrist, was trying to restore the cult of Astarte in his last years, 1918 to 1920.

At the end of Hauptmann's story the narrator sees for the first time the woman who seduced the priest. He is going down the mountain after hearing the latter's story, and she comes up the mountain toward him; he feels weak and small before her.

> There was no protection, no armor against the demands of that neck, those shoulders, and that breast, blessed and stirred by the breath of life. She climbed up and out of the depths of the world, past the wondering scribe—and she climbs and climbs into eternity as the one into whose merciless hands heaven and earth have been delivered.[6]

This sense of the divinity of woman is one of the ideas the Asconans propagated, as was the pagan significance of the Virgin. The transition from Christian Puritanism (associated with modern Europe and thus with modern science) toward pagan life-worship could be made through Roman Catholic Mariolatry, which partook of both. (There is much in the novel about the cult of the Virgin Mary as a covert worship of the Great Mother.) And the key word is Eros—with Dionysus and Pan as alternates. At the beginning, the heretic says, "'You know that Eros is older than Chronus, and mightier too. Do you feel this silent glow about us? Eros! Do you hear how the cricket is chirping? Eros!'" And when two lizards darted across his body as he lay in the sun, he repeated the word:

And, as if he had given the command for it, two strong bucks arose and attacked each other with their curved horns. He left them undisturbed, although the combat grew more and more heated. The clash of the blows rang louder and louder, and their number kept increasing. And again he said, 'Eros, Eros.'[7]

The goats are of course Dionysian, and the heretic says he would rather pray to a live goat than to a hanged man.

We know that in 1897 Hauptmann visited the little town of Rovio, which was a place very like Soana and Ascona (in the same province, with the same mountain landscape and climate, and with the same social history of underdevelopment, backwardness, and emigration). The writer had that year left his wife and three children for another woman; his wife refused a divorce, and he had to live with his new partner unmarried for the next seven years. His two older brothers, who were married to sisters of his wife, disapproved of his behavior. Hauptmann was therefore looking for stories to justify social-moral rebellion. He had just finished *Die versunkene Glocke* [The Sunken Bell], in which his hero leaves wife and home for a forest nymph because he is an artist, but that story ends tragically; the artist must pay for his happiness with his life. *The Heretic of Soana* ends happily, triumphantly. And in fact Hauptmann's health and spirits improved dramatically in his new life. He returned to Rovio four times, and wrote this story about it between 1911 and 1917. The Mediterranean south recharged his vitality: in 1900 he had a love child, Benvenuto (the Italian name is significant) and in 1907 rediscovered Dionysus in Greece (see his *Griechischer Frühling* [The Greek Spring]).

Such stories as *The Heretic of Soana*, with similar autobiographical sources and the same social message, were often repeated in the years 1900–1920. There are versions in all the languages of Europe and in all the arts. What went on in Ascona was more experimental, more extreme, more intellectual than such a simple and sentimental legend could suggest. But Hauptmann's story represents well enough the dream of "happy ever after" that animated many Asconans' efforts; and—just because it was a popular novel—it reminds us of what linked them all to the bourgeois world, at least to that part which read novels.

A complementary story, equally important to Asconans, was about the Primal Crime, humanity's Original Sin, which had been committed by Man—that is, by the patriarchal father-husband-master who dominated this new ironclad society, especially in pre-1914 Germany. This story was myth rather than fiction and was never fully told; it exists only in fragments. One of those fragments was invented by Otto Gross, the most brilliant of the Asconans, in the years 1917–1920. He had a vision of a turning point in world history when a horde of ambitious half-apes burst out of a clump of bushes and flung themselves upon the naked and unsuspecting women who had till then, in matriarchal innocence, directed human life. They enslaved these women, as wives, and with that event our history began.

He depicted these men in contemporary caricatural terms, as war-mad bureaucrats, administrators, and academics who wore professorial beards and official decorations on their breasts. That is, he saw them as being like his own father, Hanns Gross, who had been a professor of criminology and had volunteered, though in his sixties, to fight in 1914. At the beginning of our history, men like Hanns Gross hung up, in the women's innocent temples of sensual love, their weapons of war and their tablets of the law. (This version of Otto Gross's ideas comes from Franz Werfel's *Barbara* and is confirmed by Gross's own late essays.) In the avant-garde arts in German-speaking Europe, these ideas found wide acceptance. At least the faith in eroticism did. That mountain landscape of Hauptmann's glittered in the sun, and announced the silent presence of Pan to almost everyone. But the Asconans took these ideas seriously and tried to do something about them.

The idea of a sacred mountain is strange to modern Western civilization. But we keep the memory of it in Judeo-Christian teaching; Moses went up a mountain to receive the Ten Commandments, on which the rest of Judaism was built; and Jesus went up a mountain to deliver his most famous sermon. The Hindus have Mount Meru as the locus of sanctity—the place of retreat for saints and sages. It is a natural symbol: mountains are so different from the plains, so far from the cities, so high, so white, so visible, so pure. Where else should we fix our dream of Truth? Where else should we realize it, singly or communally, by prayer or by work?

In our time, an American equivalent would be Big Sur in California because of its cliff-and-ocean landscape, and because of its association with such ventures as the Esalen Institute and with rebellious spirits like Robinson Jeffers and Henry Miller in the recent past, with speculative Orientalism and with youth-cult music. In the Joan Baez film of the 1960s, *Ceremony at Big Sur*, we see young people flocking to the concert in the costumes of anarchism and protest, defying and provoking the communities through which they pass on their way, just as did the *Naturmenschen* (long hair, bare legs, sandals) who flocked to Ascona between 1900 and 1920, to dance together to the sun. Memoirs of Ascona (for instance, by Hermann Hesse, Emil Szittya, and Mary Wigman) stress their actual approach to the place, walking through villages where the people whispered and laughed behind the young hikers' backs.

The enthusiasts of Ascona were inspired by legends of Paris under the Commune of 1871, just as the enthusiasts of Big Sur were inspired by the legends of Paris in May 1968. Kropotkin wrote:

> "I will never forget," said a friend to us, "Those delightful moments of deliverance. I came down from my upper chamber in the Latin Quarter to join that immense open-air club which filled the boulevards from one end of Paris to the other. Everyone talked about public affairs; all merely personal preoccupations were forgotten; no more thought of buying and selling; all felt ready, body and soul, to advance towards the future."[8]

This was what the anarchists aimed at in our own time, too.

Some of the people of Ascona became famous in one field or another: Hermann Hesse and D. H. Lawrence in literature, Mary Wigman in dance, C. G. Jung in psychoanalysis. But others, more central to this story, are not as well known because their rebellion against contemporary culture was more thoroughgoing. They rebelled against the arts and sciences themselves, and refused to engage their talents and energies in culturally rewarded enterprises; they refused to "produce."

We see something similar among their famous contemporaries from related milieus: in Wittgenstein, who gave up the study of philosophy in search of a purer ascesis; in Kafka, who felt guilty about devoting his energies to literature. But these men *did* achieve and produce, finally. The Asconans—some of them—did not. Their works were their—usually tragic—lives, and it was others who profited by their sufferings, who rationalized and organized their idea or turned it into art. But they—those who became famous for doing that—were true heroes of culture, true rebels against the grimmer forces of civilization. The others belong to that further frontier, moving toward madness and toward true spirit, to which culture can only point. Ascona was, granted the great differences between Christianity and eroticism, a bit like a Dark Ages settlement of religious enthusiasts, each inventing new spiritual disciplines for himself, defying the Church's controls.

My title, "The Mountain of Truth," in fact belongs to Ascona's one institution. Monte Verità, or Der Berg der Wharheit, was the name given by a group of vegetarians to the hill on which they built a nature-cure sanitarium in 1900. Just because it was an institution, Monte Verità was not entirely typical of Ascona as a whole, but the name has the right resonance. The Mountain of Truth was in fact only a hill, only 150 meters higher than Lago Maggiore and 300 meters above sea level. It is cultivable right to the top, though it is faced and backed by real mountains, the Alps, those soaring summits, sheer rock faces, and avalanches. Monte Verità was a hill in fact; it could only be a mountain of Truth, and only by defying the Alpine masses of fact.

And it failed. What happened in Ascona does not matter. It was not history. History was being made in other places—Berlin, St. Petersburg, Paris, London—the antipodes of Ascona. There were remarkable men there, too, and it was they whose ideas and life-experiments set the armies moving in 1914. What they wrote conscripted men into the services in their millions and assembled the cannon and the submarines and the dynamite and the poison gas. They rationed the food, directed the factories, constructed the prison camps, and ordered the people to slaughter each other. The enthusiasts of Ascona were trying to stop all that, not just the events of 1914–1918, and not just by antiwar propaganda, but by changing everyone's idea of life.

### Romantic Ascona

"Romantic" means many things, but I have not, up to now, applied any of its meanings to those aspects of Ascona which have interested me most. To call Otto Gross, Gusto Graeser, and Rudolf von Laban "romantic" seems to blur their outlines. They, and such women as Fanny zu Reventlow, Frieda Lawrence, and Mary Wigman, transcended romanticism just as they transcended the aesthetic dimension. They were too bold, too tough, too determined to survive and succeed.

What do I mean by romantic when I make such a judgment? The best definition is by example. Let me take some images of women from English romantic poets: Keats's "La Belle Dame Sans Merci" or Isabella, Coleridge's "Christabel" or Geraldine, Tennyson's "Mariana in the Moated Grange" or "The Lady of Shalott." The three Asconan women I mentioned were too strong-willed to remind anyone, including themselves, of these figures of grief and glamour.

However, I am so reminded when I read this passage by Frieda Lawrence, about her Asconan friend, Frieda Gross:

> A strange blond "Nixe" kind of woman, living in a world of her own, abstract like a visionary, brooding in her own way. . . . She looked like an Etruscan woman. Her hair was the longest, loveliest Paula had ever seen. It was the color of wheat before it is quite ripe. She was very musical, her voice had a slow, gentle quality. . . . She was Austrian, with all the soft, cultured quality of an old race.

There are a dozen indices of the romantic in that paragraph: the old race (Poe), the Nixe (de la Motte Fouqué), the music (Coleridge), the brooding and abstraction (Tennyson). D. H. Lawrence used several of those indices in his portrait of Miriam Leivers in *Sons and Lovers*, who dreamed herself a heroine of romance. And of course the portrait of Miriam carried with it an implicit diagnosis or critical judgment—part of the dialectic of the novel. Miriam gazes into a mirror instead of engaging with life.

Frieda Schloffer Gross, wife to Otto, was the daughter of a failed lawyer of Graz, whose wife died while her daughter was very young. Frieda grew up in cultured seclusion, reading classical literature and playing classical music. A life of quietude, refinement, studies. An aunt who took the place of the girl's mother was married to a professor of philosophy at Freiburg University.

Frieda grew up an enthusiast for Wagner, dreamed of going to work at Toynbee Hall, the settlement house in London, took *Thus Spake Zarathustra* on her honeymoon. But the man she married belonged to a generation that left behind Wagner and Nietzsche. As long as she was with him, she had to be oriented toward the future, not the past.

Married, Frieda and Otto went to live in Munich-Schwabing, the liveliest center of bohemian life in Europe then, and from there they moved to Ascona. They soon ceased to spend much time together, and he persuaded her—for her own good—to live with his disciple, Ernst Frick. Her friends, Else von Richthofen Jaffe and Frieda von Richthofen Weekley, had affairs with Otto, and Frieda one with Frick, also. When Frieda Weekley eloped with Lawrence in 1912, she described him to Frieda Gross as a man like Otto and Frick, and she had a scheme whereby Lawrence and Frick (both sons of the proletariat) should collaborate on a book.

The relationship with Frick did not long succeed, and Frieda was left with her children (by him and by Gross), impoverished and in legal trouble. Her father-in-law tried to have the son by Otto taken from her, on the grounds that she was not a fit mother; and Frick was charged more than once with acts of terrorism. He left Frieda to live with a well-to-do photographer, Margarethe Fellere. Out in the woods, gathering sticks for her stove, Frieda, as in a folk tale, would meet Margarethe out strolling beneath a silk parasol.

She was a figure of pathos and resignation. But she remained also a remarkable woman, beautiful and courageous and in her way distinguished. Else von Richthofen Jaffe supported her, financially and emotionally, all her life. Loyal friends wrote and came to Ascona to see her. And men fell in love with her; for instance, Erich Mühsam and Emil Lask. The latter bequeathed her money in his will.

She was, amongst all the famous names of Ascona, the writers and dancers and so on, the one who was most permanently there. For many of the people, Ascona meant Frieda Gross. Thus when peripheral Asconans traveled through Switzerland—when D. H. Lawrence stayed in the next village and Max Weber lodged in Ascona itself—hers was one of the faces the name conjured up. Weber gave her legal advice and Lawrence sent her a copy of *Women in Love* when it appeared.

From a certain point of view she can be seen as central to the human landscape of Ascona. To the left, in a more extreme and melodramatic direction, stand the two suicides, Sophie Benz and Lotte Hattemer; to the right, in the more prudent and respectable direction, stand Else Jaffe and Marianne Weber. And insofar as Ascona was Frieda Gross's, it was romantic.

## Fanny zu Reventlow

There is quite a somewhat looser sense of "romantic," by which it means picturesque, adventurous, scandalous, scorning both pathos and dignity, and that was certainly applied to Ascona. It was summed up in Fanny zu Reventlow, *"die tolle Fanny," "die tolle Graefin"*—the crazy countess.

People named Ascona "the Schwabing of Schwabing," the place Schwabingites went to when Schwabing ceased to be bohemian enough for them—which is not to say that they then lost all claim to our interest. Fanny zu Reventlow was the prime example of that group.

She was born in 1871 and died in 1918. Her dates are exactly those of Bismarck's Reich, and her life was one long protest against it. Because of their dislike of Prussia's increasing power, her family, which was aristocratic, moved to Luebek, an independent city-republic within Germany, when Fanny was a girl. As a child she was, like Frieda von Richthofen, a tomboy and a rebel, and clashed with her mother. She rebelled against both family and marriage. At twenty-one she ran away from home and was disowned.

From that time on, she lived in Schwabing and tried to become a painter, but in fact supported herself by writing, first translations from the French, then satirical sketches, and finally novels. But her essential career was made by living the life of Schwabing.

Poets and intellectuals like Rilke and Mühsam, Derleth and Stern, Klages and Wolfskehl were among Fanny's admirers. She never lacked for lovers. But it seems likely that, as Ludwig Klages said, her mother's early withholding of love, in punishment, had created a hunger in Fanny which nothing subsequent could satisfy. She had a child, whose fatherhood she refused to divulge; she brought him up by herself, finding from then on her major emotional resource in her relationship to her child.

Her affair with Klages, a philosopher of eroticism, was the most important experience in the lives of both and seemed historically important to their friends, who declared that in their love the world of paganism would celebrate a revolutionary awakening. Klages himself called her *"eine heidnische Heilige,"* a pagan saint, which meant that she possessed the virtues to Christian chastity, meekness, and selflessness, in the same measure as the saints. She was a saint of sensuality, pride, power, life-worship, and self-assertion. With her child she was a pagan Madonna.

Her later years, after she moved to Ascona in 1910, were somewhat more comic-adventurous. She planned at one point to travel the world with a circus. She married a Baltic nobleman who was happily allied to his Italian laundress but who needed an aristocratic spouse in order to satisfy his family and get a permanent allowance from them.

There had always been this circus side to Fanny, and she loved the Schwabing festivals, like Fasching, which she attended in Pierrot costume. She had appeared as a rope dancer at country fairs. All this adds up to a different kind of pathos from Frieda Gross's.

In this aspect of Reventlow's life, she had a connection with modern art in France. She lived for a time (in 1907 and intermittently later) à trois with Franz Hessel and Henri-Pierre Roché. Hessel was a gifted novelist writing about Jewish-melancholic themes, who later went to live in Paris. He became a friend of Walter Benjamin—they were both interested in the imaginative character of big-city life—and Benjamin admired Hessel's writing on that theme. Roché was a well-known figure in the world of art in Paris, and the author of *Jules et Jim*, the novel about a German, a Frenchman, and a woman in love with each other.

This was a fictionalized account of the triangular relationship of 1907. It was a projective fantasy of what might have happened in 1910 if—as nearly happened—Reventlow had joined the two men in Paris. Hessel was Jules, Roché was Jim, Reventlow was Catherine, and their relations followed the Pierrot-Harlequin-Columbine pattern.

In fact, in that year Reventlow moved to Ascona and married her Baltic baron. But she was considering two other ways to extricate herself from her financial problems that year. One was to go into analysis with Otto Gross, her treatment to be paid for by Edgar Jaffe, Else's husband; the other was to go to Paris to work at an art exhibition. This last meant joining Roché, who knew everyone in the Paris studios—he introduced Picasso to Gertrude and Leo Stein.

Moreover, Roché later became a close friend of Marcel Duchamp, who began work on *The Bride Stripped Bare by Her Bachelors, Even* during his visit to Munich in 1912. Given that place and time, it is likely that Roché and Duchamp discussed the cult of Magna Mater—of which Reventlow was one of the most famous incarnations. If they did discuss her and it, that painting—one of the great enigmas of modern painting—can be read as a sardonic and blasphemous participation in that cult. Reventlow then represents another horizon to the romanticism of Ascona, or another center, if one cares to think of plural romanticisms.

## Otto Gross and Shelley

And, finally, there is another sense in which Otto Gross himself was romantic. His life shows a number of striking parallels with the English poet Shelley. The two men lived a century apart, in different countries, and worked in different fields—poetry and psychoanalysis. But they had similar developments, both being very precocious as children (gifted especially in science and philosophy) and also hypersensitive, morally and emotionally (both became vegetarians, in abhorrence of animal killing).

Each had a lifelong and deadly quarrel with his father (who in each case went so far as to officially denounce his son as crazy and to try to get possession of his grandson); both were important figures in the revolutionary movements of their times, as theoreticians and practical anarchists; both often helped young women to rebel against paternal tyranny; and both developed tragic relations with female disciples, who fell desperately in love with their saviors and killed themselves in that despair. Both men were unmistakably noble and idealistic, but wounded others by treating them as abstract ideas.

Not only are there many such likenesses, but there is evidence that some people who knew Gross saw those likenesses, notably D. H. Lawrence. Though he never explicitly compared the two men, he did connect them, and quite often talked about Shelley in ways that apply strikingly well to Gross. In *Mr Noon*, for instance, he describes how Johanna (Frieda) turned away from her husband toward a man of Shelley's type (Gross).

Lawrence describes this type as

the non-sensual, quite spiritual poets like Shelley. . . . Now Johanna, after Everard [her husband] was aiming in the Shelley direction, at the mid-heaven spiritual, which is still sexual but quite spiritually so. Sex as open and as common and as simple as any other human conversation. And this, we urge, is quite a logical conclusion of the spiritual program.[9]

Moreover, in the essays Lawrence wrote soon after his elopement, he developed sets of antitheses in which Shelley was an important example of a spiritual tendency, or "direction," or what at other times he calls an "infinity," which needs to be balanced against something quite opposite. These essays are to be found in *Twilight in Italy, The Crown,* and *A Study of Thomas Hardy;* they are some of Lawrence's most brilliant work and deserve more study.

One antithesis pits Shelley against Shakespeare: Shelley is pure male, Shakespeare is both male and female and therefore a better model. Another sets the Son against the Father, which means the spirit against the flesh, and freedom against authority, and therefore Shelley against all fathers and tyrants. The primary context Lawrence offers is that of Christian theology, with its distinction between God the Father and God the Son, the Old Testament and the New, the Law of Moses and the Sermon on the Mount. But in the year 1913, when Lawrence worked out these ideas, it is surely inconceivable that anyone could write on the conflict between Father and Son without thinking of Hanns Gross and Otto, for this is the year in which Hanns had his son arrested and locked up.

Thus it seems clear that Lawrence assimilated the challenge of Gross, which must have been a forceful one for him in 1912 and 1913 (such a brilliant mind, such a prophet of love, so important to Frieda, and such a dramatic fate) by blending him into Shelley, and by talking about him under the code name of Shelley. In *A Study of Thomas Hardy*, he said: "Shelley cannot properly be said ever to have lived. He transcended life. But we don't want to transcend life, since we are life."[10] That use of "we" and that idea of "life" surely prompts us to think that Lawrence might have spoken those words to Frieda about Gross—or indeed Frieda might have spoken them to Lawrence.

Also interesting, of course, is the question of what "causes" the striking similarity between Gross and Shelley. It is a shared identity, of which the resemblances are only symptoms. My answer to that is that a world-conquering civilization like ours regularly throws up the seeds of revolt against itself. It produces stresses and strains that are felt by many individuals in the form of guilts and revolts: guilt for all the other races and classes subordinated to the ruling race and class; guilt for the other genders (women and children and homosexuals) sacrificed to white male chauvinism. And rebellion not only against the State and its laws but also against the family, which is in many ways the building unit of the State, where the roles of husband and father are identified with those of master.

In times of revolution these stresses and strains are greater than at other times. And when those seeds fall into the fertile minds of boys like Shelley and Gross, so gifted, so sensitive, so pushed and promoted, so fostered and stimulated by a proud and proprietary father, so insistently summoned to carry the father's name to new heights of triumph—why then you get this radically destructive and noble self-sacrificial identity that Gross and Shelley shared.

It is an identity that many other men have doubtless shared at other times, perhaps most often men of religion. Frieda von Richthofen was always looking for a contemporary Francis of Assisi (a figure Lawrence often linked to Shelley). She thought she saw traces of him in her father and then in Lawrence. She probably saw even more of it in Gross. From this point of view, romanticism is a recurrent phenomenon and one of the largest significance for cultural history. And in this sense, too, Ascona was a site of the romantic.

### Notes

1. Ulrich Linse, *Barfüssige Propheten* (Berlin: Siedler, 1983) 13.
2. The English phrase is the work of Talcott Parsons, Weber's translator; the German phrase was *"ein stahlhares Gehäuse,"* which could mean "steel housing," as in "engine housing." Perhaps "iron framework" is as close as we can get to a natural-sounding English equivalent, but "iron cage" seems to have established itself.
3. Sigmund Freud, *Civilization and Its Discontents*, trans. J. Strachey (New York: W. W. Norton, 1962) 44, 42.
4. Peter Kropotkin, *Kropotkin's Revolutionary Pamphlets*, ed. R. Baldwin (New York: Dover, 1970) 35.
5. Ibid., 33.
6. Gerhart Hauptmann, *The Heretic of Soana* (London: M. Secker, 1923) 184.
7. Ibid., 15.
8. Kropotkin, *Revolutionary Pamphlets*, 239.
9. D. H. Lawrence, *Mr. Noon* (Cambridge: Cambridge Univ. Press, 1984) 193.
10. D. H. Lawrence, *Phoenix*, ed. Edward D. Macdonald (London: Heinemann, 1936) 459.

# ERICH MÜHSAM
## In Defense of Literary High Treason
### *Christopher Winks*

Portrait des Genossen Erich Mühsam *by Eugen Maria Karpf,* Die Aktion
*3–4 (Jan. 2, 1921)*

In 1925, after serving five and a half years in prison for his participation in the 1919 Bavarian Revolution, the German-Jewish poet,
playwright, cabaret performer, essayist, and revolutionary Erich
Mühsam (1878–1934) published an anthology of his satirical and agitational song lyrics. This collection met with such popular success
that judicial proceedings were brought against Mühsam on the
grounds that his publication "served to prepare the way for civil war."

Ironically, that same year a far more significant—and legally
sanctioned—step toward civil war was taken when Hindenburg
assumed the presidency of the German Republic. Eight years later,
Hindenburg stepped aside in favor of Adolf Hitler, who began a

crackdown on radicals the month following the burning of the Reichstag. On the night of the Reichstag fire, Mühsam was preparing to leave Germany when the SS arrested him for allegedly taking part in a 1919 execution of counterrevolutionaries. Although crippled by his jailers' tortures, Mühsam refused to capitulate. Fifteen agonizing months after his arrest, he was beaten to death in the office of the commandant of the Oranienburg concentration camp. His body was dragged to the outhouse and hung up inside to make it look as if he had committed suicide.

According to his friend Alexander Berkman, Erich Mühsam was "an idealist, a revolutionary, and a Jew—everything Hitlerism hates and denounces." Evidently, his presence still haunts the modern-day Parties of Order and their intellectual acolytes, for they have done their best to eliminate him from the history in which he played such a crucial role. Although Mühsam was highly esteemed by his contemporaries (besides collaborating with such luminaries as Frank Wedekind, Erwin Piscator, Gustav Landauer, and Ernst Toller, he was greeted by thousands of workers at the Berlin railway station after his release from prison), none of the current English-language works on either the German Revolution or Weimar culture accords him more than a passing reference. To cite a particularly egregious example of this falsification, John Willett's highly praised *Art and Politics in the Weimar Period* virtually dismisses Mühsam as a "cabaret poet." Reading Willett, one would never guess that Mühsam's monthly journal *Fanal*, which appeared regularly between 1926 and 1931, was one of the rare voices of resistance to the authoritarianism lurking behind the Weimar Republic's liberal façade.

Perhaps the reason for the neglect of Erich Mühsam and his ideas can be found both in Rudolf Rocker's description of him as an "unshakable opponent of every tyranny" and in his own statement of intent published in *Fanal's* inaugural issue: "Fanal is meant to be an organ of the social revolution. It is intended to assist in the preparation of the revolution and to give it a direction, a meaning, and a goal." Mühsam's ideas, in a word, were dangerous, the more so as he remained independent of any political party and hence free from the ideological constraints such environments impose. In the early essay, "The Artist in the Future State," Mühsam brings his idiosyncratic, undogmatic style to bear on a question that even after ninety years retains its immediacy—the role of the artist in social transformation. My decision to translate this essay and thereby to introduce Mühsam's work to the English-speaking public, was governed less by antiquarianism than by a desire to contribute to a redefinition of the bases of artistic commitment, beyond the stale clichés of "art serving the people."

By 1906, when "The Artist in the Future State" was published in Karl Kraus's review *Die Fackel* (itself an exemplary blend of anti-journalism and critical thought that illuminated the declining years of the Austro-Hungarian empire), Erich Mühsam was a familiar figure in Berlin's café life. Through his association with the New Community, a proto-Expressionist group of artists and poets, he developed a close relationship with the anarchist theoretician Gustav Landauer, whose utopian vision of complete social transformation fused naturally with the younger man's hatred for the philistine tendencies of bourgeois life. Yet Mühsam did not share his mentor's puritanical outlook on "moral" questions; in fact, his first published work was a pioneering defense of homosexuality, and in 1905 he wrote a sympathetic but critical account of his experiences on a rural artists' commune in the South of Switzerland.

Mühsam's championing of the outsider and the declassed intellectual, as well as his taste for uninhibited life, meant that the conventional socialism of the German Social Democratic Party held little appeal for him. The essay's frequent derogatory references to Marxism and Marxists should be understood in this context. Only twenty years after Marx's death, "scientific socialism" had become a socialism of university professors, whose central concept was the "future state" or "the people's state." In this scheme, the socialist republic would evolve as more and more functions were handled by the state. In the face of this "inevitable" result, social upheavals were unnecessary. Far from "withering away," state power would be reinforced. Mühsam called this notion "Bismarxism." During his membership in the Socialist Party, Landauer had already denounced the "future state" concept for ignoring the spiritual content of revolution in favor of a blind faith in progress; social change, however, meant nothing unless it was accompanied by a transformation of human relations around explicitly creative, communal principles. Mühsam, less starry-eyed and more pragmatic than Landauer, was to take this insight one step further.

Instead of propounding abstract remedies, Mühsam asked: if social change entailed personal change, how could the immoral, anarchic rebels against "philistrosity" harmonize their struggle with the more conventional, disciplined industrial class struggle? As he indicates here, such unity was still only conjectural—though it is known that Mühsam spoke frequently to workers' groups at the time he wrote the essay. For Mühsam, truly creative spirits were outsiders who did not live according to majority codes and who could not be expected to abandon their principles for even the most emancipatory collectively imposed ethic. Leaving aside his exaggerated, typically Expressionist faith in the lone artist pitted against a materialistic world, Mühsam's willingness to envision the conflicts and divisions of a revolutionary society is already far removed from standard revolutionary images of the "new world" where all tensions magically disappear. Even when the human community has been created, Mühsam said, some people will still want to live differently from the rest, and the health of the new society will be determined by how well it is able to adapt to their needs. Art serves the revolution only if the revolution serves art.

During the brief existence of the Bavarian Council Republic of 1919, Mühsam and Ernst Toller drew up a proclamation of a new revolutionary art. Amid the most perilous conditions—shortages brought on by a war-shattered economy, disunity and confusion among the revolutionaries, external opposition from the reactionaries and Majority Socialists, and internal opposition from the newly formed Communist Party, which did its best to demoralize the movement by condemning it as premature and adventurist—Mühsam added a bold corollary to the revolutionary watchword "all power to the councils": "The world must flourish like a meadow on which each can make his harvest." Six days later, he was arrested by the "official" socialist government of Bavaria. History had made Mühsam a better prophet than he would have imagined in 1906. For a single moment, his long-dreamt-of union between the "creative spirits" and the masses had been realized, only to be swept away by the same socialist philistines who had been the butt of his sardonic jibes when they were out of power. In every respect, the much-heralded "future state" had become identical to the present one.

For all his scorn for Karl Marx, Mühsam's entire life was a tribute to the principle enunciated by Marx in the preface to the first edition of *Capital*: "As to the prejudices of so-called public opinion, to which I have never made concessions, now, as ever, my maxim is that of [Dante]: 'Go your own way and let people talk.'" Mühsam never compromised his ideals—which after all he had once called the expression of his essence—for the sake of political expediency. Unlike so many "committed" intellectuals who sought salvation in the bureaucratic dictatorship of Soviet Russia, Mühsam—notwithstanding a brief flirtation with Leninism in the early years of the Russian Revolution—was quick to denounce oppression whether or not it called itself "revolutionary." In so doing, he fulfilled the responsibility of every radical intellectual—to confront power with the truth at all times, regardless of the consequences.

This may seem obvious, but the unfortunate careers of most politically engaged intellectuals in the twentieth century indicate otherwise. For all their professed dedication to the transcendent values of truth and justice, intellectuals have more often than not been willing to overlook all kinds of abuses in exchange for a seat at power's banquet table. Today, no government, be it in the U.S., China, or Cuba, can claim legitimacy unless it has its own court of prize intellectuals (and preferably, some extra public relations representatives abroad). And once intellectuals renounce their potentially greatest asset—their independence—they become incapable of really questioning anything. Their submission is bought with grants, publisher's advances, lecture tours, and lucrative positions; under these conditions, whatever spark of creativity they may possess is sooner or later snuffed out.

In the grim ebbing moments of our century, when media-created urban bohemias emerge as high-rent playgrounds for newly (and temporarily) affluent, spectacle-intoxicated minions of virtual capital and speculative finance, when nationalist and racist poisons are secreted in ever-increasing quantities, when poverty becomes most of the world's daily bread, when the concept of socialism has become either a picturesque anachronism at best or synonymous with police rule at worst, Erich Mühsam's intellectual and political journey at the cross-roads of bohemian counterculture and revolutionary subversion would seem to exemplify a bygone, unrecoverable era. Yet just as the ever-hopeful Mühsam—whose mordant sense of humor was legendary among his contemporaries—refused to idealize his comrades both in alternative lifestyles and in political struggle, or to minimize the real dangers of the fascism whose brutality and violence he would experience in his final days on earth, so also must his intellectual heirs refuse complacency and renew the difficult but necessary task of clearing away the accumulated ideological debris of the past and the present age. Perhaps if we heed Mühsam's advice to continue on our individual creative paths—while continuing to demand more space, more freedom, more fantasy at every opportunity—the seeds might yet be planted that will one day blossom into the meadow of the "romantic socialist republic" of which he dreamed so long ago, so recently.

# THE ARTIST IN THE FUTURE STATE
### *Erich Mühsam*

Für die Freiheit in den Kerker *by unknown artist,* Die Aktion *35–36*
*(Sept. 4, 1920)*

"Socialization of the means of production"—the phrase swarms through the agitational speeches, writings, and anthologies of the "goal-conscious" Marxists, as if its realization were synonymous with mankind's eternal salvation and the attainment of ultimate bliss in all earthly relations.

The legend of the Messiah, sanctified by poetic beauty, has been "modernized," stripped of its artistic purity. Instead of the Savior descending from Heaven to redeem the world from sorrow, an economic principle of utility is offered to the gaze of enslaved humanity as a new cross and church. Belief, superstition in all its unsullied childishness, has given way to a frivolous scientism. Promises of hope for future liberation through divine power have been replaced by the elimination of false consciousness from the susceptible masses, on the grounds that the "materialist conception of history" so cleverly constructed by Karl Marx must, like a law of Nature, automatically lead the development of things to salvation—i.e., to the socialization of the means of production. . . .

To anticipate my own conception: I take my socialist demands much further. I strive toward communism in its most thoroughgoing form; I want the socialization not only of all the means of production, but of all the products produced by these means. I consider the community of consumption to be just as desirable as the community of production; besides the free disposition of everyone over all the natural and artistic possibilities of work, I demand everyone's free enjoyment of all created products.

Marx, whose theory of the elimination of private property amounts to nothing else than the nationalization of capital, slips off the secure track of the economic worldview and falls into the rocky seas of political speculation. The concept of the state—correctly termed the "executive of the propertied classes" by Marx's friend, the even more malicious hairsplitter Friedrich Engels—is once again smuggled by Marx into socialist society, and from the combination of completely incompatible socialist and democratic ideas results the dreary sensation of the social-democratic "future state." This fusion, born of errors and sophistries, leads Marx to the grotesque undertaking—and here his theory is consciously violated—of yoking the romantic socialist republic to the dogma of the materialist conception of history—a completely arbitrarily devised political speculation, then, which has absolutely no internal connection with the formation of economic developments, and which with a bold sleight-of-hand attempts to force the future society, as if it were a physically necessary deduction, into a philosophical law that, for all its logical untenability, is no less ingeniously thought out.

*

The selling power of the conception of the future state consists in the fact that its realization (which may yet appear with a few extras based on personal fantasy) would unquestionably guarantee the working class a secure existence and perhaps even a few luxuries in their living standards. Dedicated as he is to the Christian ethic of the masses,

Marx even takes into consideration the need to take care of all those who are unfit for work—idiots, cripples, old people, women, and children. Father State as sole employer and monopolistic exploiter assures profitable occupation for all those willing to work, and combines under a single jurisdiction the functions of our health and insurance companies. Of course, as a result of all this a regime of officials and bureaucrats would be created that would make the Kingdom of Prussia look like a veritable orphanage—but this doesn't bother the mass of wage slaves, inured as they are to authority. All they need for their well-being and happiness is a chicken in the oven every Sunday and the firm knowledge inculcated in them by the Marxist priests that the services performed by them for the common interest will be justly recompensed by the community.

But the benevolent teachings of monopolistic exploitation and the plutocracy of state officials do not take into account that besides the idiots, old people, cripples, children, and pregnant women, there are other people who are in the medical sense "able to work" but who do not feel like submitting to the sanctified principle of *do ut des*. There are some who would passionately resist the idea of submitting the products of their activity to a tribunal of majority opinion for an assessment of their value, just so that as a result of the decision they can be told the size of the chicken to roast in their oven. There will even be individuals who are so far gone that they won't have any physically visible products of any kind of activity that could be exchanged for a piece of paper instead of the customary, more manageable coins of today.

Because these "social parasites" will never be taken into consideration at all, and because no one will ever figure out that their special art could very well necessitate the destruction of the entire system, it follows that the "future state" is an institution that would mean the crushing of all individual emotions and the deification of the "average man's" intellect, and is to be resisted fanatically for this reason alone—that the furthering of real culture is worth more than the realization of a highly questionable principle of justice.

The artist—who in this regard is a "parasite" of the first order—would be living in a society that robbed him of the possibility of private patronage and abandoned him pitilessly to physical and psychic destruction. He would be required to offer up his work—his personal credo—for sale as a commodity to the hordes of his fellow-beings. He would have to get the "value" of his creations appraised by the intercession of the inartistic "majority," and the question of whether his artistic creations would be "useful to the community" would be settled by professional assessors. And if their decision were not in his favor, he would have to get used to the idea of putting aside his art "in the interests of the general public" and play the role of toilet-cleaner or even a judge.

Not to mention that as long as history has provided us with hindsight, we have noticed that great artists have very rarely been given their due by their contemporaries, and certainly the *vox populi*, which in the future state will have been enshrined as the *vox dei*, will never be in a position to recognize genuine art; useless also to point out that every artist goes through unproductive periods, and that there are and will be artists—even very great ones—who throughout their lives achieve little more than an intuition, but this intuition, which of course cannot be measured, inspires a great many likeminded artists, and only then does it facilitate conception and production, the most obvious point to consider being the radical differences between the motives that impel the citizen to useful work and the artist to individual life expression.

\*

All statist societies are founded on ethical agreement. The ethic that has turned out to be the most powerful, and which has placed its proponents in a position to destroy all other conventions, centralizes the collectivity under the laws that derive from it. Every revolutionary movement is the insurgence of a suppressed ethic against the ruling one. The ethic that has been established by the laws currently in effect, to which we are forced to submit, takes effect at the physical expense of the laboring masses who are fighting this ethic in the name of a new ethic which decrees the absolute right of the majority and desires to establish their material interests as the collectivity's highest law. Every statist centralization is therefore the result of the violation of one ethic by another, every social order is built on ethical principles, and every action, whether within the boundaries of an existing society or on behalf of building a new one, is governed by ethical principles. So every human being's business will be judged in the most ethically principled manner by the ethically brought up and ethically thinking masses. The artist's distinguishing feature is in fact his thoroughly unethical character. His actions—manifestations of his essence—derive from personal rather than profit motives. Every form of self-expression, be it an artistic production, a declaration, or any other deed, is an act of personal temperament—it occurs without the influence of an ethic.

This does not mean that a feeling of solidarity between artists and the people is to be ruled out. Whether this feeling endures or not, however, does not depend on the artist, but on the cultural level of the people. The "cultured lands" of today, especially Germany, are definitely ill-suited to make the unethical artistic types useful to their ethical interests.

It is self-evident that the organization of a centralized democratic state cannot for ethical reasons take artists into consideration at all. Even Plato, himself an artist to the core, demonstrated his correct understanding of the ethical foundations of the state by emphasizing in his *Republic* that there could be no room for the artist in the state. Least of all, of course, can the social-democratic "future state" grant the artist such a place, for not only does it seek to surrender all decisions over material utility or harmfulness to the mass instinct of the majority, but to entrust it with the mental and spiritual evaluation of all people.

Naturally, in circumstances like these the artist will be forced into a hostile position against such a social order. His instinct for self-preservation unfailingly leads him toward decentralist, anarchist tendencies. Since I consider myself an artist and restrict my feelings of solidarity essentially to artistic individuals, I will now declare quite clearly and bluntly why I place these purely destructive feelings on the same level as the positive development of communistic society: in communist society, the artist has the best possibility of truly becoming a parasite on ethically minded social strata, more than he could ever have considered being on any social institution. The "free access to goods," the unlimited right of each to the products of common labor, is for me the distinguishing factor in considering communism the ideal social form. I freely confess that this sets me at odds with the standard theoreticians of communist socialism. Peter Kropotkin explicitly states that, *faute de mieux*, allowance must be made for those individualists who because of the right of free access claim the privilege of partaking of the common product. But even on account of these few individuals, these sponges, I have taken up a position in the line of fire, and I do not know whether I would prefer communist socialism to collective socialism, were I to limit myself exclusively to proclaiming the workers' interests, were it possible for me to ignore the artist's weal and woe.

*

The often-raised and constantly repeated objection to communism, that it would make all individuals identical, is completely untenable. As long as the leveling of economic possibilities is kept separate from all democratic influences, it will not be a reason for restricting the free development of all personalities; rather, it will abundantly further the differentiation of individuals. Because of the identity of economic conditions that the individual encounters upon his entry into life, he is in the position of participating in production as he pleases, according to the needs that depend on his psychic and intellectual conditions. It is utterly wrong to believe that if everybody could have everything, everybody would grab for everything. Even the man of our times, brought up under capitalism, finds desirable only that which is either indispensable to his needs or so high-priced that it cannot be bought by his poorer neighbor. We gaze enviously and covetously only at those things we cannot get our hands on.

In communist society, material envy will provide hardly any gratification. The struggle for possessions will be governed exclusively by needs and inclinations. What is today called "luxury" because only a few can afford it, what is now owned by those well-bred types to whom it is least well-suited, will fall into the hands of those whose innermost beings yearn for it, and in the hands of a single person, the accumulated values of culture will proportionately enhance his spiritual and psychic worth *vis-à-vis* the masses. Economic leveling entails not a simplification but a differentiation that is inconceivable in any other social order. For the artist, however, this state of affairs means the only chance he has for independent creation and independent spiritual development.

Despite these propitious conditions for an artistic life, I in no way believe, nor do I wish, that hollow peaceful coexistence and mutual esteem prevail between artists and the masses. On the contrary, the gap between them will be even wider than it is today, where thanks to private fortunes and in some cases to patrons (to whom I must grant at least a conjectural existence), artists have sufficient means of financing the necessities of life. Hence, their natural character as social parasites is somewhat hidden from bourgeois perception. With the installation of communism, however, this character emerges fully into the light of day. In a society such as communism, based purely on the ethic of mutual aid, anyone who ostensibly shuns this ethic, who one-sidedly takes advantage of the followers of this ethic without visibly giving anything in return, and who cannot be punished materially lest the entire social structure be endangered, will be pitilessly subject to social ostracism. However, this natural form of self-defense nonetheless guarantees that it is entirely groundless to fear that communism will bring into being an army of worthless idlers for whose maintenance the better portion of society will have to slave away with disproportionate exertion.

Only very strong, intensely talented natures—devoid of ethical instincts and feelings of social shame—are capable of enduring society's collective proscription. Precisely on this do I base my artistic respect for the taverns and highways, because I know people there who have fled from the holy institutions of the capitalist state in defiance of the torrent of spittle that society hurls at them. To me, the young, strong tramp I met a few years ago on a hike through Mecklenburg is a thousand times more worthy than the factory worker slaving away for a capitalist wage. When I asked him why he wasn't working, he replied, "I can't live the way I want to if I'm a worker or a consumer. At least here I can be my own master to some extent, because I don't need to have an exploiter nail down my shoes." This person has more artistic blood in him than all the kitschmakers patronized by the Berlin court put together. Hence, I am even more likely to give alms to a strong, employable beggar who crosses my path than a cripple, because the former's lifestyle does not elicit weak sympathy from me but honest respect for his genuine Protestantism.

However, I believe that the real formation of the class struggle, which today presents itself as a struggle of the propertyless against the propertied—in other words, the formation of masses against individuals—is itself in the masses' own interests. How many individuals of perhaps unimaginable worth have already perished from malnutrition on their mothers' breasts! How many children with the highest artistic ability have been prematurely killed or intellectually destroyed by the inhuman horror of the exploitation of child labor!

How many strong individuals have been forced by senseless capitalist industry down false paths entirely unsuited to their beings!

*

In all other social classes, there are of course enough exceptional people who are worth standing up for. However, the place of the artist, whose temperament leads him to participate in the transformation of things, is with the working people. Until capitalist society is overthrown, until the construction of the socialist-communist order, the artists and the masses have a single path. Once this goal is attained, the artist will go his own way. The individualistic types from the masses will follow him close at hand. For the small minority of artistic nonconformists, the resting point that the people, no longer economically constrained, occupy in order to fulfill their ethical duty of mutual aid to one another, is but the point of departure for the individual development of spiritual qualities. The socialization of the means of production, and beyond that the community of consumption, the free access to goods, is therefore for the artist not the goal of revolutionary struggle but merely the means to a goal. But this goal, since the artist is not a goal-oriented person, is he himself, the development of his faculties and temperaments, above all the most pronounced differentiation of his personality.

So the artist, then, does not compromise his work at all when he takes a stand in the struggle for a radical transformation of all social institutions, when he in all his virginal innocence believes himself to be a solitary, withdrawn hermit and rages passionately against the capitalist state that restricts his growth in a thousand different ways—and when, with redoubled anger, he opposes anyone who mentions the word "future state" to him. For such a person wishes to deny him the last possibility of breathing freely, to make him a slave to a hateful ethic, and thereby cut off the wellspring of his life and that of his kindred souls.

(1906)

*Translated by Christopher Winks*
*(Special thanks to Ron Javorcky for his assistance.)*

# SURREALISM AND ROMANTICISM
## *Marie-Dominique Massoni*

Le Gardien du Seuil *(1991–1993) by Guy Girard*

A*rcanum 17.* This is the title of the book that André Breton wrote during his exile in the United States; it refers explicitly to the Tarot of Marseilles, whose seventeenth arcanum is the Star. If the title alludes to the tarot created by the surrealists as they awaited passage in Marseilles during the winter of 1940–41, it also clearly harks back to Gérard de Nerval, the French romantic poet who wrote in his poem "El Desdichado":

> My only star is dead—and my star-studded lute
> Bears the Black Sun of melancholia.

The melancholy of the romantics—like their refusal of every-thing standing for bourgeois values—will always be read, for it will always be seen and heard, and this effort to listen to what Victor Hugo called "the voice of darkness" guided the young surrealists' experiments in automatic writing. But automatic writing is also based on the work of psychoanalysis, and Freud's discoveries offered a theoretical ground for the surrealists' investigations. The surrealists share with the romantics the desire to put empirical reality on trial; the common project is the search for true knowledge. But the surrealist adventure goes far beyond the surge of an exalted sensibility or the self-imposed schism of imagination and experience. The surrealists work from above (dreams, hypnotic trances, the simulation of dementia) and from below ("the imaginary is what tends to become reality"). For the surrealists, the task is to "rethink the world in view to its magic redemption."

The marvelous is that point where "human reason loses all control." It is the source of Anne Radcliffe's novels and those subterranean territories where initiatory spaces are constructed—spaces that would fascinate Byron and Mary Shelley as well as André Breton and the Czech filmmaker Svankmajer. If what the Frankfurt School would term "instrumental reason" designates what was already the lament of the romantics, it is the number one enemy of the surrealists. The surreal is intimately connected to what Gaston Bachelard poignantly calls the "surrational." *Spirit against Reason*, to borrow the title of René Crevel's book, is fundamentally the spirit of a reason that is yet to be, a dialectical process of opposing a dominant paradigm of reason while affirming a new intelligence in its interstices. The surrealists inherit from the romantics the refusal to perceive the world according to certain mathematical, logical, useful, verifiable, quantifiable—in brief, bourgeois—presuppositions. The hatred of Cartesianism, the philosophy *par excellence* of bourgeois science, is deep-rooted. Surrealism is a rational idealism: its major reference is the Hegelian dialectic.

In opposition to instrumental reason, the surrealists emphasize the imagination; against scientific demonstration they affirm the magic moment of poetic evidence, the metaphor whose secret networks encourage the quest for "the gold of time," as opposed to the finite gold of profit-seekers caught in the vicious circle of materialism. Just as the Gothic novel spelled the end of the English aristocracy, surrealism is intrinsically at odds with the capitalist ethic and aims at embodying a new civilization. To undermine modernity's understanding, to dynamite its morality by putting himself on the side of evil, such was Lautréamont's venture in *Les Chants de Maldoror*, one of the greatest achievements of black humor, an essential surrealist weapon to triumph over the material circumstances of place and time (*La Révolution Surréaliste, Le Surréalisme au Service de la Révolution, La Brèche*), and to empower those disabled by capitalism to use what Fourier called their *archibras* or "super-arms." If the romantic connection to politics is of an incredible complexity that defies sociological classification (Goethe is a town notable and Hölderlin a revolutionary; Chateaubriand is a royalist and Byron dies in Greece; Mary Shelley has the makings of an anarchist; George Sand is a Saint-Simonian at first, then a disciple of Pierre Leroux while continuing to be a feminist, and yet she applauds the massacre of the Paris Commune, which deeply distresses a mystical left-wing Hugo), the surrealists have an explicitly revolutionary political standpoint. Their support for the Communist Party quickly becomes a resounding outcry against the persecution of Trotsky and the Moscow Trials. But their motto, a synthesis of the revolutionary and romantic traditions, combines Marx and Rimbaud: "Transform the world! Change life!" Whether surrealists are closer to the anarchists or the Trotskyists depends on the situation and the individual. The poet Benjamin Péret, a Trotskyist, fought in Spain in the anarchist Durruti Column. Like a political movement, they produce pamphlets, leaflets, declarations.

Of course, the surrealists are atheists and anticlerical, which marks them off from many romantics whose glorification of nature and spiritual yearning were fused with religious conviction. Surrealism avoids any metaphysics that could become an ideological trap: the radical refusal of domination translates into a refusal of the best tool that mankind ever created to justify submission: God. "Change life!" does not imply that "true life" is elsewhere or that it existed in humanity's Golden Age. There is no surrealist nostalgia for a mythical past. True life, as the surrealists understand it, is a genuine possibility that awaits its historical chance. The romantic revolt that stems from the anguish of Being, from the deception of the world, demands a lucidity, a critical reflex that counters illusion and the myriad forms of subservience that are themselves caused by the fact of mystery.

The marvelous suggests that we perceive only a minute portion of reality, that we are victims of a retinal tyranny, prisoners bound by our finitude. Yet the marvelous is a moment of reality. If the surrealists try to bring to light "the real functioning of thought" by way of automatism, they also work toward the liberation of all its potential. As with the romantics, the phenomena of coincidences and premonitions are essential, even if surrealism does not consider the extraordinary a moment of transcendence. The "objective chances" that make up the magic of life represent the convergence of inner necessity with outer reality. Such moments of dazzlement have a coherence that the Hegelian dialectic is never far from making apparent.

If, however, unlike the romantics, the surrealists interpret social reality specifically in light of a transformation of the mode of production and a collective intervention in the political sphere (be it of an anarchist or Marxist character), the power of desire and of the marvelous push them to embrace hermeticism, just as the romantics had before them. Since "Entrée des Médiums," and up to the paintings of Camacho or Stejskal, the surrealists follow in the footsteps of the alchemist Eugène Canseliet and the esoteric tradition, clearing their art of the occultist hodgepodge that often had the place of honor in romantic works. "I am looking for the gold of time," reads the inscription on Breton's grave. The double reference to romanticism and alchemy is obvious. The Prague surrealist group has just shown (1997) the boards of its *Mutus Liber*, a key work in alchemy, and Svankmajer has filmed his *Faust* (1996).

"Love is the goal of universal history," wrote Novalis. The surrealists have made love their major arcanum. It is at once the wonderful isolation of lovers, that which propels the dynamic of refusal to challenge social constraints, and sublime immanence.

*Translated by Max Blechman*

# UNDER THE STAR OF ROMANTICISM
## Walter Benjamin and Herbert Marcuse
### *Michael Löwy*

*Illustration by Eric Drooker*

Romanticism is not only a literary and artistic school from the early nineteenth century: it is much deeper and broader phenomena, a powerful worldview, a style of thought, a structure-of-sensibility that is present in all spheres of cultural life, from Rousseau and Novalis until the surrealists (and beyond). One could define the romantic *Weltanschauung* as a protest against the modern (capitalist) civilization, in the name of premodern (precapitalist) values, a cultural critique of the bourgeois-industrial world responsible for the quantification and mechanization of life, the reification of social relationships, the dissolution of community, and, above all, for the *disenchantment of the world*. Its nostalgic gaze toward the past does not mean that it is necessarily regressive: reaction and revolution are both possible figures of the romantic worldview. For revolutionary romanticism, the aim is not a *return* to the past but a *detour* through it, toward a utopian future.

In Germany, at the end of the nineteenth century, romanticism (sometimes referred to as "neoromanticism") is one of the dominant cultural forms, not only in literature and poetry but also in the *Geisteswissenschaften*, where many thinkers criticize the industrial society in the name of *Kultur* against *Zivilisation*, or *Gemeinschaft* (community) against *Gesellschaft* (society). The common pattern of this romantic culture, which includes many German-Jewish figures, is the attempt—often desperate—to reenchant the world. Walter Benjamin and Herbert Marcuse both belong to this constellation. Although the affinity between them has been recognized, notably by Gershom Scholem, there has been no systematic attempt to examine the nature of their spiritual kinship.

The relationship of Benjamin to romanticism is not only manifest in his interest for the German *Frühromantik* (Schlegel and Novalis) or for such late romantic figures as E. T. A. Hoffmann, Franz von Baader, Franz-Joseph Molitor, and Johann Jakob Bachofen—or for Baudelaire and the surrealists—but by all his aesthetic, theological, and philosophical ideas. These three spheres are deeply intertwined: politics, art, and religion are so intimately linked in his writings that it is difficult to separate them without destroying the singularity of his thought.

In one of his first publications, the short notice "Romantik" (1913), Benjamin criticizes the "false romanticism" taught in school and calls for the birth of a "new romanticism," emphasizing that "the romantic *will* to beauty, the romantic will to truth, the romantic will to action" are "inseparable" (*unüberwindlich*) acquisitions of modern culture. In an essay in form of dialogue from the same year (*Dialog über die Religiosität der Gegenwart*, 1913), he acknowledges that his generation lives "very deeply immersed in the discoveries of romanticism," among which are the powerful insights on "the nocturnal side of nature." Sharply criticizing the reduction of men to working machines and the debasement of all work to technical production, he insists, in opposition to the illusions of progress and evolution, on the need for a new religion, whose prophets would be Tolstoy, Nietzsche, and Strindberg—i.e., cultural critics of modern civilization—and for a new, sincere (*ehrlichen*) socialism.[1]

The intimate association of romantic-messianic and anarchist-utopian themes is one of the central features of Benjamin's philosophy. If we examine his early speech *On Student Life* (1914), we can already find the seeds of much of his future writings. Against the "formless" idea of progress he celebrates the critical power of *utopian images*, such as those of the French Revolution and of the messianic kingdom; the real issues for society are not those of technology and science but the metaphysical questions raised by Plato, Spinoza, the romantics, and Nietzsche, under whose inspiration the student community should become the harbinger of a "permanent spiritual revolution." The anarchist dimension is already suggested by the statement that truly free art and knowledge are "alien to the state, frequently hostile to the state." But it is also present in a more explicit way, in the reference to the Tolstoyan spirit of serving the poor, whose most authentic expressions were "the ideas of the most profound Anarchists and the Christian monastic communities."[2] Utopia, anarchism, revolution, and messianism are alchemically fused and linked to a romantic cultural criticism of "progress" and pure technical-scientific knowledge. The past—monastic communities—and the future—the anarchist ideal—are directly associated in a characteristically revolutionary-romantic shortcut. This document contains *in nuce* many of Benjamin's subsequent essays, and it has a striking similarity with his last piece, "Theses on the Philosophy of History" (1940). We can perceive a basic continuity in his spiritual trajectory from 1914 to 1940—which does not mean that there were no changes or transmutations: after 1924 Marxism becomes an increasingly essential ingredient of his worldview. Communism and historical materialism did not replace his former spiritualist and libertarian convictions but amalgamated with them, forming a distinctive pattern of thought.

Benjamin's first important literary essay (1914–15) was devoted to the revolutionary-romantic Hölderlin, and after 1916, he became fascinated by Friedrich Schlegel's youthful writings, which were to be the raw materials of his doctoral thesis. In a letter to Scholem in June 1917, he praised the "infinite profundity and beauty" of the *Frühromantik* and significantly concluded that "romanticism is the last movement that has once again saved tradition for us."[3]

In 1919 Benjamin presented his thesis on "The Concept of Criticism in German Romanticism," a provocative assessment of the romantic aesthetics of Friedrich Schlegel and Novalis, as an over-coming of the "rationalist dogmas" of the eighteenth century. In a heterodox manner he discovers that the true essence of the *Frühromantik* "must be sought in Romantic Messianism," and quotes the following astonishing statement by the young Friedrich Schlegel: "The revolutionary desire to achieve the Kingdom of God is the beginning of modern history. . . ." According to Benjamin, there follows from romantic messianism a qualitative conception of *infinite time* (*qualitative zeitliche Unendlichkeit*), for which the life of humanity is a process of accomplishment (*Erfüllung*) and not simply of evolution, as in the infinitely empty time (*leere Unendlichkeit der Zeit*) of the modern ideologies of progress. Once more, the affinity is striking with the "Theses on the Philosophy of History" of 1940.[4]

One of the first occasions on which Benjamin fully expressed his libertarian-revolutionary views was in "Critique of Violence" (1921), directly inspired by that eminently romantic anarchist, Georges Sorel. Voicing harsh contempt for state institutions such as the police and the parliament, Benjamin endorses the "devastating" antiparliamentarian critique of the anarcho-syndicalists and the Bolsheviks (a highly revealing association) as well as the Sorelian idea of the proletarian general strike as an action "whose one and only task is to destroy the violence of the State." This conception, which he explicitly describes as anarchist, seems to him "profound, moral and authentically revolutionary"; however—and here Benjamin parts company with Sorel and moves into the sphere of theological messianism—he defines "pure" and "immediate" revolutionary violence as a profane manifestation of divine violence, the only one capable of breaking "the circle of the mythical forms of law . . . and therefore the violence of the State."[5]

The attempt to combine or articulate communism and anarchism is the *leitmotiv* of Benjamin's fascinating essay, "Surrealism" (1929), which celebrates the movement founded by André Breton as the most outstanding heir to the libertarian tradition: "since Bakunin, no radical concept of freedom has existed in Europe. The surrealists do have it." They are also heirs to those other "great anarchists who worked during the years from 1865 to 1875, without knowing each other, in the preparation of their time bombs": Dostoyevsky, Rimbaud, and Lautréamont, whose devices exploded exactly at the same time forty years later, in the upsurge of surrealism. Benjamin believes that in relation to the cardinal questions of the time, surrealism and communism are very close: in opposition to the mindless, dilettante optimism of social democracy, they have the same view of the destiny of humanity: "pessimism all along the line." And if the *Communist Manifesto* requires reality to transcend itself (through a "revolutionary discharge"), "the surrealists are the only ones to have understood its present commands."[6]

Instead of "progress," revolution is, according to the "Theses on the Philosophy of History," a "tiger's leap in the past," searching for the lost paradise, the archaic golden age of edenic harmony between human beings, as well as between humanity and nature. Utopia and restitution, future and past are associated in a characteristically romantic way and opposed to the present (capitalist) "hell." In a key paragraph of the essay on Baudelaire, "Paris, Capital of the Nineteenth Century" (1936), Benjamin refers to the dreams of the future as always being "married" to elements of prehistoric ages (*Urgeschichte*), "i.e. of classless society"; for him, the experiences from this archaic past stored in the collective memory "produce Utopia, by interpenetration with the new."[7]

In the 1940 theses utopia is represented by the Marxist perspective of a classless society but also by Fourier's *travail passionné*, as a dream of reconciliation with nature, in opposition to the modern, industrial-capitalist, and pseudosocialist ideology of production as "exploitation of nature."[8] Following the logic of revolutionary romanticism, nostalgia of the past becomes in Benjamin a critical energy, a subversive force, a creative source of utopian hope.

What Marcuse shares with Benjamin is not so much messianic Judaism or libertarian leanings but the *romantic outlook*, the romantic protest against modern civilization and the romantic opposition of artistic *Kultur* to prosaic bourgeois society. There is a significant similarity between his 1922 dissertation "The German Artist Novel" (*Der deutsche Künstlerroman*) and Benjamin's "The Concept of Criticism in German Romanticism." Marcuse's doctoral thesis is essential for understanding his future intellectual evolution. The central theme of the book is the contradiction between the world of idea and empirical reality, art, and bourgeois life—a contradiction painfully perceived and expressed by the romantics. Some of them, particularly Novalis, tried to overcome this duality by ignoring the empirical world, replacing it with an ideal reality—an imaginary new world dominated by love and peace, Eros and Freya. Others, like Goethe in the *Sorrows of the Young Werther*, show how the artist's idealist subjectivity leads him to a radical conflict with the *zweckhaft-rationellen* order of reality—a conflict that cannot but end with his surrender or death. And some later romantics, like E. T. A. Hoffmann, are attracted to the ancient, dark, and dissolving forces of passion that threaten to explode the existing world. For Marcuse, most of the artist novels—i.e., novels whose central hero is an artist—contain a critical dimension against the growing industrialization and mechanization of economic and cultural life, as a process that destroys or marginalizes all spiritual values. He emphasizes the burning aspiration of many romantics or neoromantics for a radical change of life, breaking the narrow limits of bourgeois-philistine materialism, and he compares them with the contemporary utopian socialists, such as Fourier.[9] Some of these ideas of *Der deutsche Künstlerroman* reappear, almost unchanged, in *Eros and Civilization* and *One-Dimensional Man*.

There is a striking parallel in the intellectual evolutions of Marcuse and Benjamin: both begin with German romanticism and the problems of art; both move toward Marxism during the 1920s, under the influence of Lukács and Korsch, and become linked to the Frankfurt Institute for Social Research during the 1930s; both are highly critical of social democracy, hope for a socialist revolutionary transformation, but refuse to join the Communist Party; and they probably met in Germany or Paris (1933). Nevertheless, to the best of our knowledge, during Benjamin's lifetime there is no mention of him in Marcuse's writings.[10] Why this silence? One possible hypothesis is that after the short Heideggerian interlude of 1928–32, Marcuse moved increasingly away from romanticism and toward an interpretation of Marxism linking it to the tradition of Western rationalism, from Plato to Descartes, and from the *Aufklärung* to Hegel.

During his whole life, Marcuse's Marxism moved between two poles: the romantic and the rationalist. For him, these poles are not contradictory. They have a common element, which is the constant of his thought: *negation*, the opposition between the idea and the given reality. There is a remarkable passage in Marcuse's 1960 preface to *Reason and Revolution* where this is explicitly stated: "Dialectic and poetic language meet . . . on common ground. The common element is the search for . . . the language of negation as the Great Refusal."[11]

For Marcuse, another link between rationalism and romanticism is their commitment to *qualitative* human values, cultural or ethical, as opposed to mere *quantitative* values of the capitalist market. But Reason is conceived as substantial, not purely formal and instrumental, which also can be found in capitalist industry, even in concentration camps. This unity of the two poles is the unity of Marcuse's *oeuvre* beyond the particular (romantic or rationalist) emphasis of different periods of his intellectual evolution.

During the 1930s and 1940s, the rationalist pole becomes predominant in Marcuse's thought. After 1924, when he published an annotated bibliography of Schiller's works, the problems of art, literature, and culture and their opposition to reality tend to disappear from his writings for the next three decades. Although in 1937 he published an essay on "The Affirmative Character of Culture," this text, far from being restatement of his 1922 ideas is precisely their *most radical negation*. According to it, traditional culture—in particular, literature—by preserving an ideal world above and opposed to the vulgarity of daily life, plays an ideological and conservative role; the beauty of the "soul" (*Seele*) is extolled as a compensation for the wretchedness of the material world:

> The freedom of the soul was used to excuse the misery, martyrdom, and enslavement of the body. It serves the ideological surrender of existence to the economy of capitalism. . . . The soul has a tranquilizing effect . . . the joys of the soul are cheaper than those of the body and less dangerous.

Marcuse seems to believe that there is a basic difference between philosophy and literature, in their relation to the established state of affairs: "The beauty of art—in contrast to the truth of theory—is compatible with the existing evil."

Therefore, to this "affirmative" cultural sphere, with its illusory freedom and happiness, Marcuse opposes the tradition of rational philosophy—Descartes, Kant, Hegel—which is alien to the concept of "soul" and committed to the critical rationality of *spirit*. While the concept of *Seele* is typical of irrationalist tendencies, from romantic historicism (Herder) to modern authoritarian doctrines (a euphemism for fascist ideology), "Hegel does not fit in the authoritarian states. He

was for the spirit; the new ones are for the soul and for sentiment."
Of course, Marcuse is aware of the one-sided character of this indict-
ment of rational art and literature in the bourgeois era; he recognizes
that they contain not only the justification of established forms of
existence, but also the pain of its existence; not only the reconciliation with that which is, but also the memory of that which could be.

> Great bourgeois art, because it . . . painted the beauty of
> people and things and a supra-earthly happiness with the
> bright colors of this world . . . deposed at the foundation of
> bourgeois life not only false consolation . . . but also true
> nostalgia (*Sehnsucht*).

This insight will become decisive in Marcuse's later writings. In
1937, however, it is integrated as a subordinate element in the general conception of culture as "affirmative": "Culture becomes a servant of the existent. The rebellious idea becomes a lever for its
justification. . . . Since art depicts the beautiful as present, it brings
rebellious nostalgia to a halt." Needless to say, such a theoretical
framework could not but alienate Marcuse from Benjamin's aesthetic
and cultural preoccupations.[12]

This rationalist orientation, which runs through most of Marcuse's
essays of the 1930s, culminating in 1941 with *Reason and Revolution*,
may explain why he ignored Benjamin's works. Conversely, Marcuse's
increasing move toward the romantic pole in the fifties and sixties may
be one of the reasons why he rediscovered Benjamin at that time. One
can trace the development of this new turn in Marcuse's thinking
through the various prefaces to *Reason and Revolution*, from 1941,
1954, and 1960. In 1941 Marcuse still praised the "American rationalist
spirit." This had a direct political translation on his activity as an (anti-
fascist) adviser for the American Office of Strategic Services during the
war. But in the 1950s, after the Cold War and McCarthyism, and after
a deeper study of American society, Marcuse grew increasingly critical
of industrial civilization and its instrumental rationality. In the epilogue
written in 1954 for the second edition of the book, Marcuse recognized
the *contradictory* character of the Western rationalist tradition:

> From the beginning, the idea and the reality of Reason in the
> modern periods contained the elements which endangered its

promise of a free and fulfilled existence: the enslavement of man by his own productivity . . . the repressive mastery of nature in man and outside.[13]

At the same time, he rediscovered the subversive virtues of imagination and art, i.e., the problematic of his early writings.

This new "romantic" period began with *Eros and Civilization* (1955), where, reinterpreting Freud, Marcuse counterposed erotic sensuousness to the rationality of the performance cycle. Art was then conceived in a completely different light than in the 1937 essay (which had opposed the truth of theory to the illusory beauty of artistic imagination): "Fantasy is cognitive in so far as it preserves the truth of the Great Refusal, or, positively, in so far as it protects, against all reason, the aspiration for the integral fulfillment of man and nature which are repressed by reason." The great German writer on whom he had worked in 1925 comes once more into the fore: Friedrich Schiller, whose aesthetic letters attain an "explosive quality" by showing that "freedom would have to be sought in the liberation of sensuousness rather than reason," or at least that "the laws of reason must be reconciled with the interest of the senses." Moreover, according to Marcuse, "Herder and Schiller, Hegel and Novalis developed in almost identical terms the concept of alienation. As industrial society begins to take shape under the rule of the performance principle, its inherent negativity permeates the philosophical analysis" (a quote from Schiller follows). This remark is highly significant: it combines in the same sociocultural "front" artists and philosophers, romantics and rationalists, and in particular two thinkers Marcuse had counterposed in 1937 as representative of the *Seele* (Herder) and of the *Geist* (Hegel).[14]

It is no accident that in *Eros and Civilization*, the first work where the romantic dimension of Marcuse's thought reemerges, is also to be found Marcuse's "rediscovery" of Walter Benjamin. He quotes, comments on, and praises an important passage from the "Theses on the Philosophy of History" (1940). When Marcuse wrote the book, Benjamin's main essays had not yet been republished (Marcuse quotes the "Theses" from a 1950 publication in *Die Neue Rundschau*). It is well known that Adorno's edition of the *Schriften* in 1955 became the starting point for a general reception of Benjamin by the Western radical intelligentsia. But Marcuse's interest in him precedes and is not related to it. It flows, rather, from the inner dynamics of his own spiritual development.

In the passage quoted by Marcuse, Benjamin writes: "The wish to break the continuum of history belongs to the revolutionary class in the moment of action." In connection with this passage and the whole content of Benjamin's "Theses," Marcuse argues: "Remembrance is no real weapon unless it is translated into historical action. Then, the struggle against time becomes a decisive moment in the struggle against domination." The memory of the past as a weapon in the fight for the future: one could hardly imagine a more striking and precise formulation of the revolutionary-romantic perspective, which is common to Marcuse and Benjamin and pervades both their political and their aesthetic views.[15]

From 1955 till his last writings, Marcuse was attracted once more to art and the romantic artistic ideal of a world dominated by Eros and peace. This ideal is one of the central features of *One-Dimensional Man* (1964), where he stressed its critical potential:

> The traditional images of artistic alienation are indeed romantic in as much as they are in aesthetic incompatibility with the developing society. *This incompatibility is the token of their truth.* What they recall and preserve in memory pertains to the future: images of a gratification that would dissolve the society which suppressed it. The great surrealist art and literature of the 1920s and 1930s has still recaptured them in their subversive and liberating function.[16]

Similar statements on the contradiction between the artistic or poetic universe and the given reality, as well as on the revolutionary dimension of surrealism are also to be found in Marcuse's subsequent books. For instance, in *An Essay on Liberation* (1969), he hails the absolute nonconformism of surrealist poets who find "in the poetic language the semantic elements of the revolution."[17] Marcuse's interest in surrealism is also documented by his fascinating exchange of letters with Franklin Rosemont and the Chicago surrealists, where he celebrates "the revolutionary heart and core of surrealism, its radical transcendence beyond the given reality principle."[18]

Marcuse insists in *Counterrevolution and Revolt* (1972) that in the most important works of art and literature since the nineteenth century a thoroughly antibourgeois stance is prevalent: the higher culture indicts, rejects, withdraws from the material culture of the bourgeoisie. It is indeed separated; it dissociates itself from the world of commodities, from the brutality of bourgeois industry and commerce, from the distortion of human relationships, from capitalist materialism, from instrumentalist reason. The aesthetic universe contradicts reality.

It is significant that among the great works of literature that represent for Marcuse the most authentic, absolute, and uncompromising form of sublimated Eros, works that, in his view—in *One-Dimensional Man*—are "beyond the reaches of the established Reality Principle, which the Eros re-uses and explodes" are Goethe's *Elective Affinities* [*Wahlverwandtschaften*] and Baudelaire's *Fleurs du Mal*—two books that are central in Benjamin's aesthetic and philosophical reflection (the first one in the 1920s and the second one during the 1930s).[19]

The relation to Benjamin occupies a very special place in *One-Dimensional Man*. As is well known, the book ends with a powerful and moving homage to him:

> Critical theory . . . holding no promise and showing no success, remains negative. Thus it wants to remain loyal to those who, without hope, have given and give their life to the Great Refusal. At the beginning of the fascist era, Walter Benjamin wrote: *Nur um der Hoffnungslosen Willen ist uns die Hoffnung gegeben.* It is only for the sake of those without hope that hope is given to us."[20]

In its original context, this passage from Benjamin's 1922 essay, "Goethe's Elective Affinities," had a deep religious meaning, while Marcuse gives it a directly political translation (in a way typical of his "secular" reading of Benjamin).

One can find here a common element, a peculiar quality of their style of thought, which could be designated as *desperate hope* or *pessimist revolutionarism*. Both Marcuse and Benjamin refuse to believe that the "natural course" of history, the development of productive forces, or inevitable social progress will lead to a rational and liberated society. For them, as Benjamin formulated it in a most remarkable image, the revolutionaries must learn to "brush history against the grain." There is no predestined and irresistible triumph of humanity and reason. Left to itself, "progress" produces only, as in Benjamin's allegory of the angel of history, a "pile of wreckage." Revolution is not "swimming with the current," but is a fierce struggle against the blind forces of history, a hard and protracted war whose end result cannot be predicted. In a postscript to a new edition of Marx's *18th Brumaire*, Marcuse wrote: "the consciousness of defeat, even desperation, belongs to the truth of the theory and its hope." Far from favoring passivity (as does resignation *as well as official optimism* in Kautsky), this brand of voluntarist pessimism is, on the contrary, the most desperate call for action, initiative, and resistance.[21]

In this respect, *One-Dimensional Man* owes much to Benjamin's "Theses on the Philosophy of History." One can therefore understand that in the same year as his book appeared (1964), Marcuse felt the need to write an essay on Walter Benjamin himself. This little-known piece is an afterword to a collection of five articles by Benjamin, among them "Theses on the Philosophy of History" and "Critique of Violence" (1921). It is not a systematic piece, but clearly reveals the common features between the two—as well as their differences.

First of all, both Marcuse and Benjamin stand for an *absolute* negation of the existing social order. Both aspire to a *radical* revolution and recognize the need for oppressed groups to use *violence* against oppressors. Commenting on Benjamin's essay on violence, Marcuse stresses that

> The violence to which Benjamin's criticism is directed, in not the one . . . employed from below against those above. . . . The violence criticized by Benjamin is that of the existent (*Bestehenden*), which obtained from the existent itself the monopoly of legitimacy, of truth and of right. . . . Benjamin took much too seriously the promise contained in the word "Peace" to be a pacifist. . . .[22]

Both men are irreconcilably opposed to all reformism and gradualism and perceive revolution as *an explosion of the historical continuum*, a totally new beginning, and not an improved version of the status quo, or the cumulative result of progressive evolution. At the same time, paradoxically, this new future implies a return to the precapitalist past: as Benjamin puts it in his famous image, revolution is "a dialectical leap of the tiger into the past." These and other *leitmotivs* of Benjamin's 1940 "Theses" are shared by Marcuse, not only in this essay on Benjamin but in most of his works of the sixties and seventies.

However, there are also undeniable differences in the understanding of revolution. In his commentaries, Marcuse ignores the anarchist component of Benjamin's early writings and tries to neutralize their religious content by presenting a thoroughly "atheological" interpretation of Benjamin's messianism. Thus, he writes

It becomes clear in Benjamin's "Critique of Violence" that messianism is the form of appearance of a historical truth: liberated humanity is only conceivable as the radical (no more the simply "determinate") negation of the existent, because under the power of the existent even the Good itself becomes powerless and an accomplice. Benjamin's messianism has nothing to do with traditional religiosity: guilt and expiation are for him social categories.[23]

This interpretation may be partly true, but it is one-sided: Benjamin's deep theological dimension, rooted in the Jewish tradition, is linked to social categories but cannot be reduced to them. Marcuse's remarks are as revealing of his own views as of Benjamin's messianism. While in 1941, in *Reason and Revolution*, he still spoke in terms of "determinate" negation of the given reality, now, in 1964, he pleads for more total negativity.

The other broad outlook shared by Benjamin and Marcuse is that both criticize not only capitalism but, more generally, all of industrial society, reified technology, alienated productivity, the destruction of nature, and the myth of progress. As Marcuse writes in his essay on Benjamin:

In opposition to the abominable concept of progressive productivity, for whom nature "exists *gratis*" to be exploited, Benjamin professes Fourier's idea of a social labor which "far from exploiting nature, is capable of delivering her of the creations which lie dormant in her womb as potentials." To liberated humanity, redeemed from oppressive violence, corresponds a liberated and redeemed nature.[24]

This is also one of the reasons why both are so critical of the Soviet Union, which failed in their eyes to generate a real alternative to the industrial society of the West, with its productivism and its technological reification.

On the other hand, both Benjamin and Marcuse recognize— each in his own way—the emancipatory possibilities of modern technology. This applies to cinema in the cultural area, for Benjamin, and to automation in the economic sphere, for Marcuse. Both try to grasp the contradictory nature of material progress and industrial technology, even if their conclusions are not the same (Marcuse, like Adorno and Horkheimer, is more critical than Benjamin of the mass reproduction of art and cultural goods).

Benjamin is once more mentioned in Marcuse's last work, *The Aesthetic Dimension* (1977), where the contradiction between art (literature) and established reality, which was the subject matter of his 1922 dissertation, again becomes the main theme of his work. Although in 1977 modern and not classic romantic writers are central, Marcuse mentions, as one of the crass errors of dogmatic Marxist aesthetics, "the denigration of romanticism as simply reactionary." *The Aesthetic Dimension* does not oppose "soul" to Reason; it shows that art is committed to the emancipation of sensibility, imagination, *and* reason—a reason distinct from the rationality of the dominant institutions. By its association with Eros against instinctual repression, the aesthetic dimension is a protest against the established world and a promise of liberation. And by preserving the memory of things past, it fulfills a revolutionary role, since "the authentic utopia is grounded in recollection."

The two references to Benjamin in this book reveal Marcuse's affinity with his friend's romantic dimension but also a certain reserve toward his views of the relation between art and politics. It seems as if Marcuse feels closer to the "Baudelairean Benjamin" than to the "Brechtian Benjamin." Although he is an admirer of Brecht's poems (one of them is extensively quoted in *One-Dimensional Man*), Marcuse is inclined to believe that, as he puts it, "there may be more subversive potential in the poetry of Baudelaire and Rimbaud than in the didactic plays of Brecht." He criticizes Benjamin's most "Brechtian" writing, "The Author as Producer," for its "identification of literary and political quality in the domain of art." On the other hand, he greatly admires Benjamin's essays on the *poètes maudits*:

The degree to which the distance and estrangement from *praxis* constitute the emancipatory value of art becomes particularly clear in those works of literature which seem to close themselves rigidly against such *praxis*. Benjamin has traced this in the works of Poe, Baudelaire, Proust, and Valéry.

There follows a quotation from a fragment where Benjamin refers to Baudelaire as an "agent of the secret discontent of his class with its own rule." Marcuse then adds this commentary: "The 'secret' protest of this esoteric literature lies in the ingression of the primary erotic-destructive forces which explode the normal universe of communication and behavior. They are asocial in their very nature, a subterranean rebellion against the social order."[25]

Both Marcuse and Benjamin were revolutionary romantics— romantic in the sense of nostalgia for precapitalist *Kultur*, a nostalgia preserved in great art as "remembrance of things past," and revolutionary because they transformed this nostalgia of the past into a radical negation of the present order and into a "desperate hope" for a radically new future society.

### Notes

1. Walter Benjamin, *Gessamelte Schriften* (Frankfurt am Main: Suhrkamp Verlag, 1977) II:22–26, 34, 46.
2. Walter Benjamin, "Das Leben der Studenten," in *Illuminationen* (Frankfurt am Main: Suhrkamp Verlag, 1980) 9, 11, 14, 16; Walter Benjamin, "On Student Life," in *Selected Writings Vol. I (1913–1926)*, ed. Marcus Bullock and Michael Jennings (Cambridge, MA & London: Harvard Univ. Press, 1996) 37–38, 40, 43.
3. Walter Benjamin, *Briefe* (Frankfurt am Main: Suhrkamp Verlag, 1966) I:138; *The Correspondence of Walter Benjamin 1910–1940*, ed. Gershom Scholem and Theodor Adorno (Chicago & London: Univ. of Chicago Press, 1994) 88–89.
4. Walter Benjamin, *Der Begriff der Kunstkrtik in der deutschen Romantik* (Frankfurt am Main: Suhrkamp Verlag, 1973) 8, 86–87; Benjamin, *Selected Writings*, 185.
5. Benjamin, *Gesammelte Schriften*, II:1, 190–194; Benjamin, *Selected Writings*, 245–250.
6. Walter Benjamin, "Surrealism," in *One Way Street* (London: New Left Books, 1979) 225–239.
7. Walter Benjamin, *Charles Baudelaire* (London: New Left Books, 1979) 225–239.

8. Walter Benjamin, *Illuminations* (New York: Harcourt, Brace & World, 1968) 261–262.

9. Herbert Marcuse, *Der deutsche Künstlerroman*, 922, in *Schriften* (Frankfurt am Main: Suhrkamp Verlag, 1969) 1:43–49, 86, 117–119, 133–143.

10. Benjamin mentions Marcuse in his short article on the Frankfurt Institute for Social Research (1938) and also refers favorably, in a letter to Horkheimer, to Marcuse's contribution to the collective volume *Autorität und Familie.* See Walter Benjamin, "Ein Deutsches Institut Freier Forschung" [1938], in *Gesammelte Schriften* (Suhrkamp Verlag, Frankfurt am Main, 1972) III:526, 683.

11. Herbert Marcuse, "Preface," in *Reason and Revolution* (Boston: Beacon Press, 1960) x.

12. Herbert Marcuse, "Uber den Affirmativen Charakter der Kultur" [1937], now in *Kultur und Gesellschaft* (Frankfurt am Main: Suhrkamp Verlag, 1970) I:67–68, 76–81, 89–94. Benjamin knew this essay and mentions it in his notice on the Frankfurt Institute (1938), where he stresses, in reference to Marcuse, the need to oppose a critical concept of culture to the "affirmative" one. For him, this "critical culture" is not identified, as for Marcuse, with rationalist philosophy and Hegel: it is made up of cultural elements that, "linked to their early times and to their dreams, do not deny their solidarity with the coming humanity, with humanity itself." Far from rejecting, like Marcuse, the bourgeois cultural tradition as "ideology," he insists on the need to "salvage the cultural heritage" and, by developing critical insights, to "make room for an authentic tradition." Compare Benjamin, "Ein Deutsches Institut Freier Forschung," III:525–526.

13. Herbert Marcuse, "Epilogue," in *Reason and Revolution* (New York: The Humanities Press, 1954) 433. Of course, it is probable that Marcuse had also been influenced by Adorno and Horkheimer's criticism of the rationalist tradition in *Dialektik der Aufklärung* (1947), but there is no doubt that he followed his own path to this conclusion.

14. Herbert Marcuse, *Eros and Civilization* [1955] (New York: Shere Books, 1969) 132, 152, 154.

15. Marcuse, *Eros and Civilization*, 186.

16. Herbert Marcuse, *One-Dimensional Man* (London: Routledge, 1964) 60 (emphasis added).

17. Herbert Marcuse, *An Essay on Liberation* (Boston: Beacon Press, 1969) 33.

18. Herbert Marcuse, "Letters to the Chicago Surrealists" (March 6, 1973), in *Arsenal: Surrealist Subversion 4* (Chicago: Black Swan Press, 1989) 44.

19. Herbert Marcuse, *Counterrevolution and Revolt* (Boston: Beacon Press, 1972) 86; *One-Dimensional Man*, 77.

20. Marcuse, *One-Dimensional Man*, 257.

21. Walter Benjamin, "Theses on the Philosophy of History" [1940], in *Illuminations* (London: J. Cape, 1970) 259–61. On Marcuse's "pessimism," see Russel Jacoby's interesting essay, "Reversal and Lost Meanings," in Paul Breines, ed. *Critical Interruptions: New Left Perspectives on Herbert Marcuse* (New York: Herder & Herder, 1970) 70–73.

22. Herbert Marcuse, "Nachwort," in Walter Benjamin, *Zur Kritik der Gewalt* (Frankfurt am Main: Suhrkamp Verlag, 1965) 99–100.

23. Ibid., 100–101.

24. Ibid., 104.

25. Herbert Marcuse, *The Aesthetic Dimension* (Boston: Beacon Press, 1979) xii–xiii, 6–9, 11, 19–20, 33, 73.

# AN EPISODE IN A FRAGMENTARY HISTORY
## Surrealism and the 1946 Revolution in Haiti
### *Michael Richardson*

*Illustration by Sergio Ruzzier*

Even though André Breton had written that "liberty is the color of humanity," when he went to Haiti in December 1945 at the invitation of his friend Pierre Mabille (then the French cultural attaché in Port-au-Prince) he little expected his presence to initiate a revolt that would lead to the overthrow of the government. Yet this is precisely what did happen. A group of young people were so entranced by what Breton said to them that they published a special issue of their journal *La Ruche*, in which they published the text of Breton's speech and adopted an insurrectionary tone. A general strike followed which was soon to bring down the government and force the U.S. puppet President Lescot into exile.

Breton was keen to play down the significance of his intervention, attributing the revolt to the objective conditions on the island. It was undoubtedly the case, as he says, that

> At the end of 1945, the poverty, and consequently the patience, of the Haitian people had reached a breaking point. You have to realize that, on the huge Ile de Gonave off the Haitian coast, men earned less than one American cent for an entire day's labor, and that, according to the most conservative newspapers, children in the suburbs of Port-au-Prince lived on tadpoles fished out of the sewers.[1]

Yet this describes a situation that is sadly hardly out of the norm for the Haitian people, and continues to the present day. While it may have been the case that an uprising would have taken place in the particular circumstances that pertained at the end 1945, there seems little doubt that Breton's presence had an impact that was decisive for the course the revolt would take. According to Haitian poet René Depestre, "André Breton's speech served as the backdrop for a pure and simple call to national insurrection!"[2] What could have caused such a reaction?

There is little in the context or delivery of his talks that would mark Breton out as a revolutionary firebrand. He was hardly a Fidel Castro or Malcom X, exhorting the crowd with brilliant rhetoric. Rather he spoke in tones of intimacy and common humanity. It was as much Breton's personality as what he said that made an impact. One of those who welcomed him to the island, the poet Paul Laraque, evokes an almost messianic atmosphere:

> With leonine head, a mane of sun, a god begotten by lightning, Breton stepped forward. To see him was to grasp the beauty of the angel of revolt. The shadows became sources of light. The storm of a life was shot through with bolts of light whose flashing blades, burst from the scabbard of night, tore through the veil of time, and restored the lost paradise of innocence to love.[3]

René Depestre was hardly less effusive:

The great poet would not disappoint our expectations. His personal magnetism fascinated us. His leonine head, his noble and majestic bearing, his air of a prophet, the sobriety of his gestures and the sumptuousness of his French tongue were to make a lifetime impression on all those like me who . . . had the honor and the poetic exhilaration to share his company in private and during the lectures he gave in Port-au-Prince.[4]

Such expressions of human warmth are remarkable and bear witness to the fact that it is not only economic and political circumstances that impel people to action. As Laraque said:

What surrealism represented to us above all was the leap into the unknown. In a world which, in the name of logic and reason, condemned them to chose between lies and despair, in a world which left those who "refused the shadow" no way out but madness or suicide, the surrealists opted for the disruption of traditional values. Beginning from total negation, it was no longer a matter of creating or inventing but of discovering. Man had been presented to himself in one of his guises to which, without any justification, he ascribed not only primacy over the other but his exclusive attention. It seemed there was a shameful part of himself which could not be talked about. The honor of the surrealist set, striking out on the trail laid by Freud, is to have relentlessly prospected mankind's subsoil. For us the surrealist coming to consciousness corresponded to the *revelation* of Breton's personality, spiritually by the mediation of his works but above all, in a way that cannot be gauged, by an entirely physical attraction. My own debt to Breton lay, above all, in his having brought me lucidity. The further I entered myself, the more the columns of shadow rose up into the light. I was not unaware that at a certain level everything is in danger of confusion but, without a doubt, there is the lance which runs it through. Little by little, I became decipherable to myself, and the world became clearer. In this sense, Breton was truly a bringer of light.[5]

That Breton could elicit such a reaction testifies to the responsiveness of the Haitian people to the revolutionary effect that the simple word "liberty" could have in a land in which the idea of an independent nation could only have been made possible through a *romantic* faith in human potentiality.

Taking shape against the backdrop of the French Revolution, romanticism fully partook of the revolutionary ardor, even if in its trajectory it may have an ambivalent reaction to it, especially in relation to its political consequences. Nevertheless, the history of romanticism paralleled the movement of revolution in Europe in the early part of the nineteenth century, its path leading from hope to a disillusion with the failure of the revolutions of 1848.

Haiti, too, was born as a nation in the same international context. It also drew an inspiration from the French Revolution that led to disillusion and ultimate betrayal. The reasons for this are different, and yet there is a sense in which the course of the Haitian Revolution equally ran parallel to the hopes of romanticism. As little as they may have known of romanticism, the maroons and slaves of the French colony of Saint-Domingue responded intuitively to the clarion cries of liberty, equality, and fraternity.

Toussaint L'Ouverture, the luminous head of the Haitian Revolution, was himself a great romantic figure, the subject of a poem by Wordsworth. The emancipation of slavery was one cause to which the objectives of romanticism could hardly fail to give support and it may be said that the Haitian revolution embodied a romanticism in action; that is, a spirit, even a contagion, of the idea of liberty as a force that impelled people forward. Haitian history has never lost its *romantic* aspirations, even if its political history is one that is undeniably horrible.

This intuitive romanticism undoubtedly accounts for the impact that Breton made in Haiti. The collective memory of the Haitian people had kept alive a belief in the possibilities of transformation in accordance with the demands of liberty, and Breton's presence and words made this manifest. The 1946 revolution—like other revolts in Haiti's history—led to no great improvement in the polity of Haitian society. Although it had the effect of loosening the iron grip within which the United States held Haiti, this undoubted achievement was double-edged, for it also made possible, a decade later, the election victory of Duvalier, and the terror he unleashed was a tangible consequence of the failure of the revolution to effect real change in Haitian society. Its epitaph may well be provided by the fate of

Jacques Stephen Alexis, one of the Haitians inspired by Breton's talks, who set out in 1961 on an ill-conceived invasion attempt to overthrow Duvalier, which led to his capture and execution. A romantic gesture whose fatal consequences do not diminish its long-term significance, the actions of Alexis manifested the human will toward a liberty whose value is not measured by its immediate results. Yet the events of 1946 in Haiti represented an episode from liberty's fragmented history that was by no means negligible for, as Breton wrote, "rebellion is its own justification, completely independent of the chance it has to modify the state of affairs that gives rise to it. It's a spark in the wind, but a spark in search of a powder keg."[6] That spark has flickered closer to the powder keg in Haiti than elsewhere, even if brute necessity has prevailed to the present day. The Haitian poet Jacques Roumain nevertheless captured the qualities that constitute the spark in a Haitian context when he wrote,

> Your heart trembles in the shadows, like a face reflected in
>     troubled water.
> The old mirage rises from the pit of the night
> You sense the sweet sorcery of the past:
> A river carries you far away from the banks,
> Carries you toward the ancestral landscape.[7]

Haitian history remains defiantly Other to Euro-American consciousness and it would be the gravest error to impute the impact of surrealism on Haitian sensibility to an influence flowing from one place to another. In no way did Haitians assume surrealist ideas and put them into some ill-fated action. Rather surrealism responded to aspirations that were already present and gave an inspiration to make the imaginary become real. Haitian history belongs to the genius of the Haitian people and its unfolding responds to the necessity of Haitian reality. Nevertheless, its surge—of which 1946 presents a most poignant moment—represents a clear will to fulfill universal cravings for a complete liberty that is inherent to the romantic attitude in which the contradiction between necessity and freedom is overcome. As Breton said: "Necessity is blind only insofar as it is not understood and liberty is nothing other than necessity realized."[8]

At the same time, though, in speaking about liberty to his Haitian audience, Breton insisted on the fact that it is something that cannot be tied down as a thing. It needs to be allowed the air in which it can breathe, it needs to be able to develop. The necessity which Haitian society remains forced to acknowledge is one which is imposed by the Western powers, most especially that by the United States, which makes any realization of the aspiration toward freedom impossible to realize. And yet the history of Haiti also embodies that desire in its generality. As the invocation of Haitian poet Georges Castera *fils*, presenting an issue of the journal *Conjonction* devoted to the theme of "Surrealism and Revolt in Haiti," has it: "Reader poets and friends,/ paradise on earth remains possible!"[9]

The 1946 revolution in Haiti was significant not for what it achieved, but for what it lays bare of the mechanics of desire transforming itself in the process of realization. A fragment from the history of a nation, it is also an inspiration toward the possibility of transformation for all peoples. In the modern world this has become almost an impossible experience since the events of the century have led us no longer to believe in the possibility of the realization of freedom. The consequence of this is apparent. As I write, news broadcasts give details of events in Sierra Leone, where nothing but resentment and a configuration of different interests appear to have led to the triumph of pure necessity and where any hope of freedom could only be burlesque. Liberty itself needs to be reinvented and the moments in which its has made an appearance in human history need to be charted. Haiti in its entire history, made manifest in 1946, offers one moments in the fragmentary history of liberty that will one day attain its effective realization.

### Notes

1. André Breton, *Conversations: The Autobiography of Surrealism*, trans. Mark Polizzotti (New York: Marlowe, 1993) 201.
2. René Depestre, "André Breton in Port-au-Prince," in Michael Richardson, ed., *Refusal of the Shadow: Surrealism and the Caribbean*, trans. Krysztof Fijalkowski and Michael Richardson (London: Verso, 1996) 232.
3. Paul Laraque, "André Breton in Haiti," in Richardson, *Refusal of the Shadow*, 218.
4. Depestre, "André Breton in Port-au-Prince," 230.
5. Laraque, "André Breton in Haiti," 223.
6. André Breton, *Arcanum 17* [1944], trans. Zack Rogow (Los Angeles: Sun & Moon Press, 1994) 89.
7. Jacques Roumain, "When the Tom-Tom Beats. . . ." trans. Langston Hughes, in Ellen Conroy Kennedy, ed., *The Negritude Poets* (New York: Thunder's Mouth Press, 1975) 22.

8. André Breton, "Evolution du Concept de Liberté à travers le Romantisme," *Conjonction* 194 (April-May-June 1993) 91. [A.B.'s talk given in Haiti.]

9. Georges Castera *fils,* "Sous le Voile Déchiré," *Conjonction* 193 (April-May-June 1992) 14.

# DEBORD IN THE RESOUNDING
# CATARACT OF TIME
## *Daniel Blanchard*

*Daniel Blanchard (l) and Guy Debord (r) (Fall 1960)*
*(photo courtesy Daniel Blanchard)*

There are moments in one's existence that stand out, as if of a
more solid texture, drawn in stronger lines contrasting with the
fuzziness and fathomless ambiguity of the rest of life. And they really
are charged with objective meaning, imparted by the movement of a
sort of historic overdetermination. Often that special quality only
reveals itself retrospectively, but sometimes, too, it is perceived
immediately.

That is what I experienced on the day, in autumn 1959, when
I first glanced through an issue—number 3, I think—of *Interna-
tionale Situationniste*. At the time, I participated in the Socialisme ou
Barbarie group, and in the journal of the same name, for which I

wrote, as was the rule, under a pseudonym: P. Canjuers. That day, as a few of us were going through the weekly mail, my eye was attracted by that sleek, elegant publication, with its scintillating cover and incredible title. I took hold of it and immediately began to explore what I gradually came to see as a new-found-land of modernity, bizarre but fascinating.

Now we, at *S. ou B.*, felt that we epitomized modernity, and I continue to think us completely justified in doing so. S. ou B. had broken with orthodox Marxism-Leninism and gone on to radically criticize the Eastern European Communist regimes, but also to reformulate the criticism of capitalism, through the analysis both of its most sophisticated forms of domination and of the most advanced experiences of the working-class movement. Among these, the revolutionary workers councils in Hungary in particular fed our thinking about what, positively, might be the content of a truly revolutionary program.

How passionate were those years of searching, their fever further intensified by the position of quasi-intellectual clandestinity to which the utter rejection of our ideas confined us! For, despite the Khrushchev report and the uprisings in Poland and Hungary, the French political scene was still essentially paralyzed by the intellectual blackmail both of Stalinists and the most cowardly *pentiti* of bourgeois ideology, such as Sartre. So we explored the deep waters Nautilus-like, almost unknown to the world on the surface, freely and audaciously, to a point that would perhaps not have been possible had we been obliged to battle foot by foot against dishonest opponents who, furthermore, had nothing of interest to say to us.

And now, looking through this perfectly singular booklet, I discovered a small group of unknown people who did have some terribly exciting things to say to us. Definitely strange things for us, with our eyes glued to the Marxist horizon, even though the point, for many of us, was to travel beyond it; totally inhabitual in regard to the messages sent out to us by other tiny groups intent on saving some vestiges of the revolutionary past from the Stalinist disaster. The strangeness was not uncanny but, rather, attractive, incredibly enticing. The criticism of art and culture led on to a utopian, liberated life, already experimented with by these young adventurers in practical poetics such as *dérives* around cities or the illustrated description of a fantastic place called the "Yellow City." And that utopia already haunted the people whose faces could be seen in a few dim photos, sitting around café tables engaged in ardent, infinite conversation that lofted them through the nights. With the frenzy of escaped prisoners, in the secret folds of the city, they too were struggling to elucidate the deepest roots of modern misery, and living, in fantasy, the upheaval that would overthrow it. And the journal was something of the tale of their efforts, in a sharp, tense style, almost stiffened in the same arrogant conceit with which we too affected to steel ourselves, both to reflect back on our opponents the scorn they inflicted on us and to convince ourselves of how radical we really were.

As I read that issue of *Internationale Situationniste*, then, I realized that what was occurring was an objective encounter, so to speak, a criticism in action of "separation," to use an expression in consonance with my emphatic feeling of the time: a meeting at the acme (no doubt hidden to everyone but us) of modernity.

Over the following months, Debord and I checked out in detail just how necessary and fertile that encounter was, during long talks in bistros and endless roamings through the city streets. In the project of self-management embracing every aspect of social life, as expressed by the workers movement at the heights of its spontaneous creativity—from the Paris Commune to Hungary 1956—resided the social and political underpinnings for the utopia of people constantly inventing their "use of life," like a perpetual composing of music or poetry. And in turn, the subversion of the artistic and cultural institution, which the Situationist International claimed to embody, came as an extension and a consecration, so to speak, in what was reputed to be the highest spheres, of the subversion of every agency of domination and exploitation. The text that we finally wrote jointly, and pompously entitled *Préliminaires pour une Définition de l'Unité du Programme Révolutionnaire* [Preliminaries Toward Defining a Unitary Revolutionary Program], definitely gives an idea of the ambition behind our exchanges, but tells hardly anything about how rich they were and even less of the friendship that was built up through that conversation.

In a restaurant on Rue Mouffetard, on July 20, 1960, we put the finishing touches on what we viewed as the guidelines of an agreement between the cultural vanguard and the vanguard of the proletarian revolution. We were very finicky about the title and its layout, designed, according to Debord, so that the document would be referred to as the *Préliminaires*—and I smiled, indulgent and foolish, knowing nothing about communication at the time. After that, we parted for the summer, each with the task of circulating the paper among his comrades. In the fall, I had to leave France for nine or ten months, and during my absence I learned that Debord had formally become a member of S. ou B, was participating fully in its activities, especially during the group's action within the major strikes that shook the Belgian Borinage in the winter of 1961. The news surprised me. His membership, I felt, exceeded the closeness we had actually achieved: and above all, it seemed useless and, in fact, in our discussions Debord had expressed the view that each group should continue, in practice, to follow its own path. The news of his resignation came as less of a surprise, since he had based it on his disagreement with the internal functioning of the group and on the role played by some domineering individuals. Apparently, he had attempted to foment a revolt among the younger members, mostly students, but that had been no more than a Fronde. The other members deliberately ignored the SI, both then and thereafter.

I have stressed the episode of Debord's relations with S. ou B. because it seems significant on several counts. First, the person I knew and loved at that time was, so to speak, a nascent Debord. Although he already had a brilliant career as an agitator in the cultural sphere behind him, the most singular traits of his personality as a revolutionary as well as the most fertile and most perspicacious of his inventions still retained a vivaciousness and an accuracy that would subsequently be somewhat adulterated by his obsession with being public enemy number one, and also by the structural stupidity of disciples, from whom he proved unable to take sufficient distance. At the time there were Khayati, Kotányi, Jorn . . . friends, not disciples.

Above all there is a need, I think, to point up the importance, for the road Debord followed, of that involvement with S. ou B.— particularly so since he and most everyone who has had anything to say about his adventure have practically systematically ignored it. The point is obviously not to stake any claim either for S. ou B. or even less for myself, as having fathered the thinking of a man who went on to become a celebrity. On the contrary, it is the objective nature of our encounter that I would emphasize once again and what it revealed about a particular moment in history. Debord did not succeed in wrenching himself from the curse that Stalinism and the bureaucratization of the working-class organizations had laid on the revolutionary movement by dint of reading Hegel, the young Marx, and Lukács. It was the insurgent Hungarian workers and the councils they created that lifted that curse, at least for those who were prepared to listen to what they had to say.

At this point in his itinerary, Debord was ready. He had broken with the Lettristes and with a criticism that remained complacently restricted to culture: in his opinion, the cultural vanguards did nothing but repeat *ad nauseam* the scene of the break with art, originally performed by the Dadaists after the Second World War. A clean break was called for, and a way of moving beyond art had to be found. Art conceived as play, as the freeing of desire, as subversion, as negation of the deathly, repressive social order, for this was the sense of modern art, as Debord saw it. The creation of "situations" was a response to that exigency: "The arts of the future will be upheavals of situations, or they will not be." There was clearly a parallel between the revolution as the invention of society and those "upheavals of situations" as the invention of daily life.

Now, the link between so radical a demand and the concrete action of the proletariat turned out to be thinkable again. For anyone intent on seeing the true situation, the Budapest insurgents—about whom Debord had learned first hand from his friend Attila Kotányi— had overthrown not only the colossal statue of Stalin but also the terrifying image of a proletariat whose mission it was, as the sadistic agent of historic necessity, to force all of humanity, once and for all, to endorse industrial discipline, the cult of the leader, the annihilation of individuals, reduced to being the masses, etc. For artists and intellectuals, that proletariat was truly a bogey man, who so many had determined to serve nonetheless, out of fear, masochism, or ambition.

In the West, by the same token, all those libertarian anarchists, antiauthoritarian Marxists, council communists, etc., who had never ceased to denounce the Stalinist imposture began to gain some acknowledgment. And among them, S. ou B. and such sister groups as Solidarity in England, Correspondence in the USA, and Unità Proletaria in Italy had undertaken a complete reinterpretation of the proletarian experience, highlighting the significance, for a liberatory movement, not only of the great moments of revolutionary creation but of the everyday struggles around the work process and the creativity with which workers combat the disciplinary industrial organization. In doing so,

S. ou B. revived the radicality characteristic of the anarchists and of the very beginnings of the socialist movement, and geared thinking about the revolutionary utopia ("the contents of socialism") to call every aspect of life into question, from the shape of cities to gender relations.

Clearly, then, there was nothing fortuitous in the arrival of an issue of the *Internationale Situationniste* in the mailbox of S. ou B., any more than in the passionate interest it drew from a young member of that group or the excited discussions that ensued. . . . And, conversely, the reader will understand that when such themes as the criticism of daily life or all-encompassing self-management became the battle cries of the SI years later, I was not overwhelmed by their novelty, and I was surely not the only one.

How is it, then, that my excitement of some thirty years ago, when I first discovered the SI, is still tingling—not as some narcissistic pleasure in reliving the vanished past but truly as the ongoing perception of an invaluable uniqueness? It is, I believe, because of the sense of form and the artistic quality that inhabited everything Debord undertook, and which contributed enormously to making him effectively subversive.

I am, of course, not by any means contending that Debord should be embalmed in museums of modern art. It is true that he boasted of being the inventor of the major modern-day cinematographic innovations. . . . And one could also argue that as a virtuoso in the collage, photomontage, and *détournement* of ads and comics, he was a great pop artist—but the only sense in doing so would be for the (mediocre) pleasure of drawing screams from his devotees. Or again he may, as late sycophants would have it, be ranked among the great French writers of this century, thanks to his resolute style and the fine boldness of his assertions. And Philippe Sollers, who is one of Paris's highest-paid literary clowns and can therefore get away with anything, even took advantage of his position to subject Debord, alive and kicking, to the insult of claiming to be his spiritual heir; shortly thereafter Sollers supported Balladur for president.

No, what I would like to demonstrate is quite the opposite: how the artistic treatment, so to speak, applied by Debord to revolutionary activity constitutes the precise, faithful expression of the contents of that activity and gives its perspective proper depth.

To call Debord an artist is obviously something of a paradox. His criticism of art, intended to be devastating, was two-faceted.

Modern art, on the one hand, with its succession of repetitious van-guards incapable of surpassing themselves, has exhausted its critical bite on alienated existence. But, on the other hand, and more deeply, art contrasts with "true life" in that it is congealed, so to speak, and therefore doomed to be no more than a cemetery of moments, pro-viding fictitious, deceptive gratification of desires.

The same alienating force that Debord would later extend to the entire functioning of society, through the concept of the specta-cle, applied, then, to the very principle of art. Art was nothing but separation from life.

Perhaps the explanation of the paradox by which the pro-mulgator of so vivid a criticism actually turns out to be an artist, and profoundly so, resides in the fact that this criticism misses its mark, leaving its object intact, in essence. In fact, to reduce twen-tieth-century art to the movement of negation embodied by those vanguards is to mistake official art and some historicizing discourse on art for art work itself. The fact that Dada, and above all Duchamp, traced the theoretical limit of twentieth-century art with exemplary clarity—namely, that in the last resort it is the signature that makes the work of art, and for anything to be art the condi-tion, necessary and sufficient, is that an artist decides it is—has in no way prevented art since then from being rich and meaningful within that limit. In striving obstinately to define what present-day art can or should be, the vanguards have succeeded only in becom-ing the *art pompier* of the second half of this century, in the per-sons of Beuys, Buren, and so many others—and in this it really has succeeded. And again, in any reference to vanguards, it is impor-tant not to align them all on any single historical trend. The Cobra movement, for instance, exemplifies a positive renewal much more than the work of negation.

This work of negation, which cannot be completed by art itself and can only achieve completion when life itself surpasses art—in "situations"—seems to rehash the old denial not only of art but of symbolization, and of mediation by signs or figuration. To condemn art—and thence signs as well, or symbols—as false, in the name of the truthfulness of life or of things themselves, is not a judgment but a pure act of violence: does that make it revolutionary? Swift derided the academicians of Lagado who replaced words by specimens of things in their attempt to reform language by doing away with its unfortunate polysemia; that is to say, its very power of symbolism: endless transports were needed to have the slightest conversation!

Symbolization has avenged itself of this violent dismissal by taking over the very field of "destructive" activity to which Debord devoted himself and by conferring the aura of the work of art on his life as well as on his writings and films. And this came about through play and style.

As we all know, nothing is more serious than play, where the exercise of freedom adventures as close as possible to material and social constraints, or to chance; it guards us, then—but at such great risk!—from the most repugnant kind of comfort: repetition—death in disguise in the eyes of Debord. But its seriousness also derives from its always, and especially in revolutionary action, being a world-play. Be it in tarot, chess, or go, the physical objects and the rules of the game compose an analogue of the world, and each game or each move reorganizes and recommences the world. In the case of a group of revolutionaries, however small, the form of its organization, the way it functions, the content and the modalities of its action all prefigure, as in a microcosm, the desired state of the world. This was one of the bitter lessons drawn from the fate of the Bolshevik party, and S. ou B. was intent on drawing the consequences and on behaving immediately, concretely, and on its own microscopic scale as we thought a free society would demand.

Debord quite naturally extended this exigency to the area in which his desire to break with the "old world" was in fact most strongly focused, and which I will not call everyday life because of the somewhat futile connotation of the term but, rather, "the use of life," use of the fleeting moments and of the most concrete contents of situations. And play was necessarily the model here, in the sense that the artist is playing when the progress of his work proposes an unheard-of, desirable modulation of the course of time or the unfolding of space. "Experimenting" with the urban environment was this sort of play: through wanderings imbued with the hues and resonances lent by the peculiar qualities of the places visited, the drinks downed here and there and the remarks exchanged. The same was true of conversation, to be taken almost in the original sense of "shared life," for it embodied something of a sensual fulfillment of friendship. For Debord it was a verbal *dérive*, the playful experimenting, by several people, of ideas, words, new fancies—and anyone who ever spent some time with him knows how his presence and talk succeeded, in these exchanges with friends, in catalyzing and freeing their imaginations, in its liveliest expression. With real opponents, on the other hand, the discussion veered to another type of game, which he called a "boxing match" but was actually more of a free-for-all since he had no qualms about resorting to every available means, including the lowliest personal attacks.

In friendship, however—and I think friendship is what really most accurately prefigured the kind of society he expected a revolution to produce—he was intent on enforcing the rules dictated, in his opinion, by the constraints inherent in the fight against the existing order and the degree of freedom required to be worthy to fight. And he often pushed that inflexible stance to the point of formalism and of arbitrariness as well, since it was he who set those rules unilaterally and most often left them implicit, the understanding being that they were self-evident. His disciples obviously were incapable of anything but an exaggeration of these practices, turning them into the most putrid fashionable snobbishness.

I myself was victim of that formalism, without even understanding, at the time, what had transpired, since the notion that relations between friends could be regulated by a code was completely alien to me. On the evening when Guy and Michèle invited me to dinner at Impasse de Clairvaux and served me a chicken-and-French-fries plate bought in some greasy joint on Boulevard de Sébastopol, I should have understood that my hour of disgrace had arrived, even if the "insult" was strangely cloaked in an apology—"we're broke"—which canceled it and which I definitely could not revile. Had I been less of a fool I would probably have read the signals more completely and understood that the mixture of chicken-fries-plus-apology was a sort of self-contradictory compromise between the will to exclude me—clearly imputable to Michèle—and a desire to be indulgent. Etc. Here, then, in any case, is the method Debord chose when he felt the time had come to put an end to our friendship, without informing me of his reasons, even in the form of insults. Too bad for me, and for him.

The May '68 retreat by the SI, calling itself the Council for Maintaining the Occupations, into the Institut Pédagogique National(!), seems to me to be an infinitely more serious perversion of this kind of play. In doing so, the SI usurped the title of council, which, in its own eyes, was supposed to designate the agency of collective empowerment of the revolutionary masses, turning it into a camouflage for a separate authority handing down judgments—that is, condemnations—of the innumerable protagonists of the May revolt and, above all, of those people who dared to defend ideas barely distinguishable from their own.

Playing, under the circumstances, would definitely have demanded that the game be waged on a much broader scope, and Debord would no doubt have lost control of it and the possibility of imparting a style to it.

No irony is intended in my use of the term "style." Style, to me, is not an affected form used to facilitate or embellish the communication of a message, the meaning of which is located at some basement level of expressiveness. Play involves style; and so does the revolutionary action of a minority group, the idea being to give shape to a vision of the world that cannot be achieved at its own small scale. Each move or combination of moves outlines a gesture or a figure, projecting an order, however fleeting, into the existent chaos. To speak of beauty or elegance in reference to play is not superficial but truly imparts the awareness that play operates in the objective world. And again, style cannot be defined as the mark of subjectivity but, rather, as the tension between the ephemeral and the utopic dimensions—between movement, on the one hand, wresting free speech from the inertia and senselessness of the pervading verbal noise to adventure, in all its vulnerability, suspended over "the cataract of time," and, on the other hand, utopia, the projection of a figure offering, by analogy, a foretaste of some desirable ordering of the world.

When a minority group acts, then, it is style more than the necessarily limited material effect that propels reality to a breaking point where open-ended time, the incompletion of history, and the possibility of revolution make themselves felt, by surprise.

In the work of art this gaping openness to time, signature of its uniqueness, is what Benjamin called the aura. He deemed relinquishment of it necessary, in the name of his melancholic subjection to modern technicity. The fate of the revolution was believed at the time to be tied to machines and the massified humanity presumably generated by them, and Benjamin, grounding his argument in the highly questionable postulate that, "One principle of works of art is that they are always reproducible. What men have done can be done again by others," hailed as liberatory, at least for the masses, the present-day possibility of having this reproducibility achieved by technical devices that made it similar to mass production. Now that we know a bit more about machines, and above all about society as a machine, it seems to me that the revolution needs to bet on the postulate that "what one man has done cannot be done again by any other," if we are truly intent on acknowledging equal dignity for all subjects, referred to here as men.

This is the postulate asserted in his practice by Debord, haunted by his horror of repetition and, what comes down to the same thing, by his acute perception of the uniqueness of each moment: "[what is] beyond the violence of intoxication . . . peace, magnificent and fearsome, the true taste of time passing."

The mirror as a figure—mirror adhering so closely to the fluctuating image of reality, but, at the same time, reversing it—acts as a deeply unifying structure for Debord's work and perhaps even for his life, from his writings to the singular critical posture he adopted, including the contents of that criticism: the concept of the spectacle.

But again, the mirror figure embodies all of Debord's ambivalence toward any mediation by signs, representation, and symbolization. It would ensnare us in alienation and commodity fetishism or in the substitute for true life that art extends to us: because it is fake, distorting, and fragmented, it is the instrument of domination through the spectacle. It must constantly be broken, to liberate "true life," to rid oneself of the petrifying hold of images and reassert authenticity, constantly to be reinvented. From *Mémoires* to *Panégyrique* [Panegyric], however, and in all of his films—down to the palindromic title marking his last film—the mirror also figures remembrance: a memory both hurt to the quick, ravaged by nostalgia, and at the same time controlled and guided by critical thinking.

In his writing, then, mirrored phrases, used as a mode of criticism in themselves, proliferate. Debord himself theorized "this insurrectional style that turns the philosophy of misery into the misery of philosophy," and that "is not a negation of style, but the style of negation": because it ferrets out the instability in the "existing concepts . . . it simultaneously includes the grasp of their rediscovered fluidity, of their necessary destruction."

On a broader level, the mirror served Debord again, as an instrument for reversing "existing concepts," in an ongoing reflection trained on the course of events, a sort of chronicle of current events, of the kind he wrote in the twelve issues of *Internationale Situationniste* and in *Commentaires sur la Société du Spectacle* [Comments on the Society of the Spectacle]. And to me, it is when he did just that, speaking within the surging movement of history, that he saw farthest and aimed most accurately. He had to defend his life and work inch by inch, against concrete, constantly repeated facts, in "the resounding cataract of time." And through that fight he drew a sort of reasoned, demythologizing portrait of present times, yielding the subject matter for theorization but still retaining the very grain of the event.

But when he came to a halt and attempted to stand at a distance to construct a theoretical battleship, *La Société du Spectacle* [The Society of the Spectacle], he got bogged down, in my opinion— but I will not attempt to explain my reasons here. The very expression, "society of the spectacle," seems abusive to me, but probably because I am captive of the existing meaning of the words. And the word "spectacle" seems right to me as a metaphor, not as a concept; that is, precisely, not as the generalization that Debord so stubbornly defended. The metaphoric power of the word, so cuttingly critical in partial applications, takes its revenge when Debord attempts to make all of social reality fit into it, and traps him; this is clear in *Commentaires*, in particular. Society is reduced to the oversimplified model of the conventional theater, and the dialectic of alienation wears thin in a pitiful denunciation of the stagehands pulling the strings behind the scenes. The society of the spectacle then becomes a society of backstage manipulations. . . . Here again, the demythologization of how domination works is reduced to the simple denial of the symbolic dimension. The concept of the total spectacle completely flattens out the sphere in which, precisely, the enormous complexity of representation, and of the alienation generated by it, unfolds.

The extraordinary effectiveness of the machinery combining commodification, the market economy, representative democracy, opinion polls, the mass media, and the social sciences resides specifically in the fact that it does not impose its discourse unilaterally, as being the law, but rather, that it is interactive. The TV commentator is not Big Brother, authoritatively proclaiming the official lie, he is John Doe, who reads your mind and utters your thoughts. The agitated clowns on the screen have our faces, our gestures, our voices, and the thundering discourse that oppresses us and drives us to despair is depicted as our own. And in a sense, it is: lies, like taxes, are levied directly at the source. It is from us that a vast scheme extorts the basic material out of which the various organs of the domination-producing apparatus, and the social sciences in particular, then proceed to isolate the active principle of the lie and to resynthesize a social discourse that is a sort of clone of our own—uncannily familiar. And, stupefied at hearing and seeing ourselves speak and act from outside of our selves, we shut up. Can there be any worse censorship?

Would Debord have agreed with an analysis such as this? Probably not. It hardly matters.

What does matter is that he denounced and described the universal lie proffered by our society about itself and the world; that he showed how this lie destroys reality by saturating everything animate and inanimate with inauthenticity and eliminating the temporal dimension, so that we circle round endlessly in the perpetual present of current events. And above all, what matters is that he detected the sickly locus of the devastating lie: the denial of death. "The social absence of death is the same as the social absence of life." "The spectator mind no longer moves through life toward achievement and toward death." "He who relinquishes expending his life can no longer admit his own death to himself."

At such depths of critical thinking, Debord was very much alone. The denial of death also inhabited the revolutionary movement, with its dire need for positivity and optimism. Around '68, it was fashionable to qualify death as "reactionary."

And, too, at such depths there can be no empty talk. Debord was not content to oppose a few statements to the key imposture of the times: his entire work and life were spurred by an awareness of the presence of death, and tensed between the ephemeral and the utopic dimensions. The "true taste of time passing" is also the taste of the true, be it in savoring wine, in certain moments, or in a revolutionary struggle. The presence of the "movement toward death" is the touchstone of authenticity, which revolution should restitute—or institute.

It is in this sense that Debord was radically an artist. In the same sense that he acknowledged that his friend Asger Jorn had remained a situationist although, when enjoined to choose between the two, he gave up being a member of the SI to continue his work as painter, sculptor, and ceramist. For, as Debord said in *De l'Architecture Sauvage*, writing about the perpetual metamorphoses effected by Jorn in his home and garden in Albisola, despite that choice, his life never ceased to be propelled by a constant spate of invention and desires.

*Translated by Helen Arnold*

### Bibliography

*Editor's note:* Many of Guy Debord's works are available in English translation; this is a selected bibliography. For a more complete bibliography, see Shigenobu Gonzalvez, *Guy Debord ou la Beauté du Négatif* (Paris: Mille et Une Nuits, 1998) and recent printings of Ken Knabb's anthology, below. See also Anselm Jappe, *Guy Debord*, translated by Donald Nicholson-Smith (Berkeley: Univ. of California Press, 1999).

Andreotti, Libero, and Xavier Costa, ed. *Theory of the Dérive and Other Situationist Writings on the City*. Trans. by Paul Hammond and Gerardo Denís. Barcelona: Museu d'Art Contemporani de Barcelona & ACTAR, 1996.

Debord, Guy. *Comments on the Society of the Spectacle*. Trans. by Malcolm Imrie. London & New York: Verso, 1990.

———. *In Girum Imus Nocte et Consumimur Igni*. Trans. by Lucy Forsyth. London: Pelagian Press, 1992.

———. *Panegyric*. Trans. by James Brook. London & New York: Verso, 1991.

———. *The Society of the Spectacle*. Trans. by Donald Nicholson-Smith. New York: Zone Books, 1994.

———. *Society of the Spectacle and Other Films*. London: Rebel Press, 1992.

———, and Gianfranco Sanguinetti. *The Veritable Split in the International: Public Circular of the Situationist International*. 3d ed. London: Chronos Pubs., 1990.

Knabb, Ken, ed. and trans. *The Situationist International Anthology*. Berkeley: Bureau of Public Secrets [P. O. Box 1044, Berkeley, CA 94701, USA], 1981.

# REFLECTIONS ON REVOLUTIONARY ROMANTICISM
## *Max Blechman*

*Collage by John Heartfield (© Artists Rights Society (ARS),
New York/VG Bild-Kunst, Bonn)*

The world must be romanticized. Then one will again find the
original conception.

— *Novalis*

### I.

In the *Grundrisse* Marx describes romanticism as the historically
inevitable counteroffensive to the "complete emptiness" of bourgeois
life—the nostalgic yearning for an "original fullness." From a bird's-
eye perspective, Marx judges that romanticism will accompany capitalist civilization "as legitimate antithesis up to its blessed end."
Situating romanticism in the context of an antinomy that contains its

resolution in a higher term, we propose to think this higher term from within the *subterranean continuum of history* and to call *revolutionary romanticism* the unsurpassed movement for the "blessed end" envisioned by Marx.

## II.

If romanticism, according to Baudelaire's definition, is a way of feeling that aspires to the infinite, revolutionary romanticism is the meeting point of the romantic voyage in the farthest outposts of fantasy with the revolutionary struggle for the highest political freedom. Just as for Baudelaire romanticism transcends all literary and artistic schools, and is the true spirit of modern art, revolutionary romanticism transcends all specific political tendencies, and is the authentic spirit of modern revolt. The utopian content of poetic adventure merges with the utopian content of revolutionary discovery; the transformation of the political sphere stands in direct relation to the transformation of the cultural sphere; the revolutionary imperative for a majesty of the people spells the romantic imperative for a universal regeneration, summarized in the unitary demand: *All power to the imagination!*

## III.

In his *Defence of Poetry* Shelley defines reason as the faculty of contemplating "the relations borne by one thought to another" and imagination as the faculty of acting "upon those thoughts so as to color them with its own light." Reason is the principle of analysis that acts on the empirical differences of things and functions as an instrument for deconstructing and organizing given quantities. Imagination is the principle of synthesis that perceives "the value of those quantities, both separately and as a whole." Inasmuch as reason is in itself a strictly analytical capacity, it is to "imagination as the body to the spirit, or as the shadow to the substance."

Considered by Cartesian philosophy as the source of error, the imagination is rethought by Shelley as the primary faculty for guiding action. Shelley's revalorization of imagination serves to recognize poetry as the essential vehicle for cultivating political virtue in society. The poet, as it were, brings to earth the beautiful and the good from the lofty heights of poetic imagination and thus materializes the timeless aspirations of culture. Poetry stems from imagination's participation "in the eternal, the infinite, and the one" that precedes the activity of reason, and which reason can only propound in doctrines or schemes. Accused of starry-eyed idealism by the regulative ethics of understanding and memory, Shelley presents a straightforward defense: "the great instrument of moral good is the imagination; and poetry administers to the effect by acting on the cause." Relocating enlightenment ethics in the matrix of the "creative faculty," Shelley construes virtuous action as depending less on reasoned maxims as such than on the feeling of a higher identity inspired by poetry, on an imagining that involves a "going out of our nature and an identification of ourselves with the beautiful which exists in thought, act, or person, not our own." Poetry, in Shelley's interpretation of the word, is the essential organ of virtue because it goes to the source of society, to the collective *sensus communis* that alone makes the whole of society more than the mere addition of its parts; it kindles the fading coals of political virtue by activating the moral magma of society, and it catalyzes liberation by expressing this moral identity in the words of the imagination.

## IV.

The critique of the moral impotence of modern rationality leads Shelley to the eminently romantic verdict that social corruption is that which first seizes the imagination "as at the core and distributes itself thence as a paralyzing venom through the affections into the very appetites, till all becomes a torpid mess in which sense hardly survives." The decline of what Shelley calls "the poetical principle"—the capacity to awaken in the imagination the desire for greater beauty and justice—inevitably accompanies the rise of an objectivism that inverts the proper relation of imagining to reasoning in the inner world of mankind. With the fading of "the poetical principle," human freedom is cut from the faculty that inspires moral action. Without an intuitively understood end, the free will does not know how to begin; bereft of origin and *telos*, it loses itself in the mechanism of a multitude of self-interested wills. In this state of uprooted willing, civil power is inevitably held by the "reasoners and mechanists" who operate the political body according to the sole criteria of utility.

But utility in light of what? Without recourse to the poetic imagination, and therefore without recourse to any collectively legitimated goals, the pleasure and the good that utility refers to are circumscribed to a circularity of needs and wants and a concomitant progress of the mechanical arts that fail to pose the question of their moral center or circumference. The "transitory and particular" forms of pleasure, those that "control the security of life," that "conciliate mutual forbearance" with the drive for personal advantage, are adopted as the principles of governance, and the "universal and durable" forms of pleasure, the arts that "strengthen and purify the affections," that "enlarge the imagination," and that "add spirit to sense," are considered private pastimes. Starting with the obscuring of the "poetical" ground for social cohesion and with the relegation of public virtues to the private sphere, the free market "accumulation of the materials of external life"—the reign of money as "the visible incarnation of selfishness"—grows in direct proportion to the perversion of the genuine needs of inner life. Having lost sight of the first principle of the imagination, blind to the instituting power of "the poetical principle" that alone allows for fulfilled political freedom, the principles of political legislation inevitably conform to the unmitigated exercise of the "calculating faculty," which can at best rationalize the dynamic it has itself brought about.

## V.

Shelley's *Defence of Poetry* can be seen as a resurgence of Dionysian romanticism in the wake of nascent rationalist instrumentalism, and as an early attempt to overcome a one-dimensional reason that intrinsically fails to effect a humanly viable freedom. From an ethically grounded perspective, Shelley anticipates the Nietzschean urgency of addressing the implications of the enlightenment abolition of metaphysical foundations, of unveiling the abyss before the feet of modernity, and of saving the human spirit from fragmented individuation. Nietzsche's definition of the "mystery doctrine of tragedy" as "the fundamental knowledge of the oneness of everything existent, the conception of individuation as the prime cause of evil, and of art as the joyous hope that the bonds of individuation may be broken in augury of a restored oneness" reads as a summary of the reintegrative function of poetry defined by Shelley. It is no coincidence that Shelley was also a great admirer of ancient tragedy. Believing that the health of political institutions is dependent on the heroism of those who bring drama back to its principles, Shelley went so far as stating that drama, as the essential public medium of poetry, embodies "the energies which sustain the soul of social life." Similarly, the Nietzschean hope for "a new birth of Dionysus" expresses the aspiration for an incredible union of art and social life through which "not only the union between man and man is reaffirmed, but nature which has become estranged, hostile, or subjugated, celebrates once more her reconciliation with her prodigal son, man." As with Shelley, the Nietzschean enchantment of life through art replaces the metaphysics shattered by the enlightenment, or, rather, it redefines metaphysics as artistic activity: "art is the highest task and the proper metaphysical activity of this life." Inasmuch as the Dionysian intoxication aims at a liberation of aesthetic experience, it also envisions a radical transcendence of disenchanted social reality: "Now the slave is free; now all the stubborn, hostile barriers which necessity, caprice, or 'shameless fashion' have erected between man and man are broken down . . . in song and dance he expresses himself as a member of a higher community."

The ontological conflict of the Apollonian-Dionysian duality— of the divided many and the primordial one—that the Greeks put on stage did not occur in a social vacuum. It was performed in the context of a crisis of meaning and legitimacy that parallels the crisis of political legitimacy that begins with the bourgeois emancipation from political theology. Nietzsche points out that Dionysus saved reason from nihilism twice in human history: in sophistic Greece and at the end of the enlightenment. Euripides' tragedies were conceived during the rise of skepticism and the closure of the mythologized reality that defined its political institutions, and Dionysus—"the coming god" according to Euripides—resurfaces in romantic art and thought at the very moment that the enlightenment had supposedly done away with this god of wine and poetry. Inverting Hegel's version of Christianity as the dialectical culmination of all past religions in their absolute truth, for Schelling the whole mythological process of the past is there to prepare for the coming of Dionysus. In this sense, as Schelling writes, "all is Dionysus," and "the coming god" is not the quintessential god of mythology but a new consciousness of the activity of mythological thinking itself. Dionysus, who according to legend first appeared as a traveling singer from the Orient to rehabilitate Greek civilization from skepticism, becomes in the context of the *Frühromantik* the symbol for a "new mythology" that will overcome the modern decomposition of reason. Inspired by the French Revolution, discouraged by the social vacuum it ultimately produced, the early German romantic call for the poetry of life is also a plea for rethinking the terms of human emancipation.

## VI.

Thomas Mann interpreted the enlightenment ambition of bypassing the mythological structure of thought as an absurdity that could only provoke the return of the repressed with disastrous consequences. For Mann, it is the task of literature to "rip the myth from intellectual fascism" and to "give it a human function."

In the same vein Ernst Bloch sees the major failure of communism as the failure to effect the romantic detour through the myth to envision a new future. Bloch criticizes orthodox Marxism for having adopted the intellectual *tabula rasa* of Cartesian rationalism and for having lacked the political imagination to connect sensuous feeling with utopian vision in revolutionary struggle; modern revolution demands far more than what the platitudes of Marxist realism can offer, and its practice needs to be as radical and imaginative as its utopian vision. In Bloch's analysis, the failure to achieve an aesthetic radicalism is specifically what left the door open for fascism: the primordial myths of fascism can be fought only with those ideals that refer to an event or a condition "that has never happened because it has never fully come, whose utopian content overflows the limits of the present and maintains for this reason its power of subversion." Bloch is in search of a utopian *praxis* for political action that goes beyond rational foresight; for Bloch, as for Benedetto Croce, empirical history is only of the past, while the charting of future historical events is imaginative and mythological. Revolutionary history is a product and consequence of those who do not hesitate to discover the psychological subsoil from which new social conditions may sprout. Since revolutionary engagement operates against the sanction of empirical history, the images informing revolutionary action are found through the imagination. In this respect, Bloch's revolutionary romanticism harks back to the revolutionary syndicalism of Georges Sorel, who wrote in reference to the myth of the general strike: "the myth must be judged as a means for acting on the present; any attempt to discuss how far it can be taken literally as future history is devoid of sense. *It is the myth in its entirety which is alone important.*"

# VII.

There is no Sorelian pretense that *mythos* should be grafted on the imagination as an objective truth. The point is that the integrity of action depends on the moral viability of the idea behind it and not on any notion of its empirical reality. For all intents and purposes, the idea may well be a fiction, in somewhat the same sense that Schlegel referred to the principles of freedom as "fictions" when thinking the "Concept of Republicanism"; that is, as the functioning of the idea in the mind and the passions, the practical "X" of emancipatory representation. "Realism" cannot be a viable prolegomena for political action of any kind, not only because of its epistemological untenability and its necessarily monological form, but because it determines limits before these limits are themselves known and is as such a hindrance for free and creative action. Despite obvious philosophical differences, Sorel shares Kant's disdain for "the very miserable and pernicious pretext of impracticability" when thinking political freedom, and he knew that this question had indeed been settled by Kant in the *Critique of Pure Reason*: "it is the destination of freedom to overstep all assigned limits between itself and the Idea." In short, any notion of how wide must be the chasm between human nature and the Idea are problems that will always remain insoluble. Sorel's sublime myth of the general strike and the abolition of the master class—which was not properly speaking *his* myth, but the myth of thousands of revolutionaries in *fin de siècle* France (or for that matter, the myth of millions of workers and students seventy years later in a "romanticized" France)—acts as a ground for action in a way analogous to the Idea of "the highest good" that acts as an operative cause in Kantian practical reason: as the "necessary idea" of "the greatest possible human freedom."

Taking his distance from even the most radical transcendental ethics, Sorel hits the nail on the head when he considers people as passionate beings and not as supersensuous moving powers, as the spontaneous creatures of desire and not as the rational wheels of doctrine. Convinced by Bergson's philosophy of "integral knowledge," Sorel maintains that the question of political freedom finds its answer at the moment the idea of freedom becomes *vital;* that is, at the moment the idea becomes a *living image* that coheres with the organic performance of human psychology. Rousseau's truism that sentiment and not reason propels action is in fact the basis for the whole Sorelian imperative to better connect the *idea* of freedom to the *desire* for freedom through the strengthening of emancipatory imaginary significations. Imagination is the sole faculty whose tie with human passion can effect a rupture with social mechanism; it alone can break the chains of parched tradition. For Sorel, the passions inspired by the myth of capitalism can be surmounted only by the myth that represents its radical negation, and "in a country where the conception of the general strike exists, the blows exchanged between workmen and representatives of the middle classes have an entirely different import, their consequences are far reaching and they may beget heroism."

Adam Ferguson had already gone to the root of this problematic in his writings on the history of civil society in the late 1760s: rather than thinking the history of political institutions according to the schema of planned political foundation, he instead saw political history as the uncertain result of the mobility of conflicting passions. The health and the corruption of political life are the permanently possible results of the conflict between the passions of heroism and public virtue with those of calculation and private egoism. As an empirical historian, Ferguson did not measure the decline of political institutions according to a fixed idea of what constitutes a free regime, but according to the loss or perversion of the passions required for *effective* political freedom. Thus Ferguson's pessimistic analysis of the emergence of the market economy: transformed into the fundamental principle of social relations, in modern society the passions of interest progressively dominate virtuous passions and therefore the very possibility of political freedom.

Sorel's argument only starts where Ferguson's pessimism left off: the health of a political body is the result of the stimulation of those passions that are aligned with freedom; it necessitates a poetical power that sparks the virtue the laws of economy repress; it needs the wings of imagination reborn, the stimuli of symbols redeemed. *Freedom demands a mythology of emancipation.*

## VIII.

The creation of revolutionary mythology through renewed imagination was the project of surrealism. Described by André Breton as the "prehensile tail of romanticism" and by Herbert Marcuse as "dream realization through revolution," surrealism intensified the early romantic revolt against flattened prosaic existence in the form of a revolutionary avant-garde with internationalist aspirations. Transforming everyday life through poetic practice, the surrealist groups refused to confine poetic inspiration to the poem, just as they were careful not to confuse revolutionary hope and action with strategizing for *le grand soir*. Far from devaluing written poetry (Péret, Prévert, Breton, Char, Eluard, Soupault, Desnos, and Mansour were talented poets) or making it one medium among others for expressing political ideas, the surrealists claimed for poetry an ontological significance; the insights and wonder of poetry are the spiritual mainspring of human existence. The revolutionary content of poetry is not realized by making it political but by seeing how poetry is *de facto* revolutionary in relation to functional knowledge, an intrinsic opening to the repressed possibilities of life and to the magic of the universe as a whole. Poems do not need revolution as a subject matter because they are in themselves symbolic testimonies of its possibility, the *a priori* experiments of its beginning. Taking its point of departure from the movements of art and literature opposed to the First World War, combining libertarian and Marxian theory with a philosophy of the unconscious, in 1925 the surrealists proclaimed:

> Wherever occidental civilization reigns, all human attachments are channeled through the determinations of interest. . . . For over a century, human dignity has been choked down to the rank of exchange value. . . . We do not accept the law of Economy and of Exchange, we do not accept the slavery to Work.

The revolt is therefore total, the very heart that pumps the blood to the organs of alienation is under attack. The surrealists were in effect responding to the unfolding of Baudelaire's prophecy: "So far will machinery have Americanized us, so far will Progress have atrophied in us all that is spiritual." Slipping past the machinery of progress, the images found by the imagination are not an unreal escape but the only meaningful reality that can counteract the oppression of outer fact. The surreal vision expressed through poetry is not a refuge, because the vision represents an immanence that is asserted in the form of a confrontation with a blinded world, a process of reassertion and rejection. The surrealist engages in *poeisis*, in making, but transforms only that which is imaginatively discovered. As opposed to instrumental making, poetic making is least of all an act of the conscious will; it is, to borrow an image from Breton, a non-act of following in the footsteps of the imagination. The steps followed are not those that lead to a positive and self-transparent given but those that lead to challenging everyday patterns of thought, to undermining instituted meaning with stolen rays of poetic insight. As a visionary "thief of fire" who sailed his *Drunken Boat* straight to the barricades of revolutionary contestation, Rimbaud embodied the essential dynamic of poetry as the surrealists understood it.

The great hope of the surrealists was that by arming the power of the imagination through the power of poetic images, a new sensibility would gather, provoking an infinite desire, an unmasterable revolutionary tendency. They sought a revolution that would not only be political, but would be absolute in the sense that it would redefine not *how* to live but what it *means* to live. Artaud's 1936 quest in Mexico for "the foundations of a magical culture that may still be bursting forth from the Indian soil," was inspired by this vision of revolution as experience, by this global surrealist exigency: "Simultaneous to the *indispensable* social and economic revolution, we expect a revolution of consciousness that will allow us to rehabilitate life."

## IX.

The Situationist International was the pinnacle of the revolutionary avant-gardes of romanticism that began with the *Frühromantik* and that end with their autonegation. The S.I.'s explicit *détournement* of surrealism and the romantic legacy consisted in the direct construction of the "authentic life" implicitly demanded by art itself: "we are artists only insofar as we are no longer artists: we come to realize art." The position of the situationists in relation to the inherited history of revolutionary romanticism was paradoxical from the outset: "We will be revolutionary romantics to the exact extent of our failure." The surrealist synthesis of art and life was considered *passé* insofar that it progressively became a movement of individual artists rather than a movement for the worldwide realization of art. Introduced to the ethics of revolutionary autonomy by Socialisme ou Barbarie, the situationists understood that the desired conflagration of revolt needed its veritable fuel and that the political transcendence of the romantic tension between dream and social reality, between art and alienated life, had to be concretely organized rather than poetically prepared, a planned *Aufhebung* that would liquidate the romantic tension at the same time that it would announce a new phase of human existence. Marx's dictum, "the proletariat is revolutionary or is nothing," was translated under their pen to "the proletariat must realize art." The achieved goal of history is envisioned as "direct communication," the end of all forms of domination, and therefore the end of art as separation: "When our perspectives are realized, aesthetics (as well as its negation) will be superseded."

The dialectical viewpoint of the situationists meets Marx's: romanticism is coterminous with the division of consciousness caused by capitalism and inextricable from it. The romantic struggle for the social integration of public imagination comes to its term only with the transformation of the social conditions that cause the division of consciousness. A movement "more liberating" than one that remains within the matrix of revolutionary romanticism (i.e., surrealism) "cannot be easily formed" specifically because "its liberatory essence now depends on its seizing the more advanced material means of the modern world." In other words, the fundamental content of romanticism necessitates the transcendence of art as a separate activity in the social sphere, and this can only be accomplished through the appropriation and transformation of the means of production by a now collective poetic imagination. The situationists saw themselves as the most advanced strategists of a movement that would effect the definitive end of alienated consciousness through total revolution, or "poetry made by all." Thus they considered the deliberate construction of revolutionary situations the true fulfillment of romanticism at the same time that they saw situationist action as being romanticism's living negation. For the situationists, world revolution alone is the realization and suppression of romanticism, in the same way that Marx's "abolition of philosophy" is an argument for achieving in practice what idealism could only formulate in theory.

If the surrealist hostility to "the indifference of art" was about realizing radical imagination as well, if ultimately there is little that differentiates the surrealists from the situationists considered from the angle of their fundamental program, the situationists nonetheless sharpened a blade to sever surrealism from the subterranean continuum of history because they believed the antithesis to bourgeois life represented by surrealism was dragging its feet, and that a *pas de deux* would be therefore impossible. Yet just as the veritable fulfillment of romanticism would in the SI's own words signal its closure, the *sabotage* of the revolutionary romantic intervention in the political sphere—the French Communist Party's recuperation of the May '68 general strike—points to romanticism's perseverance as "legitimate antithesis" until the foundations that obstruct its realization give way and founder.

In the last analysis, the failure of the great romantic revolt of '68 does not only suggest how *revolutionary* romanticism must yet be; it also indicates how *romantic* the movements for changing the world must yet become. We may appreciate the dialectical intelligence that led the SI to believe "the goal of surmounting our conflict with the world is not romantic." The SI correctly understood that the destiny of romanticism is its transcendence *qua* divided consciousness. However, the situationists incorrectly believed that romantic split consciousness could be transcended by negating romanticism itself. By refusing romanticism in their effort to realize its truth content, the situationists were forced to locate their principles in the false dichotomy of "revolution or romanticism," even as they themselves implicitly challenged this dichotomy by thinking revolution as the qualitative integration of poetry. Such is the veritable *aporia* of the last revolutionary romantic avant-garde, and such is the major contradiction that we may now creatively bypass. At the beginning of the twenty-first century, thirty years after the demise of the SI, we are in a position to radicalize Marxian dialectics, to move forward with our gaze set on the horizon of an incredible synthesis, to apprehend the whole spectrum of revolutionary romantic struggles over the last two hundred years as the subterranean antithesis to bourgeois civilization striving toward consciousness, as the politics of the black sun of melancholia, as the tearing desire for truer light, as the dream of dreams that shocks objective truth through the presentiment of freedom. *La révolution sera romantique ou elle ne sera pas.*

## X.

The capacity for autonomous criticism carried the human understanding out of its state of self-incurred immaturity to the light of rational understanding, to paraphrase Kant, but mature reason has developed its own mental cage, and the twentieth century realized forms of "self-incurred immaturity" that do not bear mentioning. Today we witness what the age of analysis failed to foresee: the emancipation of reason from religious bondage has given way to a rationalist bondage that mutilates the social fabric of the mind as efficiently as it demolishes the natural texture of the earth. The revolutionary movements in romanticism tried to break with this negative dialectic of emancipation by arguing for a conception of human autonomy that would have poetic imagination as its center. If the poet, according to Novalis' dazzling phrase, is "the prophet of the imagination of nature," a collective renaissance of poetic imagination represents the crux of what is now needed for the social universe to be transformed from an automated seesaw of exploitation and consumption to a living totality of mutual respect and marvelous exchange. Is this problem not what Schiller had in mind when he contrasted "the most perfect of all works of art, the building up of true political freedom," to the "ingenious piece of machinery, in which out of the botching together of a vast number of lifeless parts a collective mechanical life results"? Is it not the intuition of a regressive reason, hostile to the subversion of aesthetic sense, that provoked Schiller to write that "to solve the political problem in practice" we must "follow the path of aesthetics"? Is this not what Walter Benjamin tried to think when he envisioned "a kind of labor which, far from exploiting nature, is capable of delivering her of the creations which lie dormant in her womb as potentials"? The romantic high argument for the "new mythology" (Schlegel), the "new religion" (Michelet), the "myth in which Socialism is wholly comprised" (Sorel), the "religion of action, life, love that makes people happy, redeems them and overcomes impossible situations" (Landauer), the "unified spirit of creative action, eros, and youth" (Benjamin), the "myth that evokes the society we deem desirable" (Breton), presents precisely this kind of extraordinary challenge to the modern "I doubt, therefore I am." Revolutionary romanticism knows itself as the free exercise of the imagination in its coloring of the ideal of universal *libertas* —"no one bidden to be anyone's *servant*, everyone scorning to be any man's *master*" (Morris)—a coloring that emphasizes the spiritual dimension of existence precisely in order to rethink freedom in its difference from the idol of utilitarianism. Perhaps revolutionary romanticism should be viewed as a political version of the "Kierkegaardian leap" or as a poetic rendering of the "Pascalian wager," given the heroism of the mind it inevitably demands. However one considers it, in light of the human and ecological catastrophes that conformity to social reality will ineluctably deliver, nothing short of such heroism will suffice. Without a cognitive leap into a whole other way of thinking, there is truly nowhere to go, and without making the bet that there *will* be a new future, nothing worth winning can be won.

"All science," in the words of Freud, "comes in the end to a kind of mythology." The task is to see the masterful legends for what they are, *and to see romantic activity for what it is*, to heed the "unknown" forms that surface through poetic activity and utopian desire, to nourish them against the *doxa* of instituted rationality . . . and to unhesitatingly *launch* the movement of romance, free from what Hegel called "the frozen capital of discursive knowledge." Euripides' "coming god" is none other than the coming god of human kind's poetic imagination, and to liberate Dionysus from his cage is to awaken a regenerative power that will find its lucid contagion. The revolutionary movements of the future begin as the springs of life wash over enervated social functioning—and the world is transfigured through the torrent of consciousness regained, "where all things flow to all, as rivers to the sea."